PENGUIN
THE PERFE

A devotee of Sai Baba of Shirdi, Ruzbeh N. Bharucha is one of the most influential spiritual writers of our times. He is the author of fourteen books, including the bestselling *The Fakir* trilogy, which has been translated into several languages. In 2014, *Rabda: My Sai . . . My Sigh*, published by Penguin Books, was an instant bestseller.

Formerly a journalist, he is also a documentary film-maker. His documentary *Sehat . . . Wings of Freedom*, on AIDS and HIV in Tihar Jail, was selected and screened for the XVII International AIDS Conference in 2008. His collaboration with Zambhala—India's yoga, music and life spirit festival, the first of its kind—gave birth to a series of powerful videos called 'Ramblings with Ruzbeh Bharucha'. His articles have been published in various publications, including the *Times of India*, *Free Press Journal*, *Indian Express*, *Maharashtra Herald*, *Sunday Observer*, *Jam-e-Jamshed* and *The Afternoon*.

His book *My God Is a Juvenile Delinquent* has been included in the reading list of all judicial academies.

Ruzbeh is also the 110th Master for 'The Speaking Tree' where he writes an immensely popular blog on spirituality.

His Facebook page has reached out to thousands in a very short span of time. The daily affirmations and messages are a source of inspiration to many. https://www.facebook.com/ruzbehbharucha. Twitter handle @ruzbehnbharucha. Website www.ruzbehbharucha.net.

He lives in Pune with his family.

THE
PERFECT
ONES

RUZBEH N. BHARUCHA

PENGUIN
ANANDA

PENGUIN ANANDA

Published by the Penguin Group

Penguin Books India Pvt. Ltd, 7th Floor, Infinity Tower C, DLF Cyber City, Gurgaon 122 002, Haryana, India

Penguin Group (USA) Inc., 375 Hudson Street, New York, New York 10014, USA

Penguin Group (Canada), 90 Eglinton Avenue East, Suite 700, Toronto, Ontario, M4P 2Y3, Canada

Penguin Books Ltd, 80 Strand, London WC2R 0RL, England

Penguin Ireland, 25 St Stephen's Green, Dublin 2, Ireland
(a division of Penguin Books Ltd)

Penguin Group (Australia), 707 Collins Street, Melbourne, Victoria 3008, Australia

Penguin Group (NZ), 67 Apollo Drive, Rosedale, Auckland 0632, New Zealand

Penguin Books (South Africa) (Pty) Ltd, Block D, Rosebank Office Park, 181 Jan Smuts Avenue, Parktown North, Johannesburg 2193, South Africa

Penguin Books Ltd, Registered Offices: 80 Strand, London WC2R 0RL, England

First published in Penguin Ananda by Penguin Books India 2015

Copyright © Ruzbeh N. Bharucha 2015

The copyright for individual illustrations vests with the respective illustrators

The essays in this book have previously appeared in the blog www.speakingtree.in

ISBN 9780143423843

Typeset in Sabon by Manipal Digital Systems, Manipal
Printed at Thomson Press India Ltd, New Delhi

A PENGUIN RANDOM HOUSE COMPANY

To
The Universal Mother Goddess and our Creator
Sai Baba of Shirdi
All Divine, Perfect, Ancient, Ascended Masters
Archangels and Angels
Celestial, Terrestrial, Physical Warriors of Light
The Oneness Family

Contents

1

Sai Baba . . . My Sigh . . . My Sai

Illustration by Pooja Bangia

What do I write about Baba Sai of Shirdi? Hasn't everything about Him been written, expressed and experienced by millions of His children? How do I begin to describe my love for Him? When I hear others talk about their love for Sainatha, I feel humbled by their love for, devotion to and knowledge about Him and wish my love for Him, too, would make Him happy and make Him less tired and maybe put a smile on His regal face and a twinkle of joy in His eyes.

I truly don't know where to start from and how to write this essay. There is so much written about Him and even now countless books published nearly a century after He took samadhi on 15 October 1918, at 2.27 p.m. Yes, books mention Baba took samadhi at 2.30 p.m. or 2.35 p.m., but one of the first things He had revealed through channelling was this time of Him leaving His body and I couldn't have known, as I wasn't aware of the day or time. He decided to leave us all orphans.

So on my phone, every day, the alarm rings at 2.27 p.m. and wherever I am, whatever I am doing, for those few seconds, I remember my Baba living in the body, taking samadhi and continuing to love, bless, help and even serve us, each moment of our existence. Thus, every day, for me, I am reminded of His life and all that He did, does and will do for His countless children.

Don't we serve all those we love? Be it our parents, or children, or loved ones. Our love is like *seva*. Baba Sai was one such master, God incarnate, who would time and again say that, 'I am the slave of my devotee.' Most masters say that 'a true devotee becomes happily a slave to his or her master', but here we have our Old Man, this sweet-tempered fakir, who says that He is our slave and that He was and is and will always be in the loving clutches and hearts of each and every child of His who loved Him and looked up to Him.

What do I write about Him? When you love somebody so much, words become meaningless.

I have always seen Him at home. He, along with Prophet Zarathustra and other gods and goddesses, were always present in frames and statues at my maternal grandmother's home. Every room had Him looking at me, keeping an eye and His gaze of protection on me and my cousins. I remember there was an old calendar, with His enlarged face, hung on the wall, and nobody once thought of replacing it, as He looked so majestic. The calendar must have remained in the same place for years. Cleaned by a muslin cloth, faded, jaded, the king remained. I would have difficulty in sleeping and everybody would be snoring away and there was a soft glow coming from a Mother Mary statue and the reflection would set Baba Sai's face aglow and I would look at both of them, and feel comforted knowing They looked at me, wide awake.

I clearly remember the first time I went to Shirdi along with my cousins and maternal grandmother. I don't remember much about my childhood, but I don't know why this trip is etched in the recesses of my soul. It was in winter. We reached Shirdi in the early hours. It must have been 9 a.m. or so, I truly don't remember the exact time. But I remember, we got out of the bus, teeth clattering, went and had a bath, and then we entered the temple and there He was, the rockstar, already awake, with that cleft in His chin. Those days He wasn't much into fancy stuff or gold and all that; simple, but royal as always.

I looked at Him and I gave Him a broad smile, sort of telling Him, yes You and me, as usual awake at this odd hour. There weren't many people around. I noticed tears trickling down my granny's cheeks. She was a tough woman, born in Iran, but living in India since the age of one. She had seen deaths, poverty, struggle, but she always smiled, always loved, was always filled with life. I went close to her and held her. I used to hold her and sleep and then watch Baba and Mother Mary for a long time while awake. Here I held her and watched Baba Sai and wondered what the old man had done to make my sweet grandmother, who was all of four feet two inches, tough as nails and tender as a dew drop, cry.

Three years back, one of my last conversations with her, before she passed over, was about Baba Sai. She was over ninety years old, riddled with illness, but the same jovial and tough woman. She would still do the housework and her eyes were bright and her laugh was contagious. That day when she spoke to me she was tired and she told me, 'Tell your Sai Baba I am now tired and He has stopped listening to me . . . tell Him now it's enough . . . it is time He called me to Him . . . tell Him it is enough now . . . tell Him, as He listens to you my son . . .' And then I heard this message deep in my heart and told her, 'It is a matter of a few weeks, before your birthday you will be with Him, Ma' and I could hear her sigh and say, 'And tell Him that I will not go to the hospital and not die in the hospital. I am going to fight with Him when I meet Him . . . I have only loved Him since a child and now He doesn't listen to me. But promise me before my birthday . . .' and I promised her.

Two days before her birthday, my grandmother woke up, washed up, did some housework, had a cup of tea, spoke to my childhood friend who'd come to visit her after years (and I know for sure seeing my friend my grandmother remembered me and spoke of me . . . it feels at least a little good that she must have remembered me minutes before she passed over, as I was not in Mumbai then, but in Pune) and then she said she was tired. She slept and never woke up. She went peacefully in her sleep.

So that day, I clearly remember, I stood with my granny in front of Sai. I remember Dwarka Mai, where Baba Sai spent nearly sixty years or more of His life, converting a dilapidated mosque into a Mecca and a Vrindavan, burning the eternal fire, making it a haven of spirituality and burning down the rigidness and pettiness that the false interpretation of religions has brought about. How cool was He? He didn't care about who said what. He went about in His own silent way, bringing all religions together, saying aloud either 'Allah Malik' or 'Raja Ram'. That day when I saw the fire, it was blazing. There was a bamboo fence preventing the overzealous from getting too close to the fire, but it was blazing. The fire that He had started around hundred and fifty years ago still blazed. (Baba Sai first came to Shirdi as a sixteen-year-old in 1851 and then returned to Shirdi in 1858 to remain here till His samadhi, and it is supposed that the holy fire in Dwarka Mai was started latest in 1860.)

Of course, now one can't even go near the fire. The fakir who didn't care about His clothing, food, His physical comfort, for whom money only meant to be given to those who needed it, He who slept on the floor, and begged for His food, now is adorned in gold and is made to live in a grandiose prison. The fire that blazed and warmed each of His children cannot be approached, no offering can be personally made to the holy fire, small packets of *udhi*, the sacred ash, are dished out to one and all, more to those who have personal contacts or very important people. Shirdi, the small home of our Baba has become the third or the fourth largest pilgrimage revenue-earner in the world and thus the fakir who cared two hoots about money, gold, comfort, discrimination between the rich and the poor and pomp and show and opulence, now is sadly confined and imprisoned into all that which Baba all His physical life, in this avatar, opposed.

Reminds me of my Prophet Zarathustra, who all His life opposed idol worship but now if you go to any fire temple you will see He is worshipped with huge portraits of Him adorning a place of prominence.

Anyway, enough of my irrelevant ramblings; we get back to Baba Sai.

While returning from Shirdi, I remember I began to weave stories in my mind. Thus, to the unfortunate unsuspecting world, the genesis of me penning thoughts on to paper or now on the screen of my battered laptop, and writing books, began from that day when I was called by our Baba to Shirdi.

Through my years of channelling His energy, I have learnt a few things about Baba Sai. This is my reality. Need not be yours.

First and foremost, He truly believes that wealth is for sharing and helping. He is big into feeding the poor. He believes one should keep a part of one's earnings to help those in need of help. He has a soft corner for those who go through their lives and their karmic cleansing with calmness, grace and humour. He is keen that one recognizes his or her true essence, 'I am the spirit in the body . . . I am not the body.' He truly would like each of us to make the Creator or one's master, one's sole and soul priority. He advocates taking the master's name or a mantra or a prayer, through the day, so it would throb within one's soul, through the night too.

He believes that one must first follow one's religion; pray the mandatory prayers advocated by one's religion and then take His name. (This is what He had told me clearly . . . if you do not say your prayers then do not take my Name.) He is big on prayers and chanting and charity and compassion and calm acceptance of one's lot. He believes each one of us must give each moment our very best and then leave the rest to one's karmic blueprint and the grace and wisdom of one's master.

He believes that each situation has three alternatives. The first, if a situation is unpleasant, give it your best to change it to the overall well-being of all present. If after giving your best the situation still hasn't changed, then you have the option of walking out. But often, a situation may not change and the option to walk out may not be possible or practical. Then one should make peace with the situation, and calmly try to make the best out of all that which is possible. The third alternative is not really an alternative. Which is, one cannot bring about positive change to the situation, one cannot walk out, but one refuses to make peace with one's lot; instead, one stews and rots and burns. This is the worst of the three alternatives and Baba Sai, on and on has advised those who come for channelling, to avoid this third path, as it leads to further worsening of the karmic blueprint, bringing forth pain, negativity and eventually taking one further away from the path.

He doesn't like slandering. It really saddens Him. To Him, those who backbite or indulge in slander are similar to pigs who relish eating dung and excreta. He is known to have said, 'Your conduct is similar (to the pig which eats dung and excreta). You go on reviling your own brethren to your heart's content.'

He doesn't like His children to get into arguments. He believes one can state one's point of view calmly but firmly. Arguments and fighting is like cutting one's nose to spite one's face. He advocates one and all not to come from a state of reaction. Do not react, as then you are influenced by external factors and one has no control over external factors. Thus, one would spend one's entire life reacting. He advocates one to come from centredness—not *react* but to *act* from a state of calmness, so that one is in control of one's action and words.

Time and again He has told one and all in channelling that the most effective mantra, the king of all mantras, is the mantra called 'shut up'. He believes most of our problems take place with what goes inside the mouth and what comes out of the mouth. If one were silent and spoke from the state of calmness, rather than a state of reaction and action, most of our problems would either be solved or would be far less exacting and tiresome.

Silence is the most effective springboard to connect with the master and eventually to realize one's own self and then one's own Godhood.

He wants each of us to give and give and give. Help those in need. If one cannot give materially, one can give via a kind word, a tender smile, compassion, love, blessings and prayers.

He wants each one of us to know our strengths, weaknesses and limitations, and then, to act from our strengths and keep a distance from our weaknesses. As much of a distance that is possible. He doesn't want us to flog ourselves when we fail or succumb to our weaknesses and limitations, but to first bring about a distance from the failings, slowly and steadily, till the distance is so far and distant, that one has nearly conquered it, rather than suppressed it.

He loves Mother Earth and wants us to give as much as possible back to Her, rather than keep taking and receiving from Her. He has a very soft corner for animals and all living beings.

He loves a good laugh and is not shy of abusing. Baba Sai wants us to be centred, whether in a place of worship, workplace, home or café or wherever. He believes that if one is with one's master in thought and breath, it doesn't matter where you are. Wherever you may be, you have made it your place of worship, as you are with your master, and wherever your master is, that place automatically becomes a place of worship.

He advocates that the best way to connect with your God, Goddess and master is via the breath and combining the breath with the name. He advocates approaching our God, Goddess and master as a child and not as an adult. A child can get away with a lot. Adults, by and large, are a lost cause.

He advocates prayers for one's ancestors, family and friends who have passed over. He is most happy when one prays for all those who have passed over and a special prayer for all those who are earthbound.

He gets happy when one remembers Him or one's master before eating or drinking even water and not only to thank Him or one's master for the food or drink but also a small prayer that nobody goes hungry or thirsty, for food, water, clothing, shelter or any other necessities. He says time and again that simple prayers, from the heart, make a major difference to the cosmos and the energy and vibration in the cosmos. In fact, time and again He has asked a number of those who have come for channelling to pray for all of creation. The mantra He has asked them to chant is, '*Ya Sai sarve bhramand sukh shanti krupa*' (Oh Sai, let there be grace of peace and joy in all of Creation). He believes that if each of His children were to chant this prayer, the vibration created would bring about peace and joy to the lives of innumerable people and also to all of Creation. Each individual can make a difference. It may be a small difference, but drop by drop, the ocean, too, is filled.

The other mantra He has given is '*Aum Sai rakshak*' or '*Ya Sai rakshak*' (Sai protect me). This prayer is very powerful as not only are we asking Sai to protect us from the external world, but also, to protect us from the wrong use of free will, which then creates karma that returns to haunt us, for that particular life, or sometimes for all of eternity.

So through years of channelling, these are the few things that I have realized that matter to Baba Sai.

I know one thing, He truly is with us. I know that. But the question is how much are we with Him? Like He so often says in channelling, 'The night doesn't descend because the sun has shown His back to the Earth, but because the Earth has shown Her back to the sun.'

He truly is with us. Believe this.

One very important thing is He wants each one of us to go beyond His physical body. He has often told those who come for channelling and those who plead that they want to see Him, 'I have come many times, taken many incarnations . . . those who focus on this body of mine, this body that lived in Shirdi, would then never recognize Me if I were to come to them in any other body I had occupied in my other incarnations . . . but if you were to focus on My spirit . . . My energy . . . My true essence . . . you will recognize Me in any body I wish to show Myself to you, be it in a human avatar or even that of an animal, bird, fish, or a butterfly.'

All His life Baba Sai lived for the poor. He helped the rich to become more giving, generous and compassionate to the plight of the needy; and the poor to live a life of dignity even in their state of poverty and hardship. He loved us so much that though once He had left His body for three days and was declared dead, He came back to serve and love and be amongst us in the flesh.

In 1886, Baba told Mhalsapati to protect His body for three days and if He did not return, to bury His body at a particular spot and put two flags for all those who wanted to come and pay respect to their Sai. Saying this, He left His body and medically He was declared dead. Mhalsapati did not get up for three days. With Baba's head on his lap, he dared any of the authorities to come close to Baba. Baba's other disciples guarded Baba's body. Baba had been suffering from severe asthma and His body had taken a toll from serving His children, day and night, those physically present and those not in Shirdi, but under the protection of Baba.

Sri Ramakrishna Paramhansa, the sublime child of Maa Kali, too, had been very ill during that same period. Baba Sai came back to His body and said, 'I went to Allah to be there forever, but My friend Gadhadhar (Ramakrishna Paramhansa) wanted to reach Allah too, so I came back.' It is said that as soon as Baba Sai woke up from the three-day period of samadhi, Ramakrishna Paramhansa took samadhi.

Ramakrishna Paramhansa used to sing a song about Sai Baba of Shirdi, which when translated went as follows, 'Such a noble fakir has come that the Hindus worship as God and the Muslims worship as a Pir.'

So Baba Sai came back to serve once again and lived in His physical body for the next thirty-six years, and is still selflessly serving even after leaving His physical form.

Serving one and all, bringing about peace amongst followers of various religions, serving the poor and the destitute, Baba Sai took samadhi on 15 October 1918, at 2.27 p.m.

He had predicted His passing over two years prior to it. A few weeks before He took samadhi, Baba Sai sent a message to a Muslim saint in Aurangabad, 'Allah is taking away the lamp He placed here.' The saint began to weep hearing this swansong.

The day Baba took samadhi was Moharram, Buddha Jayanti and Dusshera.

He was tired by then. He was exhausted. He had taken on the suffering of His children for more than eighty years. Nobody knows when and where Baba Sai was born, though now there are conjectures, but Baba Sai never told anybody.

Though Baba Sai had virtually stopped eating food nearly a month before He left His body, He till almost the last few days, continued to beg for food from five families. He would offer some food to the holy fire, put some food in a pot where animals and birds would feast on it and then He would have a morsel and the remaining would be distributed as prasad.

On the last day He lived in His physical body, even though He was truly unwell, He allowed devotees and visitors to take His blessings. Yes, there were times when Baba Sai would be in a rage, abusing one and all for the benefit of all of Creation, often going into a few hours of seclusion and not seeing anybody, but that day, the day of samadhi, He allowed all to come and take His blessings. Then He called His inner circle and individually told them a few things. Nobody was aware that these were the last few hours they would be spending time with their Sai, their 'be all and end all'.

All those who attended the last *arti* performed to Baba Sai while He was in the physical body were humbled due to the fact that Baba's expressions changed and appeared in different forms and avatars. It is said that He appeared as Lord Hanuman, Lord Rama, Lord Krishna, Lord Vithal, Dattatreya Guru; the Muslims thought they were looking at their Mecca and Medina; and Christians said Baba Sai looked just like Jesus Christ.

He then asked all to go and have prasad outside Dwarka Mai. He then gave Laxmi Bai nine coins, explained the significance of the nine rupees. Imagine, He was minutes away from samadhi and Baba explained to His dear devotee the significance of the nine rupees, each rupee signifying the quality of a devotee. To be free of ego, jealousy, worldly desires, envy, self-boasting and finding flaws of others, and to serve the needy, be of a peaceful temperament, have the desire to know the real truth and complete, total, absolute faith in one's guru and master.

He then told Bayaji that His body should be kept in Butty Wada, the same place where for years Baba single-handedly converted a swamp into a beautiful garden of jasmine and other flowers. Then our king, our father, the 'be all and end all' of our existence, rested His head on Bayaji's body and took samadhi.

Baba came to various people of His inner circle, in dreams or made them hear His loud voice, giving them instructions of what to do after His samadhi. Baba left His body on a Tuesday. On Wednesday at 4 p.m., His inner circle bathed His body. Baba's limbs were still taut and numerous hours after His samadhi, a little blood trickled down His nose, which is medically impossible.

After a bath, applying rose water and other aromatic water, Baba was placed in His physical body's final resting spot, along with His faithful broken brick, a *satka*, spices to preserve His body, an old cloth bag which had a green *kafni* and a cap which Baba did not allow anybody to touch, His chillum, His needle and cotton, with which our Baba would keep stitching and mending His clothes till they resembled a patchwork of repair. The king's body was laid to rest.

Where an idol of Krishna was to be consecrated, Baba Sai's samadhi came about.

Most people insist that Baba is either a Shiva avatar, or a Rama avatar, or a Krishna avatar. Muslims believe Him to be a Persian Sufi saint. For me He is my Sai Baba. How does it matter whose avatar Baba Sai is? I mean, does Baba Sai have to be an avatar for one to feel and recognize His greatness? Can't Baba Sai just be our Sai? Our old man. Our fakir. Our father. Our temperamental loving guru. The One who performed and keeps performing miracles at a drop of a hat. The One who, as promised, will always be with us and if we called Him, then He would come running. The One who says, 'Take one step towards me and I will take hundred steps towards you.'

Why does He have to be somebody's avatar. Sai is Sai. He sometimes said, 'The universe is Me and I am the universe' and most of the times called Himself the servant and slave of the fakir. He could control the elements of nature but lived in the most humble way and laughed, sang, danced, cursed, loved, served, lived amongst His children.

Do we really need Him to be some avatar? I want my Sai. All of creation on one side, including God, and my Sai on the other side—I want Him.

What do we do with heaven and paradise if Sai Himself is some place else serving the needy? I want to be with Him. I am sure you do too.

He called the masjid Dwarka Mai, telling one and all the importance of the Goddess—that He lived in the shelter of the Goddess. He was so loving; only a mother can be this loving. If you have Baba Sai, then you have the Mother with you too.

What have we to do with all this avatar business? Just love Baba Sai for being Baba Sai.

The one expression that I believe completely in is what Avatar Meher Baba said of Baba Sai of Shirdi. He said, 'Baba Sai is *Qutub-e-Irshad* . . . Master of the Universe.'

As long as Sai of Shirdi, the old man, this darling of a fakir remains for eternity as our master, *sab theek hain, fikar not.*

Allah Malik. Raja Ram. Sai Rakshak.

2

Nav Durga Namho Namho

Illustration by Pooja Bangia

There are nine manifestations of Goddess and Mother Durga. I have done my best with my limited knowledge and the utmost research possible to write below about Her origins and life. The victory of the Goddess over the demon Mahishasura and also the inherent evil within us—if we truly consider Maa within us and working hard at assisting us to destroy the muck within us, bringing us to salvation—comes for me at a price. My Baba Sai of Shirdi took samadhi on Dusshera day. So yes, it is a victory for all, but He left His body, thus it is a strange day. The world celebrates and all Baba lovers keep silent.

I have channelled through Baba Sai prayers for each manifestation of Nav Maa Durga. At the end of this essay there is also a prayer as one composite beseech to the Mother Goddess.

Be blessed.

Maa Shailaputri

Goddess Parvati is Maa Shailaputri. Her first incarnation was that of Maa Sati.

From the time Maa Sati was a child, She had only one focus and aim in life, Lord Shiva. As She grew up Her love and devotion for the lord grew deeper. She began Her penance to please Lord Shiva and She pleased the lord, and the lord manifested in front of Her to grant Her a boon.

Maa Sati asked the lord for His eternal companionship as man and wife. It was granted.

But there was a catch. Maa Sati's father Daksha Prajapati for some odd reason wasn't too kosher about this heavenly union. When he organized a major puja-havan (those days they called it a *yagna*), our man Daksha Prajapati, on purpose decided to call all the Gods and Their progeny but did not invite Lord Shiva. Maa Sati was furious and told Lord Shiva that this was an insult which She would not tolerate and expressed a desire to confront Her father and give him a piece of Her mind. Lord Shiva tried His level best to talk Maa Sati out of this meeting but to no avail. He warned Her that this meeting could lead to disaster but Maa Sati was furious and would not listen to reason. Eventually, Lord Shiva gave in.

When Maa Sati entered the place of the yagna, to her disbelief, She realized that Her father, along with a few of the household staff and Her sisters too, were bad-mouthing Lord Shiva.

Maa Sati, who loved and worshipped Lord Shiva all Her life, could not take the humiliation and the harsh words directed to the lord. Already angry, this was the final straw. She, through Her *yog shakti*, engulfed Herself in fire.

When Lord Shiva came to know that His beloved Sati was no more in the body, He ordered His army to destroy the place and went into silence for a long time.

Sati Maa's love was so pure and innocent that She was reborn as Maa Parvati and is also known as Sahilaputri. She is the daughter of the Lord of the Mountains, Himalaya. Maa again won Lord Shiva through Her love, devotion and penance, and on the first day and night of Nav Ratras, Maa Shailaputri is worshipped. She is the first form of Nav Durga.

Maa holds the trishul in the right hand and a lotus in the other. Her vehicle is the bull, Nandi.

According to yogis and other spiritual practitioners, Maa Shailaputri represents the root chakra or the Muladhara chakra and it is considered the first or initial platform for all spiritual practices to commence.

The prayer for Maa Shailaputri given by Baba Sai of Shirdi is given below.

I worship Goddess Maa Shailaputri,

She who has a crescent moon on Her head, rides on a bull, carrying a trishul and is ever known,

Bless me with the same love and devotion Thou had for Your Lord,

Let me always be filled with Thy fire of oneness

You are the first one, Thy name is Sati,

I chant Your Name, worship You, praise You forever more, Maa Shailaputri.

Brahmacharini (Tapasyacharini)

In reality Maa Brahmacharini is once again Maa Parvati. This second form of Nav Durga is the one related to the most severe penances connected with Devi worship. This form of Maa Durga is connected with the penance done by Maa Sati and Maa Parvati to get the boon of eternal companionship with Lord Shiva. But this form is related more with Maa Parvati's penance for Lord Shiva which went on for thousands of years.

We are already aware of why Maa Sati set Herself ablaze in the holy fire. She takes birth again as Maa Parvati. One day Lord Vishnu's eternal disciple, Sage Narada, visited the kingdom of King Himalaya. The moment He saw Maa Parvati, who was then a very young woman, the revered sage bowed down to Maa Parvati. Himalaya and his wife were astounded as to why Sage Narada would bow down to their daughter. It was then that Narada revealed to her parents the true origin of Maa Parvati and how Maa Parvati in the former form of Maa Sati had won over Lord Shiva, became the lord's wife and how She couldn't bear the humiliation meted out to Her by Her extremely strange father and thus immolated Herself, and now, here She was, as Maa Parvati.

I am sure the very energy behind Her past incarnation, which was spoken of by Narada, must have evoked long lost memories and Maa Parvati requested the sage to reveal how She could win over Lord Shiva again. The sage revealed that now, for Lord Shiva to again accept anybody as His wife and companion, Maa Parvati would really have to raise the bar of asceticism and penances.

So Maa left Her parents, the palace, the comforts and began Her quest for pleasing Lord Shiva. Her penances are considered the most severe. For the first thousand years, Maa meditated and prayed to Lord Shiva and lived on fruits and roots. Then, for the next three thousand years She lived on only leaves and then only on water, disregarding Her physical state or the elements of nature. It was but natural that She became skin and bone, and being the spouse of Lord Shiva would have been Her only emancipation.

Maa's penance eventually forced all the Gods and sages to approach Lord Brahma who then blessed Maa Parvati that She would become the divine spouse of Lord Shiva. He also blessed Her, through which She regained her health and beauty, and titled Her 'Brahmacharini', which means 'The one who is a celibate woman'.

Lord Shiva then married Maa Parvati.

All the severe penances and fasts *(upvaas)* that women do and keep are to please Maa Brahmacharini who is none other than Maa Parvati who is none other than Maa Sati who are the forms of Shakti or 'woman energy'. Thus, They are all One, and worshipped as the second form of Maa Durga.

Maa as Brahmacharini wears simple white though in some places She is shown to be wearing a pink saree.

Maa carries a *rudraksha* mala or rosary in Her right hand and in the other hand a *kamandalu* (a pitcher carried by sages). She appears very calm, serene and is always in the state of meditation. She stands for renunciation, patience and penance; and endows Her devotees and disciples with dedication, willpower, focus, courage, strength as well as well-being and eternal peace.

Yogis and spiritual practitioners who pray to Maa Brahmacharini focus on the third chakra, which is below the navel, the Manipura chakra. This chakra is thus associated with Maa Brahmacharini and according to Baba Sai of Shirdi, this is the chakra where all the powers and strengths reside.

The prayer channelled by Baba Sai for Maa Brahmacharini is as follows. If you want the original Sanskrit version and meaning, as I say often, we have God and then we have Google.

O Goddess Maa Brahmacharini,

Bless me with purity, dedication, courage and perseverance.

Bless me with Your devotion to achieve a merger with Thou and my lord and master.

Never let me be afraid to make Thou happy and proud of me,

Never let the world distract me from my highest goals.

Bless me, Maa Parvati, to shake the very heaven with my faith, dedication, love and need of a merger with Thou.

Chandraghanta or Chandra-khanda

Maa Durga in Her third avatar for the first time shows Herself as the 'Ferocious One'. Maa Chandraghanta (Maa has a bell-shaped half moon on Her forehead, thus the word *ghanta*, meaning bell). She is worshipped on the third day;

She is ten-armed and rides a lion. She is worshipped by those who want the help of the Goddess to ward off opponents, foes and those who resort to corrupt and evil means.

In this avatar, Maa is always ready for war against all which is evil and the dark side of Creation. Those who pray to this form of Maa Durga, experience fearlessness merged with tranquillity. It is said that all mental and emotional fears are eradicated when one prays to Maa Chandraghanta and the devotees are further blessed with a powerful aura and blessed speech.

The devotee is enveloped by Maa's aura, and thus, develops confidence and exudes strength and power, as well as has a charismatic pull over all he or she interacts with. Though Maa's appearance might look ferocious, She is ever loving, always merciful and most tender to those who pray to Her.

Many believe that one can look into the future with the grace of Maa Chandraghanta and get Divine Fragrance or hear sounds, which herald Maa's presence in your life. Maa's very shout can make Her enemies, demons and those who indulge in evil tremble, and go back to where they have come from.

Maa Chandraghanta's prayer, as Baba Sai of Shirdi has given, is:

O Goddess Maa Chandraghanta, riding a tiger,

Protect me from my enemies, those visible and those unseen, make me as noble and brave as Thou,

The one who holds many weapons in Her ten hands, keep me and my loved ones always protected and bless me with Your favour.

Kushmanda or Ashtabhuja

Maa Durga's fourth *swaroop* or divine form is that of Kushmanda. Maa is considered as the mother of all creation, all planets, stars, galaxies and the universe. The sun is Her home and dwelling. Kushmanda means 'The One who created the universe as a tiny celestial egg'. She has created the universe and thus is also known as the 'Primordial One', or as 'Adi Shakti'. Many consider this *roop* of Maa Durga as the Creator. She has breathed life into all things and beings; and by praying to this form of Maa, the devotee is bestowed by Maa Kushmanda with resplendent glory, fame and well-being. As She resides in the sun; and only She can reside in the sun, as She has created it all, Her form is luminous and resplendent like the sun. In fact the very sun gets its warmth and radiance because Maa dwells in it. She has eight hands and thus is also called Ashtabhuja.

Maa Kamandalu has in seven hands a vase of nectar, a discus, a bow, an arrow, a lotus (the lotus is so important to the Goddess) and a mace. But it is what She holds in Her eighth hand which is most important for yogis and spiritual aspirants; She holds a rosary that can grant the eight all-important *siddhi*s (knowledge/wisdom of all one needs to know) and nine *niddhi*s (powers and wealth of all types). Maa is seated on a lion. Having created the sun along with all of creation, those who have a malefic sun in their astrological chart must worship Maa Kushmanda.

Maa Kushmanda is seated in the heart chakra; Anahata. For a long life, success, fame and prosperity, Maa Kushmanda is appeased with purity, love and dedication. (I guess all mothers are appeased with purity, love and dedication.)

The prayer one can chant to appease Maa Kushmanda, according to Baba Sai is:

Maa Kushmanda,
Shine through me like the sun.
Let Thy radiance permeate within me and through me to all of creation,

*Let my name, fame and glory be attached with Thou
and with eight siddhis and nine niddhis, bless me, Maa
So that I can serve and spread Thy radiance.*

Maa Skanda or Chaturbhuji

Skanda Maa is the fifth manifestation of Maa Durga. She
is also called Skanda Mata, the mother of Skanda; the
name is derived from Her son, Kartikeya, who amidst other
names is also called Skanda. Lord Skanda is also known as
Subramanya and Murugan.

Lord Skanda/Kartikeya/Subramanya/Murugan was
appointed as the chief commander of the Gods and Their
Army to fight against the demons.

Kartikeya is the brother of Lord Ganesha, thus logically,
Skanda Mata, who is the fifth manifestation of Maa Durga
is Maa Parvati who is Maa Sati who is Maa Shakti.

Maa Skanda is seated on a lotus, thus, She is also called
the Goddess with a lotus-seat. Her mode of transport is
the faithful lion. She is seen carrying two lotus flowers, a
kamandalu again, and a bell. With one hand She blesses
everyone and with the other hand She holds Her son
Kartikeya or Skanda.

When Skanda Mata is worshipped, Her son, Kartikeya,
is automatically paid homage and obeisance to. The
importance of worshipping Skanda Mata is that She desires
pure, dedicated, selfless love and devotion, and thus happily
grants the devotee/disciple prosperity and well-being. I
think in this roop, Maa seeks disciples rather than devotees.
A disciple is one who has surrendered to his or her lord,
Goddess and master. A devotee worships the one but still
hangs on to his or her own ego. It is said that with the grace
and blessings of Skanda Mata and Lord Kartikeya, the
disciple gains salvation.

Skanda Mata represents the Visuddha chakra, which is the throat chakra. Skanda, as a child in the lap of Skanda Mata basically signifies the purity of a child or, in this case, purity of the mind.

The prayer for Skanda Mata—once again, none of them are traditional prayers, but what comes forth from Baba Sai of Shirdi:

Skanda Mata, mother of Lord Kartikeya, seated on the lotus, in the world, but still detached from it;

The one on the lion, make my heart and mind, childlike, completely immersed and surrendered to You,

With Thy son Kartikeya Subramanya's grace make me face my lower energies and the world like a warrior

Like Your child, take care of me and my lot,

Oh Mother Skanda, may Thou and Thy son, Lord Subramanya, the Skanda, be always pleased with me and my loved ones.

Maa Katyayani

This is the sixth form of Maa Durga, which is most commonly and widely known—the destroyer of Mahishasura. Maa Katyayani's name is derived from a sage called Kaatyaayana. Sage Kaatyaayana was a devotee and disciple of Maa Durga. He worshipped Her with love, dedication and sincerity. Maa Durga, pleased with Him, appeared before Him and told Him to ask for a boon. The sage asked Maa to be born as His daughter. Maa blessed Him.

When Mahishasura began to play havoc with the Gods and all of Creation, Maa Durga took birth as Sage Kaatyaayana's daughter, and thus, was called Maa Katyayani, the daughter of Kaatyaayana.

Legend says that Maa Katyayani was worshipped by Lord Vishnu, Shiva, Brahma and all other Gods for three days, in order to give Her all the power to destroy Mahishasura.

Sage Kaatyaayana was overjoyed, but Maa showed Him Her true form. She became huge and resplendent. Maa let Herself be worshipped by Sage Kaatyaayana for three days, and then She went and gave Mahishasura the pink slip by relieving His spirit from His body.

Maa carries a sword, a shield and a lotus. She blesses with one hand and her vehicle is the lion. Maa Katyayani can be easily pleased with love and devotion, who then destroys the sins of Her devotees and grants them material well-being, luxuries, pleasures and liberation.

The prayer given by Baba Sai of Shirdi to appease Maa Katyayani is as follows:

Maa Katyayani, the destroyer of demons,
Free me from my lower energies,
Destroy all that which Thou doesn't approve of within me and around me,
But do so tenderly, Maa
Bless me with protection, prosperity, success and courage.

Maa Kalaratri or Maa Shubhankari

This seventh form of Maa Durga is very close to Maa Kali. Maa is dark-skinned, violent and to those who don't go beyond Her physical aspect, Maa can seem very daunting. This aspect of Maa is ferocious, and God help Her or Her devotee's or disciple's enemy! She is atop a donkey, and She has a sword, a trident and a noose. She is very clear about Her intentions. No hide and seek here. Some scholars profess that this is the dark side of Maa Durga—that life has its violent, cruel and dark side. Maa Kalaratri has three eyes on Her forehead. The strange part is that though Maa is depicted as dark-skinned, black would be the right word, luminous rays of Light emit from Her body.

The more terrifying Maa Kalaratri's appearance, She is in reality that much and more tender and merciful. Thus, She is called Maa Shubhankari, meaning, 'The One who does good and auspicious things for Her children'. If one goes beyond the body, one sees Her tenderness, and She is ready to give and help and heal and absolve the sins of Her children. Like Mother Kali, Maa Shubhankari/Kalaratri is the most tender of all mothers. She wants you to go beyond the gross, beyond the physical, beyond the darkness and glitter, and focus on Her love and Her mercy.

Maa Kalaratri is prayed to, asking Her to destroy black magic, demons, ghosts, voodoo, the evil eye (*nazar*) and all the dark alleys of the spirit world. Her very blessing makes Her child fearless. Who the hell in Creation is going to oppose or get into a battle with Maa Kali and Maa Kalaratri? Maa Kalaratri wants Her children happy, moving towards liberation by going beyond the external gross body and material objects. Maa wants us all to go beyond fears and obstacles created by the world, the planets, the unknown, the dark side of one's own mind and in all of creation.

Maa Kalaratri is associated with the crown chakra or the Sahasrara chakra, giving the invoker the siddhis and niddhis (knowledge, wisdom and power) of the universe.

Baba Sai's prayer for Kalaratri Devi:

Kalaratri . . . O Maa Kali
You cannot scare me as You are my mother,
A child is never scared of the mother
But the one who harms Your child is destroyed.
Be always tender with this child of Yours,
Protect me from black magic, the evil eye, the manipulator and the one who You do not favour.
Surround me and my loved ones with Your presence,
Bestow love, grace and well-being

And let the world know I belong to You.
Jai Maa Kali. Jai Kalratri. Nav Durga namho namha.

Maha Gowri/Maha Gauri/Kanya/Kumari/Chaturbhuji

The eighth manifestation of Nav Durga, for many people, is the most important manifestation of Maa Durga. She is represented as a young eight year-old girl.

Due to thousands of years of penance undertaken by Maa Parvati to appease Lord Shiva, Maa Parvati's complexion became dark, virtually black in colour. When Lord Shiva was convinced of Maa Parvati's devotion and love, He bathed Maa with the water of the Ganga that flowed through His matted locks. Maa regained Her former complexion and radiance, and thus, Her name became Maha or Maa Gauri, the one who is extremely fair or radiant.

Maha Gauri is always worshipped in the form of an eight-year-old girl. Whoever worships Her, is granted happiness, prosperity and well-being. Yogis and sages worship Her to be blessed with dedication, devotion, courage, to continue to pursue their spiritual aspirations. Those who meditate on Her, worship Her and seek to be blessed with Her patience and Her single-minded focus of merging with the Lord and master, are freed from the cycle of life and death and attachments to the external world.

Maha Gauri is always dressed in white with jewellery. She sits on a bull and has four hands, thus the name Chaturbhuji. She grants Her devotees and disciples wealth and well-being, and also salvation to yogis. She is tender at heart, and thus forgives easily.

The prayer to Maha Gauri given by Baba Sai of Shirdi is:
Maa Maha Gauri,
Bless me with Your devotion and child-like love,

The way you appeased Thy Lord, bless me that I may
appease mine too,
Grant me, when in the body, health and prosperity of
body, mind and heart
And when in spirit back with You, liberation from the
cycles of birth and death,
Make me innocent as a child and as wise as a sage,
So be it as I pray.

Maa Siddhidayini . . . Siddhidatri

As the name suggests, Maa in the ninth manifestation is the
giver of all siddhas and siddhis. This is the final manifestation
of Maa Durga; but in reality, creation as we know of it,
evolved from Maa Siddhidayini which is Maa's ninth form
or roop of Nav Durga.

When the universal mother, the Creator of all Creators,
created Lord Shiva, legend says, that Lord Shiva prayed to
Maa Supreme to bestow on Him all boons that would lead
to perfection. Maa Durga or Maa Shakti or Maa Parvati,
whichever name one would like to call the primordial
Goddess, from Herself created Maa Siddhidayani.

Maa Siddhidayani blessed Lord Shiva with *ashtasiddhi*s,
eight siddhis while some claim eighteen siddhis (powers
and/or states of perfection). From here Lord Shiva created
Lord Vishnu, who created Lord Brahma.

Then there came a halt. For creation of the world, one
needs male and female energy. So Maa Siddhidayini made
Lord Shiva into male and female energy, half-God half-
Goddess, called Ardhanaarishwara. It is through this that
Creation followed.

Thus, all that which is perfect comes from Maa Siddhidayini.

Maa Siddhidayini is prayed to and worshipped by all those
who seek siddhis and niddhis (powers, perfection, wisdom of

all kinds). She is prayed to by the Gods and the demons. She grants all boons connected with the occult and the paranormal. Those who pray to Her are granted boons for material and spiritual well-being, and the state of perfection. She sits on a lotus, holding a mace, a discus, a lotus and a book (the *Akashik* records or the history and destination of all and everything).

Baba Sai of Shirdi's prayer to Maa Siddhidayini:
Maa Siddhidayini make me perfect,
Make me realize Your perfection in myself,
Bless me with the gifts You wish to bestow
As I am ignorant of my wants and needs,
Let the God and Goddess energy within me be in harmony
First Your love and blessings, then siddhis and niddhis
First Your protection and grace, then the occult and all else
Be with me for now and for eternity.

Baba Sai's prayer in praise and worship of Nav Maa Durga

I worship Goddess Maa Shailaputri,
She who has a crescent moon on Her head, rides on a bull, carrying a trishul and is ever known,
Bless me with the same love and devotion Thou had for Your lord,
Let me always be filled with Thy fire of Oneness
You are the first one, Thy name is Sati,
I chant Your name, worship You, praise You forever more, Maa Shailaputri

O Goddess Maa Brahmacharini,

Bless me with purity, dedication, courage and perseverance.
Bless me with Your devotion to achieve a merger with Thou and my lord and master.

Never let me be afraid to make Thou happy and proud of me,
  Never let the world distract me from my highest goals.
  Bless me, Maa Parvati, to shake the very heaven with my faith, dedication, love and need of a merger with Thou.

O Goddess Maa Chandraghanta,

Riding a tiger,
  Protect me from my enemies, those visible and those unseen, make me as noble and brave as Thou,
  The one who holds many weapons in Her ten hands, keep me and my loved ones always protected and bless me with Your favour.

O Maa Kushmanda,

Shine through me like the sun.
  Let Thy radiance permeate within me and through me to all of creation,
  Let my name, fame and glory be attached with Thou and with eight siddhis and nine niddhis, bless me, Maa
  So that I can serve and spread Thy radiance.

Goddess Skanda Mata,

Mother of Lord Kartikeya, seated on the lotus, in the world, but still detached from it;
  The one on the lion, make my heart and mind, child-like, completely immersed and surrendered to You,
  With Thy son Kartikeya Subramanya's grace make me face my lower energies and the world like a warrior

Like Your child, take care of me and my lot,
   Oh Mother Skanda, may Thou and Thy son, Lord
Subramanya, the Skanda, be always pleased with me and
my loved ones.

Maa Katyayani,

The destroyer of demons,
   Free me from my lower energies,
   Destroy all that which Thou doesn't approve of within
me and around me,
   But do so tenderly, Maa
   Bless me with protection, prosperity, success and courage.

Kalaratri . . . O Maa Kali,

You cannot scare me as You are my Mother,
   A child is never scared of the mother
   But the one who harms Your child is destroyed.
   Be always tender with this child of Yours,
   Protect me from black magic, the evil eye, the
manipulator and the one who You do not favour.
   Surround me and my loved ones with Your presence,
   Bestow love, grace and well-being
   And let the world know I belong to You.
   Jai Maa Kali. Jai Kalaratri. Nav Durga namho namha.

Maa Maha Gauri,

Bless me with Your devotion and child-like love,
   The way you appeased Thy lord, bless me that I appease
mine too,

Grant me, when in the body, health and prosperity of
body, mind and heart
    And when in spirit back with You, liberation from the
cycles of birth and death,
    Make me innocent as a child and as wise as a sage,
    So be it as I pray.

Maa Siddhidayini,

Make me perfect,
    Make me realize Your perfection in myself,
    Bless me with the gifts You wish to bestow
    As I am ignorant of my wants and needs,
    Let the God and Goddess energy within me be
in harmony
    First Your love and blessings, then siddhis and niddhis
    First Your protection and grace, then the occult and all
else
    Be with me for now and for eternity.

Jai Mata Di. Glory be to the divine mother . . .

Illustration by Aparna Bangia

3

Archangel Gabriel . . . The Master's Voice

Illustration by Nilufer Marshall

Archangel Gabriel is the voice of the Creator. Every prophet from the beginning of time, eventually, was embraced by Gabriel's energy, not only to become self-realized but also to become the medium for the Lord's words. Every scripture written or passed down through the word of mouth was delivered by Gabriel to the prophet.

Let us give a more human approach to the whole working of the big boys up there.

So you have the corporate house, started by a very reclusive and elusive thinker. S(H)e is the CEO of the organization. Let us call the company Universal Illusions. So the head honcho is the CEO (Chief Everything Overlord) nicknamed God. S(H)e has appointed extremely able Managing Directors, known as Perfect Masters. The day-to-day functioning is segregated into various Departments of Light.

Why 'Department of Light'? It is because as we humans are made of five elements (actually most of us humans are made of six elements if you count stupidity as an element), angels are made of divine light.

Thus, you have Archangel Michael, Head of Security, Protection and, Records and Documentation. Head of Well-being and Health, Archangel Raphael. Head of Communications and Chief Spokesperson of the CEO, Archangel Gabriel. There are more, but for now let us focus on Archangel Gabriel.

Archangel Gabriel is the face to the voice of the elusive CEO, who is never seen, loves to play the harp which requires tuning, and only communicates with the managing directors and the heads of the various departments.

All communication is handled by Archangel Gabriel. Remember the archangels came before religion. Archangels are not Christians. Zoroastrians have been praying to archangels and angels called Haft Ameshaspandans (Seven Archangels) and angels called Yezatas, thousands of years before the birth of Christ and long before Moses. The Hindus have Sapt Rishis (Seven Sages) who are as ancient as the archangels mentioned by Prophet Zarathustra.

I believe that the Seven Sages are the Archangels. I am of the opinion that even Christianity believes in Seven Archangels as do the Muslims. The number seven is important in the world of spirituality, the occult and the paranormal. Seven chakras, seven notes in music, seven colours to the rainbow, seven dimensions, seven figures taken home by movie stars to promote a soap that gives no lather, and so on and so forth.

But I don't believe there are only Seven Archangels. I believe that there are many who work, whose names are not revealed or revealed to those mediums who keep silent or go about working with the archangels, known popularly, or silently, as the archangels don't desire anything but to serve the Lord.

You have Zoroastrians, Hindus, Jews, Christians, Muslims and other religions who believe that the Lord created archangels and angels to oversee the functioning of creation and help the psychotic species with a self-destructive DNA called mankind to move towards the light.

Archangels follow the word and directive of the Lord. Christianity doesn't advocate praying to archangels while Zoroastrians have detailed prayers seeking them, seeking Their intervention, help and love.

Many believe that Gabriel is not an archangel as often there is a debate that in the Bible, the New Testament, only Michael is called an archangel. But I wonder how it matters, as here you have Gabriel who is the voice of God.

Back to Archangel Gabriel.

Thus, when S(H)e wants a message to reach somebody, a personal intimate message, could be a word or a complete document, Gabriel delivers the communication. It is thus believed that Prophet Moses was visited by Archangel Gabriel and given the commandments. Mother Mary was informed by Archangel Gabriel that She would, through immaculate conception, bear within Her womb, Lord Jesus. The entire Koran was dictated by Archangel Gabriel to Prophet Mohammed. Hafiz (Avatar Meher Baba's favourite poet), who Himself was a Perfect Master, was twice visited by Archangel Gabriel and given the good Lord's message.

During channelling sessions with Baba Sai of Shirdi, often it has come through that the voice of the Lord can be heard only via the soul and that the soul should be so clear, so light, so open, that even a sigh of a dying dewdrop can be heard. The soft voice of the Lord is for all but unfortunately, most of us are so caught up with the loud sound of power, ego, money, lust, jealousy, envy and fear, that the poor Lord can speak till His spiritual toes become maroon in colour, but we ain't going to hear a damn.

Also, each one of us wants to put a face to our Lord. The Lord is complete pure energy, with no shape, size or wardrobe. One can ask why would prophets need Archangel Gabriel to communicate the Lord's message? They are pure, Their soul pristine, always on the wings of the eternal divine song.

True, but remember that the language of the Lord is through the soul. Even prophets need a sign, a voice, a persona, to assuage the doubt tearing within Themselves that They are not imagining something, that They are not going nuts, that They are not going mad (as this is repeatedly told to them by the public that doubts, accuses, ridicules Them). Prophets don't have it easy. They stand alone during Their time and era, speaking something unheard of to people who want to cling on to prejudice, superstition and false age-old upbringing. The prophets don't have it easy. They are anyway already ridiculed, beaten and spat on because of what They believe and speak. They, too, need more than soul talk. They need to believe that They haven't lost the plot. Thus, most prophets have gone away into seclusion and come back enlightened. Of course false prophets have gone into seclusion and come back either stoned or completely nuts, but we are talking of the big boys.

In Their meditation and seclusion, Archangel Gabriel has come through and spoken to the master or child of God. Sometimes He has come often, like for Prophet Moses. Gabriel came for decades, slowly dictating the Koran, while to Mother Mary He came through once and told the Mother of the immaculate conception and arrival of Christ through Her.

Every time you and I beseech our God, Goddess, master to come through, the words come through via the Archangel Gabriel (each religion may have a different name for archangels, but all focus on His energy, which is important).

Each time you want a word from God, Goddess or master, beseech Archangel Gabriel to intervene and put forward your appeal to the elusive CEO and trust me, the message will be delivered, some way or the other; in prayer, meditation, dreams, even via the mouth of a child or the badly edited newspaper.

Gabriel comes through when one writes, talks, sermonizes the word of God. Thus, for those into spiritual writings, calling out to Archangel Gabriel is truly important. For all those in communication seek the help of Archangel Gabriel. Psychics, healers, mediums, those in the realm of light work, call out to Archangel Gabriel and you will see, hear and feel the divine presence.

Each one of us who wants a message some time or the other, a confirmation of being loved and heard, doubts to be assailed through a word, a thought, a dream, call out to Archangel Gabriel. When life becomes unbearable and there seems to be no light even at the end of the tunnel, a soft word of hope, is like finding an oasis in the desert of life.

Also being the messenger of God, one can seek glimpses of the future if one calls upon Gabriel. Also when fear, doubt, hopelessness, clouds the light, call upon Gabriel, as a word from the harpist can clear darkness and the feeling of defeat, helplessness and the futility of existence. Gabriel is called upon when one needs guidance for the future. Michael who is in charge of all the *akashik* records works in tandem with Gabriel, and thus, a glimpse into the future, a good word from the Lord and darkness flees, dewdrops of hope spring forth and a spring to one's faith envelopes us with comfort, strength and most important of all, hope.

I know for certain that when one channels, it is Archangel Gabriel who comes through. It is He who speaks the master's or the Lord's words. Explains, counsels, heals and guides. The Lord and the master speak through parables, thus a line can mean so much more. It is the archangel who then explains the meaning via the medium or the writer or the counsellor or healer. Archangel Gabriel is the one who then articulates the words and the meaning.

I was told just the other day in channelling by Baba Sai of Shirdi that the books that speak on God and the other side and the realms and dimensions, all are spoken through Archangel Gabriel. The master in a few lines details what needs to be passed on and it is the archangel who goes through the labour of slowly making the book take shape and also sees to it that it reaches the desired people who need the word.

Enough of my two-bit rambling. Archangel Gabriel is also called Gibril and Jibril. Many believe Gabriel is a woman just as Archangel Michael is a man, but how does gender enter the realm of archangels when it is very clear that archangels are made only of light. How does one put gender to divine light.

Gabriel means 'God is my strength'. So, first there was the word and through the word everything followed and it is His word or the eternal truth which shall set you, me and everybody free. The word is the truth which will set us free. Archangel Gabriel carries the word and thus God is my strength, as, in the word of God lies all the strength and freedom.

Damn, I have begun rambling again. Not good.

In both the Old Testament and the New Testament, Archangel Gabriel is mentioned. In the Old Testament, Archangel Gabriel comes forth to Prophet Daniel, explaining to Daniel the meaning of certain visions which the prophet had seen and needed more clarity on them.

Gabriel appeared to Zecharias predicting the birth of John the Baptist and as mentioned above, to Mother Mary, announcing the birth of Lord Christ. In Islam, Archangel Gabriel who is called Jibrai'il, dictates the Koran to Prophet Mohammed over a few decades. In fact, it is said that the very manner in which Muslims pray all over the world, their posture and all that they do was first taught and shown by Archangel Gabriel to Prophet Mohammed. He tells Prophet Mohammed, 'I was ordered to do so (to show exactly how the prayers are to be done to Prophet Mohammed).' Who could have ordered Gabriel but the Lord?

There is the beautiful passage where Prophet Mohammed tells one and all about His spiritual, astral and causal cleansing. 'While I was at Mecca the roof of my house was opened and Gabriel descended, opened my chest, and washed it with *zam-zam* (holy water) water. Then he brought a golden tray full of wisdom and faith and having poured its contents into my chest, he closed it. Then he took my hand and ascended with me to the nearest heaven . . .'

In 1 Enoch 40:9[6], when Enoch inquires who the figures standing in front of Him are, He is told, 'This first one, is the Holy Michael, the merciful and long-suffering. And the second, who is in charge of all the diseases, and in charge of all the wounds of the sons of men, is Raphael. And the third, who is in charge of all the powers, is the Holy Gabriel. And the fourth, who is in charge of repentance and hope of those who will inherit eternal life, is Phanuel.'

So, as you can see, Gabriel is in charge of all the powers, as first there was the word and all the power comes from the word and Gabriel delivers the word of God and thus Gabriel is in charge of all the power that comes from the word.

How casually we take our words and how often we slander and waste the breath of God and Gabriel. Hmm . . . not good.

One of the most beautiful and profound stories I read while going through the works on Gabriel is His intervention and His presence in the life of the poet and Perfect Master, Hafiz. It's a love story that for once doesn't end in divorce or lifelong spiritual growth, which is a polite term for the long-misunderstood institution called marriage.

Hafiz, it seems, was considered very small in stature and would be ridiculed for His looks. Many were even petty enough to call Him ugly. He was twenty-one years old and had already memorized the complete Koran. He had begun to write poems under a pen name. He worked in a bakery though He was well versed in many languages and was very good in both mathematics and astronomy. He worked all day and studied at night. Since He was thirteen He had read most of the works of famous poets and also read and studied the lives and works of the Perfect Masters. His colleagues at the bakery knew about His writing poems and men being daft and filled with a certain false sense of bravado and ill-placed manhood would make fun of His poems and the way He looked. So it is suffice to say that Hafiz was not happy.

One day He was asked to deliver bread in a locality infested with the very rich. There He saw this beautiful woman. Her beauty took His breath away. Her name was Shakh-i-Nabat, the literal translation being the 'branch of a sugarcane', and why anybody in God's name would name their daughter a sugarcane or a branch of it is a topic of debate best left for another essay, but Miss Shakh was awe-inspiring to look at and Hafiz could barely breathe. This usually happens to me when I sit with my chartered account and he tells me how much I owe the government of our beautiful country in the form of income tax.

Hafiz, since that moment, could do nothing but think of Miss 'Branch of Sugarcane'. He began to write poems about her. He knew His chances of having this ethereal beauty love Him were not very promising but He could little help Himself. When your own heart no longer belongs to yourself what can one do? To make matters worse, Hafiz bhai came to know that His love was to be married to a prince.

It was then that He remembered Baba Kuhi and the promise He had given to His followers. Baba Kuhi was a Perfect Master and a poet who lived in Shiraz and took samadhi in 1050 or there about.

The promise Baba Kuhi had made was if anybody could stay awake for forty days and also forty nights, but the nights spent by His *mazar*, would be granted the gift of immortality, poetry and anything that the heart desired. Hafiz, so much in love with the lady of His dreams, decided that the only way He could win the woman, was to spend forty nights near Baba Kuhi's place of eternal wakefulness. I am not sure if each night one had to light a lamp or *diya* but that could be so.

Thus, He would work at the bakery, pass by the house of Shakh and spend the night, awake, most often praying, near Baba Kuhi's samadhi (and light the lamp, I think, each night). Now a strange thing took place. Shakh-i-Nabat had heard a few of the poems Hafiz had written in praise of her. She had begun to observe Hafiz pass by her house each day, and she realized that with each passing day He seemed more tired but there was something about Him which made her slowly yearn for Him.

Virtually on the thirty-ninth day, when Hafiz had to spend just one more night awake next to Baba's samadhi, she walked up to Him and told Him that she would rather marry somebody who loved her the way He did and who was profound in His work and expression of the heart and soul than marry a prince. But Hafiz was in a daze. He looked at her, nodded but walked on. He had to finish the forty-day spiritual vigil and light the lamp. I can only imagine how difficult it must have been for Him to move away from this woman who He loved so much that it hurt.

Forty nights eventually passed and Archangel Gabriel came in front of Hafiz in all His glory. It is said that Gabriel gave Hafiz a cup to drink which contained the water of immortality (thus Hafiz, His poems and His spirituality will remain immortal) and by drinking the water He was also granted the blessing of eternal poetry. Now came the time for the third wish to be granted. Anything Hafiz wanted Gabriel had to grant.

Gabriel asked Hafiz what He wanted. Hafiz looked at Archangel Gabriel and realized that this was true beauty. Gabriel, who according to me is covered in golden rays, (though I am aware many say He is covered in white) looked so majestic, so beautiful, so comforting, that Hafiz forgot all about Miss Sugarcane. All He could think about was if Archangel Gabriel is so beautiful, how truly beautiful our Lord and Creator would be?

Hafiz looked at Archangel Gabriel and said, 'Give me God. . . . I want God.'

Gabriel, hearing the words of Hafiz, smiled and directed Hafiz to go to a particular place in Shiraz, to a shop which sold perfumes, owned by Mohammed Attar, who was a Perfect Master, but preferred nobody to be aware of His spiritual stature. Gabriel promised Hafiz that if He would serve Mohammed Attar, selflessly and unquestioningly, a day would come in the future that Hafiz would become God-realized.

Mohammed Attar, the Perfect Master, was awaiting Hafiz. As soon as He saw Him, He embraced Hafiz and told Him to keep writing poetry, keep Mohammed's Godhood as a secret and to obey Him, no ifs and buts.

Henceforth when Hafiz wrote about His master and praised Him, He never mentioned His name but once called His master, rose-coloured.

For forty years Hafiz served His master but His anguish for being away from God and realization of God, had ravaged His very soul. What He thought was a journey of a few years had gone on for four decades.

One day Hafiz could take it no more and He wept near His master and Mohammed Attar asked Him the reason for such anguish and tears and Hafiz cried out that for forty years He had served and served without a doubt and question, and what had He got in return? The master smiled and told Him to be patient and He would get the answer and Hafiz looked at His master and said, 'I was certain You would tell me exactly this.' He got up and left the shop.

Ironically, forty years hadn't passed but exactly forty days were left to complete the forty-year period after Hafiz had met His master for the first time. Hafiz went home and drew a circle around Himself. He had decided to remain in the circle for forty days till He got what His very soul yearned for.

This is something that Sufis, including Avatar Meher Baba's father, have done or tried to do, to obtain spiritual grace. It is called 'Chehel-a-Nash-ini' where the spiritual seeker sits in self-imposed confinement, never leaving the circle, no matter what, for forty days, no food or water, for no reason, in the hope that when the forty days are over, God grants any and every spiritual desire sought.

Once again Hafiz succeeded and managed to remain in the circle and Archangel Gabriel was sent by God, to yet again meet Hafiz.

Gabriel was aware why Hafiz had drawn the circle and what His heart truly desired, yet He asked of Hafiz: what did the great, noble, renowned poet want? And Hafiz smiled and said, 'I only want to wait on the pleasure of my master's wish.' In other words, 'I only want to love and serve my master and His wish is my command.'

Hafiz ran out of the circle and reached the home of His master, who was waiting for Hafiz. The master embraced His child and made Him drink wine that was two years old. The moment He drank the wine, Hafiz became God-realized. Hafiz lived in the body for another eight years, a God-realized soul.

Three things are clear from this above narration. Hafiz eventually realized that the master comes even before God and nothing comes before loving and serving the master. Second, both times it is Archangel Gabriel who comes forth, not Baba Kuhi or the Creator, to grant Hafiz's wish, which shows in the hierarchy of archangels, where Archangel Gabriel truly stands. Third, the two-year-old wine—they don't make that wine no more.

How many Archangels are there, the good Lord above knows, but I am certain, if you call out to Them, with name or without, They will be there, standing by you, nurturing you, protecting you, healing and counselling you, helping you to move towards the light. Archangel Gabriel is the one who speaks the word of the Lord. Call out and be silent and hear the words pour through, into the very silent abyss of your soul and higher self.

Archangel Gabriel, like all angels, belongs to nobody but anyone who truly yearns, believes and calls out with faith to him, the archangel comes forth in all divine glory.

It is all about faith. The foundation of heaven, with God and Goddess, masters and archangels and all light workers, are balancing on the pillars of true love and complete faith.

All else is shadow boxing.

A prayer Baba Sai of Shirdi has given for Archangel Gabriel is:

I beseech You, Archangel Gabriel, to help me hear the Lord's voice.

The sound of the world has silenced the voice of the Lord.

Help me hear the words that come from Him, the source and comforter.

I pray to You, Archangel Gabriel, that what I speak be the words that make the Lord happy and proud of us,

Let His voice and mine speak the same language of love, faith and surrender.

I beseech you to make His words resound in my very soul thus helping me speak what He wants of me.

Archangel Gabriel, the way You showed the path to the prophets and to the mother of Christ, Mary,

Show me the path too, am lost, flawed and weak.

Strengthen me with the comfort that comes forth from the Lord, our Father and Mother, who are in heaven and in our very soul.

Help me, Archangel Gabriel, to live a life that is pure and truthful, but brave and courageous too.

Do not let me go astray from the path but always guide me with your calm and strong words to walk the path.

When wrong, show me the way,

When lost let me hear Your guidance,
When weak let Your words strengthen me,
When proud, Your sigh humble me,
When astray lead me back to the Lord, our Father and Mother, in Heaven and in our very heart and soul.
Give me the power of speech,
Give me the power of divination,
Give me the blessing to guide myself and my loved ones,
Give me the selflessness to voice Your words for the weak and downtrodden,
Let the words of the Lord be my words through You, Archangel Gabriel.
Say a good word for me, my loved ones, my ancestors, for the weak, ill, aged, lonely, abandoned and all those in the spirit plane and those who are languishing in between.
Archangel Gabriel, who stands close to the Lord, speak for the dumb and the mute,
A word from You will set right all that which has gone wrong
Be by my side Archangel Gabriel,
By the side of all those who work for the Light and the Lord.
So be it as I pray,
Archangel Gabriel, the voice of God, the strength of God, the master's voice, be with me, now and forever, beyond the beyond.
Amen . . .

4

The Silent Avatar . . . Meher Baba

Illustration by Pooja Bangia

The first time I saw Avatar Meher Baba's photograph was at Dr Meheru Vagchhuipwalla's clinic. An elderly man, with a broad smile, hands folded, as though in prayer or beseeching all of mankind not to worry and be happy. Often when I used to sit in her clinic, waiting for our turn, I would look at Him and no matter how tired or troubled I was, I couldn't help but smile back at Him and I would often tell Him, 'You keep smiling while I have the shit kicked out of me.'

One day Meheru asked me to place an advertisement in one of the Zoroastrian newspapers. It was the Avatar's birthday and it was a simple advertisement wishing Him and seeking His blessings. Financially, I wasn't doing too well those days but for some reason I didn't have the heart to take money from her and I lied to her saying that the publishers didn't charge me anything. She loved Meher Baba with all her pure heart. Her love for Him was humbling. It was obvious when you heard her talk about Him.

So around twenty years ago by default, I wished Avatar Meher Baba a very happy birthday. About seven years later once again by default, I landed up being commissioned to write a book on the paranormal. Now when I look back, I realize that there are no defaults or coincidences. If somebody is truly daft, like me, the cosmos has to rub his nose into the ground, to create circumstances to bring about change or to put the buffoon on the right path.

It was then that I met Vira Kheshvala, a medium to Avatar Meher Baba. The first day I met her, she looked at me and said, 'Are you not too young to write about the paranormal?' and I told her, 'I do not know about being young or not but I know one thing, I am certainly not too young to be bankrupt.'

The next week she called me over and said she had communicated with Meher Baba and He had informed her that as she and her group of mediums weren't taking the responsibility of writing a book about Him and the paranormal, He had sent me to write the book and that is how *The Last Marathon* came about.

So for nearly a year, every Wednesday evening, we all used to assemble at Frenny aunty's house, and via the planchette, communicate with Meher Baba. Often I had to bunk the séance and thus I was called by Meher Baba, 'My absconding author'.

It was during this period I not only researched about Meher Baba, Guru Nanak, Kamu Baba, Swami Narayan and my boss, Baba Sai of Shirdi, but also completed the book and as I was anyway researching on the paranormal, I wanted to know if this was mumbo jumbo or the real stuff, so I began to channel Baba Sai. I remember once I was going through a truly disturbing period. I had been told a number of not very pleasant things by very close family members. I was trying my best to keep my chin up and not slide into depression. That night I sat—while the hyperventilating family, the extrovert tortoise and a temperamental dog slept—looking into the sky (in Mumbai it gets difficult to look at the sky, so let me rephrase, I sat looking at the sky through various buildings and neon signs) when I picked up a book on Meher Baba.

I looked at Him and He looked back. The hurtful words were playing havoc within me and I softly told Him, 'Do you agree with what all these psychos have accused me of . . .

am I all that they say?' And then I opened the book. There was just one sentence on that page and all it said was, 'I know who you are and you have a special place in my heart . . . believe no one as you are mine.'

I read this line and shut the book and my tears began to flow. I think after years I must have cried so loudly but then my blasted dog came and began to chew my ankle; the mutt.

The first time I went to Meherabad, I had gone in a bus, packed to the gills mostly with members of my community; lots of laughter, food and abuses. The next day was Meher Baba's day of samadhi. I remember seeing the flag fluttering from afar. There was no place in the old dormitory. Thousands of devotees were present. We got down from the bus and stood in a line to pay our respects and our surrender to the Avatar.

It was cold and as usual I hadn't packed right. So our group waited to reach the samadhi and I could hear whispering around me; some spoke about food, some about the cold, some about how they should have booked in advance. Then I saw a number of buses enter and park. Devotees from Andhra Pradesh had arrived. Most of them were poor and so much in love with Meher Baba that I felt humbled in their company. Imagine driving all the way from Andhra Pradesh, in buses. Only Meher Baba's divinity could have held together, leave aside traversing such a long distance, absolutely basic travel conditions; and they stood in the line and all of them were in prayer. Babies in arms, old people, the handicapped, pregnant mothers—all stood quietly and prayed.

I entered the samadhi cottage and He took my breath away. It was a surreal feeling. It always is a surreal feeling. It is always silent.

Even amongst so many people there was silence. Of course I don't believe Meher Baba would have wanted a grave-like silence. If He insisted on silence, I am certain He meant silence of the mind, heart, lower energies; some caretakers can go absolutely outright nuts, trying to maintain silence. I mean a child is a child and to expect a child to be silent is something Meher Baba would have voiced His opinion about in a very unbiblical manner. That night I sat in the open seeing thousands of devotees sitting and praying and suddenly I was asked if I would volunteer for an hour or so. I agreed.

I was taken to the cottage next to His samadhi, where the hospital stretcher on which He was placed and other of His personal effects are carefully preserved. All I had to do was to let a family enter, and after they had paid their respects, allow the next family to enter. That's all.

I began to do so. I would welcome them with 'Jai Baba', a phrase I use for Baba Sai and Meher Baba. After a while something strange happened. The poor people began to touch my feet. I nearly had an out-of-body experience. For the life of me I couldn't understand what was happening. I looked around for help. I saw other volunteers, and they were official volunteers and nobody touched their feet. Why would these poor people touch my feet? I was far younger to most and it kind of overwhelmed me.

After an hour or two, an official volunteer came over and thanked me and I found a place under the sky and sat down. With me were a few people who I knew and I guess they, too, had noticed the poor touching my feet. I inquired if this feet-touching stuff was customary and one old man looked at me and said something which I will never forget. He said, 'These poor people who are here haven't ever been treated with love and respect by our so-called class of people. Seeing you treat them with so much love and respect, they could only show their love by touching your feet.'

Imagine going through life being treated without respect so that the slightest sign of love and respect makes the poor feel obligated to touch the feet of a perfect idiot.

Thus, on that day, nearing dawn, on 31 January, exactly thirty years after Meher Baba took samadhi, without speaking a word, He taught me the importance of oneness, love, humility and respecting all; but as is His style, in complete silence.

Avatar Meher believed and demanded two things from His disciples and those who claimed to belong to Him. First and foremost, complete obedience. His word was the law. His philosophy was simple. An avatar or a Perfect Master knows what is best for His or Her child, not only for this lifetime but beyond the beyond. There are no ifs and buts where surrender is considered.

As Baba Sai of Shirdi in channelling so often has said that, 'One cannot be partially pregnant, either, you are or you are not, thus, faith and surrender too can't be done in measures. Either you have faith and surrender or you don't.'

Thus, Meher Baba who was tenderness personified would not expect anything but complete surrender and obedience. He was a hard taskmaster. His inner circle, called the *mandali*, who lived with Him for over forty years, did not have it easy. If He said wake up at four and have a cold water bath in winter and then set a timetable of dos and don'ts, either you obeyed or you were free to get on with your life, and come and visit Meher Baba as a normal devotee.

A devotee lives in the world, with the master or avatar, as an integral part of life. In the five-course meal, the master is one dish. It may be the most important dish but there are four other dishes—family, career, social obligations and friends, dreams, desires and aspirations. Thus for a devotee a master is all smiles, tenderness, calmness, and softness. The avatar or master is aware that in the scheme of things the person has his or her plate full and still clings on to the master, due to love, faith or fear. Most often that is why the devotees always feel that the master is gentle and like a loving, kind parent or grandparent. Most books written about avatars or masters are for devotees and usually written by devotees.

For a disciple, if life is a five-course meal, then the master is all the five dishes. Or there are no five dishes, there is only one dish, often cold and uncooked, and sometimes most delicious, all meant for the highest good of the disciple. For a disciple, life begins and ends with the guru. No ifs and buts. His or Her word is the law and commandment. If the disciple isn't staying with the master then too, the master is the 'be all and end all'; there is nothing beyond the master, everything revolves around the guru.

But, if the master or avatar is in the body, and the disciple is one of the inner circle, then for the disciple there is no family, career, likes, dreams, aspirations, wants; there is nothing but the master. His or Her word is the law. The disciple has left the world to follow and merge with the master. Here, at times, the master will be more tender than the morning dewdrop, and at another time be far harder than steel or the strongest blasted metal discovered or not discovered by mankind. Sometimes like a glass of cool water whilst walking through the desert and sometimes like hot embers under your feet. Often the master might appear even cruel, like a tyrant, but if the master is genuine, then the master comes from mercy, hard love . . . knowing what is best for the child or lover or disciple.

Meher Baba is the Avatar, so He took surrender to another level. The hardship that His inner circle experienced itself can fill a volume or two. Like all masters, Meher Baba, before He decided not to speak any more, had a vociferous vocabulary of swear words. He could abuse them and next minute pamper them, love them and drive them up the wall, embrace them and thrash them. What He expected out of them was humanly not possible and often exasperating. He would test them, say one thing and then say something which was completely the opposite, hours or months later. He would make them work to construct a building and drive them up the wall and be merciless Himself, and just when everything was virtually complete, abandon the building and move lock, stock and barrel to another place, no explanations given. But the fact that the inner circle gave up family, comfortable lifestyles, name, society, money, reputation, everything, to follow Him for the rest of their lives, shows how much they loved Him and recognized who He truly was.

Remember Meher Baba never stopped anybody from maligning Him. He stopped His lovers from defending His name. He would never say a word against anyone who thought ill of Him or abused Him. He said one needed 'negative and positive' to light a bulb and thus the negative was as important for the light to spread. Articles were written ridiculing Him and He would smile and say even the one slandering Him was doing His work. It was all well for Him but His inner circle found it hard to take it in such a Christ-like manner. Not only was He being maligned but they were being ridiculed too.

Then, the need to travel in the most basic way, always third class (in those days there was a third class compartment which was also called 'cattle class' by many people). Meher Baba always travelled in the most humble manner even though sometimes there were people who were willing to sponsor a more comfortable manner of travel for Him. He travelled the length and breadth of the country and the world, but always in the manner of the poorest and then His need for all to fast or observe silence.

Thus, one needed to completely annihilate one's ego and one's upbringing and one's way of thinking if one wanted to be with Meher Baba and be included in His inner circle. Remember, most of the people who belonged to His inner circle were educated and from middle or upper middle class families. They were well read and also were people of the world, but they readily gave up everything to follow Baba and His word.

So when the Bible says, 'first there was the word', I guess it means that first there was obedience and surrender.

Along with complete surrender, Baba expected complete and selfless love. His disciples and inner circle obviously loved Him to an extent that nothing and nobody mattered but Him, but Meher Baba expected even His devotees to selflessly love Him. He was clear about one thing. He wanted nothing and nothing at all but selfless love from those who followed and worshipped Him.

Even here, He didn't make it easy for anybody. He was clear that He wasn't in the body to perform miracles. The greatest miracle is to love the avatar or the master or the Creator (whichever name one chose to call Him or Her) without seeking anything in return. If only you can love your master without wanting anything in return, not even liberation, and love Him or Her because you truly love the master, then that love is noble and selfless. If there is an iota of want in that love, then it's like mixing a drop of lime juice in milk; the milk curdles; and you can only hope you like lots of cottage cheese.

That is why He operated mysteriously and mystically and behind the curtain. Unlike Baba Sai of Shirdi and Tajuddin Baba, who went about creating miracles countless times a day without an iota of fuss or false grandeur. The departments and memorandum of understanding are always different for masters. Some operate behind the scene, when nobody but a handful of disciples are aware of the master and some are out in the open, temples, adulations and all; thus the portfolio and the working manual is different from master to master.

Meher Baba was clear, if you loved Him, except for annihilating your ego, clearing your karma and giving you

God-realization, don't expect anything else. During His last public appearance, which I think was during the East and West meet, He had made sure pamphlets and letters were sent out to His lovers, through which He made it clear that if anybody came to see Him for better health, the poor bastard would fall more ill. If anybody came for money, bankruptcy would result. Only come because you love Meher Baba and want to see Him with and through love. No ifs and buts. Don't come otherwise. Just come because you can't love and live without seeing Him.

He performed innumerable miracles but never openly. So many people have been put on the path that it is unimaginable. One must know that He had educated people from all over the country and the world as His children and He had lepers and the poorest of the poor as His children and devotees.

All He wanted was love and devotion. He spent countless days and nights in isolation. He always said His main work took place in other dimensions and when in isolation. He went without food for weeks and months and lived in the most basic and humble habitations, the weather irrespective. He worked and toiled ceaselessly but nobody really could fathom His greatness or intensity or His Godhood.

Before He took samadhi, He suffered for seven days and nights. The spasms lifted His body, which made it mandatory for four men from the inner circle to hold Him so that He was not lifted off the bed. He called it His crucifixion.

To stop speaking for forty-four years of one's life; not say a word even when He went through two major accidents (which He had forewarned His believers and followers about) that left His body handicapped and battered; never to speak when He had the most beautiful voice and commanding diction; no longer to sing when He could mesmerize the very angels Themselves, is not something for the mere mortal. Only the Avatar can do all this and that too happily, jovially, and still be able to bring out volume after volume of books on the esoteric nature of spirituality and the very essence of creation and the how and why of spiritual and paranormal life.

I don't think there is any avatar or master who has given such intricate details on life and beyond the beyond and the very nature of creation, the way Meher Baba has.

Another fascinating thing about Meher Baba is that the Perfect Masters, gurus, saints, sages, *mast*s, all recognized Him as the Avatar. All spoke most highly of Him. Whether it were the five Perfect Masters (Sai Baba of Shirdi, Baba Jaan, Narayan Maharaj, Tajuddin Baba and Upasani Maharaj) or the God-intoxicated men called masts (who rarely spoke to anybody, but when They came in the presence of Meher Baba, praised His divinity). They all recognized Meher Baba's Godhood.

But people also doubted Him and laughed at Him. He was so accessible most often that even His devotees did not truly grasp who He was and is and will be so eternally. So often even His disciples and inner circle forgot His Godhood and divinity and thus, often Meher Baba had to remind them, 'I am not this body I am the Avatar'.

I guess when you are not dressed in the uniform of spirituality, when you play and joke and interact with one and all; when there is no pretence; no false grandeur; when you are cleaning the toilet and building a cottage; when you are like one of them; people don't take even the avatar seriously. One needs to live in the Himalayas, speak seriously, not cohabit with too many people, create a mysterious vibe about the self, materialize diet Coke from the air, then, maybe people begin to take the avatar seriously.

According to Him, Zarathustra, Abraham, Rama, Krishna, Buddha, Jesus Christ, Prophet Mohammed were avatars. Meher Baba all His life, I feel had to remind people who He was, the Avatar, not because He cared for adulation but because He wanted His people to take solace and advantage of His proximity; to drink from the spring of Godhood.

Even now, how many people in India know of Meher Baba and worship Him? Does He have temples everywhere? And this is the same *hasti* or personality who was praised by every living master and Perfect Master of His time as being the Avatar, 'God in human form'.

One must understand one thing clearly, that, even when Lord Rama was in the body, except for a few sages (some say seven sages, while some say twelve) nobody recognized Lord Rama as an avatar. Of course the greatest tragedy was that even Lord Rama was unaware of His Godhood. Lord Krishna, too, was known as an avatar while He was in the human body. He had to convince Arjuna of His Godhood by showing Arjuna His divine universal *swaroop* or self. Jesus Christ was scoffed at and eventually crucified because He revealed that He was the son of the Lord. All these spiritual rockstars were not recognized or worshipped then, when They were in the human body; but centuries later, we all accept Their Godhood.

Similarly with Meher Baba, a time will come when the world will realize who He truly is. Anyway, enough of my ramblings.

So who is Avatar Meher Baba?

Meher Baba's father, Sheriar Mundigar had spent His entire life in search of God and His own spiritual evolvement. He had travelled to India (which included the country of Pakistan, a part of India then), Afghanistan and His own land, Iran. Born a Zoroastrian, He had lived and travelled and yearned to be enlightened.

One day out of sheer frustration He decided to do what numerous seekers had tried and most of them had failed. He drew a circle around Him and sat down. It is said that if you say your prayers, voice your affirmation, draw a circle around yourself and sit for forty days, without food and water, not stepping out of the circle, your greatest wish and desire is fulfilled.

The seeker goes through various stages of discomfort and hallucination and visions which force the seeker to step out. Meher Baba's father sat in the circle for thirty days and eventually He could not remain in the self-enforced circle. He went to quench His thirst and fell down unconscious.

A voice woke Him up telling Him that what He sought He would receive through His son. Sheriar felt He was still hallucinating as He had no intention of marrying. But some time later, He married Shireen, the daughter of His sister's very close friend. There was a big age difference but They lived happily and humbly. They settled down in Poona, now known as Pune.

Merwan was the second of seven children and was born on the 25 February 1894. He was into sports and games, loved detective stories and did well in studies too. He was nicknamed Electricity due to His vibrant nature. To help the poor He and His group of friends would bet on horses, win money and help the poor. That is why Meher Baba all His physical life loved cricket and horse racing. In fact when Karl Umrigar, the talented young jockey passed over, Meher Baba embraced Him in the spirit world and even now Karl communicates with various mediums, serving and loving Meher Baba.

One day when Meher Baba was in college, a Muslim fakir, a Perfect Master called Baba Jaan beckoned Him. She, who never liked anybody touching Her, hugged Merwan and for the next seven to nine months, Merwan spent hours sitting near Baba Jaan.

Often Baba Jaan would ask Merwan to rub or scratch Her back for hours. One day in January 1914, while He was about to leave for home, Baba Jaan again hugged Merwan and kissed Him on His forehead (on the third eye chakra).

She told Him, 'Merwan, You are My beloved son who will shake the world and do immense good for all humanity.'

For the next nine months Merwan behaved like a zombie, completely or partially unaware of His surroundings. What Baba Jaan had done was to initiate the ascent of God-realization and Godhood in our Avatar Meher Baba. She had made a hole in the wall that separates Godhood from the state of duality, revealing His God-consciousness. It was an excruciatingly painful process and Meher Baba used to bang His head against the wall or on the floor with the pain. His father understood the signs but His mother thought Baba Jaan had done some black magic on Her son. She would go to Her mother with the intent of fighting with the Queen Jaan, but forget Her grouse in Her presence and sit for hours discussing Iran, reach home and realize 'What the . . .'.

As Merwan began to slowly get used to the tearing of the veil of duality, He began to spend time with Baba Jaan and She sent Him to Tajuddin Baba and Narayan Maharaj, both Perfect Masters. They both greeted Him with garlands and roses and treated Him with such love that all those who were physically present witnessing this, were shocked at the way the Perfect Masters greeted this young man. Each of Them helped the Avatar's descent into the confines of a man.

Before Merwan was kissed by Baba Jaan, He was a man unaware of His Godhood. Baba Jaan initiated the process of His Godhood—God in human form and Tajuddin Baba and Narayan Maharaj accelerated the process, each one giving Him the help and power that was needed.

Eventually Baba Jaan told Merwan that She had given Him everything but the final key was with Baba Sai of Shirdi, as He was the head of the five Perfect Masters. He holds the supreme power.

When Merwan went to meet Sai Baba along with His friend, they reached Shirdi at night and He was stopped by

muscular men who were instructed to let Baba Sai rest as
He was exhausted by the multitudes of devotees thronging
to meet Him and get blessed by Him. When Baba Sai was
told by Merwan's friend that Baba Jaan had sent Merwan
to meet Him, it seems Baba Sai said, 'No, no, no, it's not yet
time.' He seemed very agitated.

But the next morning He was calm and when He saw
Merwan, who prostrated Himself in front of our Sai, Baba Sai
saw Meher Baba and uttered the word 'Parvardigar' thrice,
which means God and the sustainer of creation. Saying these
words Baba Sai gave Meher Baba, supreme power.

From there, Merwan was directed inwardly by Baba Sai
to go and meet Upasani Maharaj, who was living in the
Khandoba temple according to the wishes of His master,
Baba Sai. The moment Upasani Maharaj saw Meher Baba,
He threw a stone which hit Meher Baba on the exact spot
where Baba Jaan had kissed Merwan.

Thus, Upasani Maharaj concluded what was started
and worked upon by the other four Perfect Masters. Hit by
a stone Meher Baba accelerated the process of Godhood in
body-consciousness and it was then that Meher Baba became
conscious of all spheres including that of the physical.

Meher Baba spent seven years with Upasani Maharaj
regaining all worldly-consciousness, while retaining
consciousness of creation and God-consciousness.

According to Meher Baba, Baba Jaan blessed Him with
infinite bliss, Sai Baba with infinite power and Upasani
Maharaj with the infinite knowledge of God-realization.
'There are five Perfect Masters who sustain Me from eternity.
In every age, when I come, They sustain Me. Sai Baba made
Me what I am; Babajan made Me feel what I am; Upasani
Maharaj made Me know what I am. And what I am, I am!'

In 1921, a group of youngsters deeply in love with
Merwan formed His mandali. They lovingly called Merwan,
Meher Baba. The mandali left their family and comfort

and surrendered to the will and love of Meher Baba. A year later, Meher Baba and His mandali lived in a home named *Manzil-e-Meem* (House of the Master) in Bombay (Mumbai).

The followers realized how difficult it was to surrender to the master. Meher Baba was a hard taskmaster and it was here that the men were separated from the boys. Those who survived the ego crushing, pride numbing, small self-annihilating experiences remained with Meher Baba all their physical life.

In 1923 or so they all moved to a beautiful place a few miles away from Ahmednagar and called it Meherabad meaning 'the master flourishes always'. It was during this period that Mehera Maa, too, re-entered Meher Baba's life and would be Radha to the modern Krishna.

Life was hard. Water was always scarce. The funny thing was that the mandali had to face severe water problems but if farmers came from far pleading for water and rains, Meher Baba would bless them and their water scarcity issue would be over. They would come to thank Baba and the mandali would look on aghast that all Baba had to do was bless them with water and lo, there was water, but they had to go through excruciating discomfort without water and the master would smile and bear the discomfort too, but there would always be a shortage of water. This is Meher Baba. He never made His life easy and those who loved Him realized that in one lifetime every karmic debt of theirs would be squared up; there would be no comfort but yes, they would always have the master with them going through the same or more discomfort.

On 10 July 1925 Meher Baba began His silence, which ended according to certain members of the inner circle a day before He took samadhi. His logic was simple. He had come countless times and spoken and spoken but nobody truly heard Him. This time He would make His lovers hear

Him loud and clear through the power of silence. For a while He used to write. He gave that up and began to use the signboard and eventually gave that up too and used sign language. The strange thing was that His followers understood everything He spoke silently. The power of silence is louder, clearer and permanent.

He opened various institutions but after a while would shut them, as His logic was clear. The work done on the physical plane was a mini model of the larger work being done by Him in the spiritual and paranormal arena. If that was completed He had no interest in being tied down to anything. He didn't care for what anybody thought about Him. He was only interested in the complete well-being of all of creation.

His seclusions began. He would fasts for months living in a small cage or hut, without water or electricity, not coming out, doing His work in various planes. At the most He would have one cup of tea in the whole day and fast like this for months. All the while His mandali were given orders to do certain work, or fast or serve and He expected His orders to be obeyed.

In the 1940s, He began to work with masts or God-intoxicated people. To the lay person They look like mad men but in reality They are so intoxicated with the love for God and dwelling in that love that They have lost all grip on physical duality and reality. They were like the most talented musician who has lost His senses to play music but still lives in the world of ethereal music. Meher Baba would bring Them down to a state where They could use Their powers in helping Him in His astral and causal spiritual work. It was like channellizing Their raw power into constructive use. The mast would and could get violent or abusive, but a whisper in their ear, that Meher Baba had called Them, and They became like sheep and would praise Baba to one and all. They recognized His Godhood.

Baba would bathe Them, feed Them, nurture Them and then spend hours and nights sitting with Them and doing His work with Them. His favourite mast was called Mohammed who took samadhi in 2003. I was fortunate to meet Him and spend half an hour with Him. I remember being told that He could be really temperamental but for some reason when I met Him, He held my hand for a while and smiled. His hand felt as smooth and cold as a slab of marble. He even allowed Himself to be photographed with me and another friend. I wish I still had that photograph.

Baba also spent lot of time taking care of lepers. He would bathe them, wash their feet often, dry their feet and kiss their feet and present them with clothing and blankets and food to eat.

He travelled the length and breadth of the country and went to America and United Kingdom, where He was courted by Hollywood too and He remained who He was, calm, jovial and always clear that the purpose of mankind was to help those in need and seek their own realization.

In 1949, He embarked on a journey called 'The New Life'. He selected twenty followers who were called companions to join Him on a journey of complete hopelessness, helplessness and aimlessness. During this period of a few years they begged for their food and lived and travelled like paupers. He did this to share the suffering of countless poor people all over the world. If the Avatar starves, countless eat. If the Avatar is homeless, innumerable are sheltered. If the Avatar is naked, limitless are clothed. I wonder if the twenty companions really knew how privileged they were. But there was only one rule. The boss is always right and must be obeyed no matter what.

He had also made it clear to all His followers all over that, if by chance they would meet Meher Baba, they should turn and walk away. Not to talk to Him and not to try and help Him and ease His discomfort and the most important rule for those who had joined Him was that all should be in a state of complete acceptance of all the circumstances and situations in their new life, be in a state of perpetual cheer and happiness no matter how harsh or humiliating the difficulty or experience. He wanted to teach the world that even if one was the poorest beggar, one could still live with joy, happiness and dignity.

The darn giants have gone.

He ended the New Life with a completely exhausting phase of seclusion and then once again entered the public glare, meeting His devotees and travelling.

He had two major accidents. He had told one and all that His blood has to spill on foreign land and in India. The first accident took place in America, bang in the centre of America, Oklahoma, where seconds before the accident Baba seemed to be directing the entire event. He was thrown out of the car and landed on His back in a ditch with blood flowing from His broken nose, a broken arm and a leg while Mehera Maa was hurt the most with a very severe gash on Her head. Doctors were surprised She lived through the accident.

The second accident took place in 1956 while after watching a cricket match He and His few inner circle people were returning to Meherabad. Baba seemed to be aware both times of the looming accidents as His mood before the accidents was intense and sombre.

Fifteen miles outside Satara, just minutes before the accident, His fingers were at work, His face serious. The car seemed to lose control and there was a major collision. Baba was covered in blood. His hip bone was fractured, His tongue was torn, and there were bad bruises on His face and legs. But when Vishnu, one of those who was least hurt in the car, went towards Baba, he saw a brilliant light emitting from Baba's face—as though some very important work had been accomplished.

'I have never in my life seen such utter radiance and lustre as was on Baba's face then! He was like a king, a victorious king who had won a great battle. Lord Krishna must have looked like that in his chariot on the victorious battlefield. The radiance was blinding! I could see nothing else, not the car, nor the surroundings, only Baba's face in glorious triumph!'

Eruch, Pendu and Nilu, Baba's inner circle, had been thrown out of the car. Nilu died and Pendu was unconscious with his leg broken. Nilu had always told Baba that he wanted to die in Baba's presence and his death should be quick. So be it.

Obviously, Baba had taken on immense suffering for all mankind, but remember, those who had vowed to love and follow Him, too, had partaken in the universal work. Many times people assume that if they are travelling or living with the master they are protected and secure. The damn fools. Once the master enters your life your real problems start, as the master is only interested in cleaning us up. He is the biggest dhobi.

Baba never really recovered after the second accident. The doctors were sure that He would never walk again, but our Avatar did walk, though always with a limp and His physical body deteriorated after that, but He was happy. A very important job had got accomplished!

He had warned all about this accident jokingly saying that they may all die in a few days. Nobody took it seriously.

Strangely, a short while after this accident, two of Baba's close friends and spiritual brothers passed over, Saint Gadge Maharaj who loved Meher Baba immensely took samadhi and six days later Mast Ali Shah left His body.

Often people would ask Baba as to how to live a life that would not add on more karmic baggage and also free oneself from karma and bring about liberation and merger with Him, the Avatar.

He would say the simplest way was to take His name (or one's master's name) fourteen times every day, 'Not more, not less than fourteen times. Then you will come to Me. Even fourteen times is difficult.'

He meant to take the name fourteen times, with complete love, devotion and surrender was difficult for most people.

'If you cannot do this, then do this much. When about to breathe your last, repeat My name, and come to Me. This too is hard to do unless you start repeating it or loving Me from now on, every second of your life. If you do not do it, you will not be able to remember Me in your last moments. Even if this is not possible, there is a last recourse which might help you. It is to do selfless service for others, as I am everywhere, in all and in everything. Service for the sake of service is selfless service. If you do this, under all circumstances and regardless of what happens, it will bring you to Me.'

He was also of the opinion that God can forget the most horrendous sins but there is one thing even God cannot forgive. 'Remember one thing: God is all-merciful. He is eternally in bliss. He cannot forgive one thing, and that is posing. Being a scoundrel, if one pretends to be a saint, God will not forgive it.'

In 1969, after the middle of January, His health began to slowly deteriorate. He was already aware of His passing over as He had jokingly asked His mandali whether it was fine if He gave darshan to the thousands of His disciples and devotees lying down with his head slightly raised. There was a big gathering taking place in some time and all were worried if He would be able to stand the strain of such exertion. Nobody realized that eventually He would give His darshan lying down, head slightly raised, in a state of samadhi, just a few days from then on.

The spasms began. They sometimes went on for hours with seconds or few minutes of respite. His body would virtually be lifted off the bed. His inner circle was with Him and nobody could see the pain. He would keep reminding the mandali that He was not the body but He had to take the pain and suffering of all His children. He said to them that as Christ, He was crucified once, but in this present form as the Avatar, He was being crucified countless times in a day.

But strangely when Mehera Maa would come to see Him, Baba would be all smiles. No spasms during Her visit to Baba. The moment She would leave, the spasms would start. It was as though He did not want Mehera Maa to see His suffering, but His suffering too was at His beck and call. He had already passed Mehera Maa the message, 'Mehera be brave.'

Also, as usual, when the doctors would walk in He seemed fine. This was a trend through the two accidents too. When the doctors would come, He would be fine. The moment they left, the pain would begin. It was as though He wanted to suffer unhindered.

It seems Baba uttered two words in these seven days and they were '*Yaad rakh . . .*' which means 'Always remember . . .' and He gestured, 'I am not this body.'

In the morning, on the 31 January 1969, hours before He took samadhi, Baba called for the board on which Baba's favourite poet Hafiz's three couplets were written.

I am the slave of the master who has released me from ignorance; whatever my master does is of the highest benefit to all concerned.

Befitting a fortunate slave, carry out every command of the master without any question of 'why' and 'what'.

About what you hear from the master, never say it is wrong; because, my dear, the fault lies in your own incapacity to understand Him.

Baba's body was kept in the Samadhi House, open for seven days. Thousands of His followers came to have a

last glimpse of their beloved Avatar. The trains passing by
would sound their horn in honour of the silent one.

He had kept His promise of giving His darshan to His
lovers, lying down, head held high.

Avatar Meher Baba Ki Jai.

5

Lord Mahavir

Illustration by Pooja Bangia

I truly wonder how this essay is going to shape up. Lord Mahavir stands for serious self-discipline and hard core austerity. He is the master of asceticism and I hold a very coveted portfolio in the Department of Indulgence.

Thus, I was in two minds to write on Him. Not because of any other reason but darn it, it is like telling an intellectually challenged yak to write on the Laws of Relativity.

I could only read about Him in awe; He was so focused on self-realization, so detached from the body and from all the pull and push of the senses and in complete surrender to whatever karma had in store for Him, as long as the jar of cause and effect got completely empty, not even a crumb was left. Yes, I am certain, there are yogis who go through various austerities for years if not decades, but usually they are defrosting in some swanky cave in the Himalayas, far from the prejudiced glare and temperament of people.

I have known only one Jain family and they really treated me well and welcomed me in their home, in spite of the fact that they were pure, pure, pure vegetarians and in those days I was religiously a dedicated carnivore. I remember being told that the eldest living member of the family, who lived some place else, ate food and drank water only till the sun shone in the sky, so unlike most youngsters nowadays who only wake up to eat, drink, SMS, MMS, surfing and the Facebook, Internet and vegetate when the sun has left the sky; in a very Laloo Prasad Yadav default way, same difference.

I was very young when I was taken to a friend's house and there were many people who were in awe of this extremely handsome man. He actually glowed, and he was on a fast, having had just warm water for over seventy-odd days and he looked at me and smiled and I stood looking at him, in absolute wonder of a man who willingly went hungry for so many days. My friend came and told me that he was starving as he hadn't eaten for three hours, which was loud enough for folks living in the adjacent building to hear. I looked at the beautiful glow which emitted from this man, wanting to apologize for my friend's absolutely unnecessary and unexplainable existence on planet Earth, and he smiled once again at me, and I gave him a smile and walked out of the house with my friend and then swore at him in five different languages. We all have our strengths, I guess.

For Lord Mahavir lived a life of luxury till the age of thirty, to give it all up, and for twelve years to go about without even a bowl of food and water and also without a stitch of clothing on Him, notwithstanding the extreme weather and the ridicule and physical abuses of society was remarkable. Just being within, always in a deep search of 'who am I', I mean when an individual goes beyond His limited self, what a miracle mankind can be!

It is said by the sages and wise men and women in the know, that we are an accumulated mass of karma. Baba Sai of Shirdi often in channelling mentions that a human being is a composition of his or her own karma, inherent nature carried forward through lifetimes and DNA. Now we are said to have three bodies. The physical, the astral and the causal; our karma is encased in the causal body—cause and effect body; our emotions and desires and inherent self are encased in the astral body; and the physical body encases, apart from piss and pus, other parts of the anatomy. Mankind is so full of shit that God in His wisdom had to make our large intestine seven metres or twenty-one feet long, all curled up. I mean why do we need a twenty-one-foot long intestine if we weren't so full of ourselves!

It is believed that all our actions, thoughts, desires, words and intentions lead to the accumulation of karma; good and not so good. Thus, through every lifetime that we have lived, we have accumulated karma, which necessitates one to keep taking birth to go through the karmic grind or karmic fruits. Baba Sai says that when an individual realizes that the only way to stop the accumulation of karma is when an individual stops operating from attachment and results, and starts operating from oneness and complete detachment from the consequences, the results and the gains. When one operates from *seva*, that is, to serve the Lord who exists in every living being and non-living thing, tangible or intangible, and becomes one with the co-existing throb of creation, then the individual stops accumulating karma.

But what is to be done about the accumulated karma, which already exists and which we carry along in our causal body? For that, prayers, charity, meditation, are a must. The divine fire that ensues through prayer and meditation and also by helping those less privileged (but without expecting any reward, including blessings, and without the thought of it erasing the karmic sludge) slowly burns away the karmic balance sheet.

Lord Mahavir understood this law and thus undertook suffering by leaving Himself in the hands of the cosmos to do as it wished with Him.

There is a lot of debate regarding Lord Mahavir's life. Two schools of thought prevail about everything related with His personal life.

So I will write my stuff from my understanding. Whether He came from a princely family or a very rich and powerful family, the fact is that Lord Mahavir was born in an affluent and well-known family. In fact, He was very fortunate

for His father, as, at the moment that He was conceived
the family fortunes increased and thus He was named
Vardhamana, which means 'continuous increase in wealth'.
He was born in the sixth century before the birth of Christ.

He was very brave, strong and well educated. He must
have been very courageous and good at sports as He was
then named Mahavir—'the great warrior'. Why would He
be named by the good people of His town as a great warrior
if He was not great at warfare?

He was very intuitive and took interest in the well-being
of all those around Him. It seems He was married at an
early age to Yashoda and had a daughter by the name of
Priyadarshana, though another school of thought says He
wasn't. But if He lived with His family till He was thirty
years old, I guess it makes sense to believe He was married
and had a child.

He always wanted to go away and find His true self
but the obligations of the family and the insistence of His
parents were like chains around His feet. By the time He
turned twenty-eight, both His parents passed over and His
brother somehow managed to persuade Lord Mahavir to
give up the thought of renunciation. But at the age of thirty
Lord Mahavir told one and all to go boil their heads as He
had had enough of the worldly life and He wanted to leave
everything and go in search of the eternal truth.

When all logic, emotion and money failed to convince
Him, eventually the family had no choice but to agree to His
need for renunciation. So He distributed His share of gold
and land to the poor. The day of His going away was done
in a lot of style and He tolerated it all until a point when He
got down from His carriage, and sat under an Asoka tree,
removed all the rings and chains He wore and forcefully
plucked out His hair. The people still surrounded Him and
then I guess He must have politely told one and all to leave
Him alone. When left alone, He meditated under the tree

for two days and then attired in a simple robe He left to find Himself and the eternal truth. It is not sure when Lord Mahavir did away with the robe too. Some say after the two-day meditation itself, some say after one year and one month. Whatever be the truth, the fact is that Lord Mahavir did not want to own anything, didn't want anything to come between Him and the eternal truth, and thus didn't want anything to do with the material world. He discarded His clothes which were a part of the material world, and for the rest of His life He was naked.

One must understand that Lord Mahavir did not start Jainism. In fact He was the twenty-fourth guru or Tirthankara. Lord Mahavir's family followed the Jain Tirthankara called Parsva, who was the twenty-third guru or Tirthankara.

Now, Parsva had laid down four laws for those who took up *sanyas,* and not wearing clothes was not one of them. Lord Mahavir thus initiated this fifth law and thus even now you have Jain sages who go about Their life with not a stitch on Them.

Without clothes and even a begging bowl, He roamed about in deep contemplation. When He sat for meditation, and He could sit for days, insects clawed up His body, bit Him, and though often in severe pain, He took the pain as the cleansing of His karma. Seeing Him naked, and those days there were innumerable sages roaming about but none naked, the people ridiculed Him and hit Him and threw stones at Him, but He did not mind or say a word to anybody. He was in pain. He was not oblivious to pain. He observed silence for months at a stretch (though the Digambara school of thought insists that He didn't speak for twelve years) and if He got food He ate and if He didn't get food He starved but He took everything as a blessing and as a mandatory requirement for Him to be cleansed off all karma and thus bringing Him closer to the one.

The problem was that Lord Mahavir did not interact with people; He often observed silence. Thus, He didn't speak and when spoken to. He was a naked man walking about with no care about His appearance and hence He was thought of as deranged and thus He was given serious grief by mankind at large.

So, He went through penances to clear off all His karmic backlog. He barely spoke to anybody and to make His life more difficult He had rules about what He ate and drank.

It is said that first and foremost He preferred eating stale food as He wasn't depriving anybody of that food. Then, He accepted dry or cold or moist food, old beans or grain gone bad. If He saw animals, birds, beggars, wanting or waiting for food, He would not beg there, as that would mean that He would be depriving another being of food and hence He would go away from there. He would eat once in two days or three days or four days or five and often went without drinking water for two to six months.

He would meditate night and day and in winter sit in the coldest spot available and in summer the hottest. He wanted to get detached from every discomfort, pain, angst that His body could feel or evoke with Himself. He was hard core.

But the most important part of it all was that He was always calm and had no anger or pride within Him. It was as though He had squeezed out all the filth that accumulates within all of us, in the body, mind and heart and excreted it all and thus was empty of attachment to anything and anybody.

Once some native idiots hit Him badly and then set the dogs on to Him. The dogs bit Him but He didn't retaliate. I mean, where do these masters come from? Truly, there must be some special place these giants come from.

Once the villagers pelted Him with stones and abuses and then once some folks from our country with an ancient heritage of over five thousand years cut Him with sharp objects and pulled His hair out of the roots and Lord Mahavir kept calm and didn't say a word.

The problem which Lord Mahavir faced was not only from the masses but also from other so-called spiritual seekers. They could not understand how a man could live completely naked and also go through so much pain and hardship with complete detachment. So they made His life more difficult.

The ascetic orders followed a few basic laws. In the rains, the ascetic tribe stayed at one place which is something Lord Mahavir would follow most often. Hoarding of anything to eat was a no-no and taking life was obviously out of question. There were certain rules of begging and the usual sacrifices depending on the sect and this was generally it.

Lord Mahavir took sacrifice or *tapas* or austerities to another level. He was clear that austerities didn't have to do only with the physical body but also the mental and emotional. Chastity and meditation were mandatory as only then would the immense backlog of karma be burnt away and He was very forceful regarding not creating new karmas, which very often were made not only by the mind and heart but often by the tongue. Speech was meant to be observed and controlled.

Though Lord Mahavir refused to give importance to taking a bath or living in caves or under a tree and was against eating roots and flowers, He wasn't much into fire worship or smearing the body with holy ash. Thus, there were issues with the ascetic community too. But He remained silent and calm.

If this wasn't enough, the warrior had another dimension to deal with. Lower energies tried their level best to harass Him and waylay Him from His path. He was often physically assaulted by the lower energies and He went through serious physical torture and pain while He would sit for meditation. In His eleventh year or when

He reached the eleventh dimension of His spiritual journey, the lower energies (the Buddhist and Jain people call these lower energies lower God but it doesn't appeal to my limited demented mind . . . I mean God, higher, lower or medium, is God . . . I don't think God would try to harass His own. So I will stick to calling these energies lower energies) went all out to confuse, harass and torture Lord Mahavir.

Often the lower energies entered weaker human beings and gave Lord Mahavir grief. Once it entered an individual who met Lord Mahavir and the former professed to become His devotee. To create hell, our chap, the lower energy bugger, stole something and fair and square laid the blame on the master who as usual quietly allowed many to beat Him up. Another time Lord Mahavir was arrested because he was accused of being a spy. I mean Lord love a defrosted duck, how could anybody arrest Lord Mahavir as a spy? But knowing the workings of a demented and disgruntled negative dimension and mankind, He was arrested and then later released.

Thus, He basically went through hell and back till His twelve years of wandering ended with His entire backlog of karma burnt away and He was filled with the powers of divination and most importantly, that of oneness. Even the Buddhists of those times acknowledge Lord Mahavir's powers of prophecy. He could divine the past, present and the future of anybody, not only those in the physical plane but of those in the spirit and those in between as well.

Some say in the twelfth year and some say in the thirteenth year, Lord Mahavir became self-realized and thus enlightened. For the next thirty years He spread His teachings and created the ground work for Jainism to flourish and also set up a guide book for all those who wanted to follow the path. The most important aspect of Lord Mahavir was that He not only set up a guideline for ascetics but also for families and the common man. He gave importance to women and also gave them the power and realization of following the path.

He was clear that every soul is an independent identity and no two souls are alike, superior or dependent on another being, and that focus on the spirit and detachment from the body is the only way forward. Time and again He emphasized that every being has to blame himself or herself for being miserable. God has nothing to do with all this. Our old man is just an observer. He has made the rules and regulations and whoever follows them gains and who doesn't gets another hole in the anatomy. Burning away one's karma will eventually lead one and all to Godhood, but this is also if the focus is on the spirit and self-realization. He was very tender at heart and thus often said that every living being abhors pain and thus one shouldn't give pain to any being. The practice of non-violence in thought, heart and action is the highest religion. More power to ahimsa.

As a guru He was tender but practical and He wasn't emotional. He answered any and every question and He spent time answering till the doubt disappeared. He wasn't the kind to spend time on chit chat and have light moments. He was always in observance of not creating any karma. He was different. I doubt anybody like Lord Mahavir ever walked this beautiful and abused planet of ours. But He was clear that one did not need an intermediary to achieve godhood. One didn't need to speak in a different dialect. God was within. Burn the karma away and realization is a sigh away.

Lord Mahavir took samadhi when He was seventy years old. He had a community of over fourteen thousand sadhus or monks, thirty-six thousand or more women disciples or nuns, nearly six hundred thousand householders of which more than half were women. So that everything would run smoothly, He appointed eleven chief disciples. He laid the rules and guidelines for each and every thing for each and every body and thus nobody had to use their discretion. All was set by Him. Now follow.

Even now all over the world Jains pray the Navkar Mantra. It's a beautiful prayer.

Namo Arihantanam: I bow to the enlightened souls.
Namo Siddhanam: I bow to the liberated souls.
Namo Ayariyanam: I bow to religious leaders.
Namo Uvajjayanam: I bow to religious teachers.
Namo Loe Savva Sahunam: I bow to all the monks of the world.

Remember when the prayer mentions religious leaders, teachers, monks, the prayer is talking about those who work for the 'oneness family', with true and selfless devotion, the true religious leaders, teachers and monks—not those who do business in the name of the Creator.

A simple prayer by a giant warrior of light—Lord Mahavir.

6

Sarkar Makhdum Shah Baba

Illustration by Sheetal Gandhi Tandon

The first time I heard of Sarkar Makhdum Shah was from a noble man, a good friend, who I call Captain P. A devout Muslim, a very kind-hearted man, my friend was undergoing the worst possible karmic cleansing ever and getting the shit kicked out of him. He would spend hours at Sarkar Makhdum Shah's dargah.

One day I visited him at a friend's place and he looked at me and said, 'You look as though you have gone and done the Haj pilgrimage.'

I kept silent. I physically had not done the pilgrimage but a night prior to that, I had dreamt I was standing in front of the Holy Kaaba.

Okay, before I narrate a few dreams and incidents, I would like to make it clear that I do so only to share my experiences. I take no spiritual credit (I have none, the lawyers of my ex and my very family will vouch I have not a straight bone in my body) and I have no powers (if Sant Dyaneshwar could make a cow, buffalo or a bull, recite the Vedas, then, I guess I too, can see a few dreams and undergo a few oddball spiritual experiences).

Enough of my ramblings.

So, Captain P asked me to describe the dream and I did. I was standing near the Kaaba, and I could feel the texture of the cloth which covered the holy structure. There were two or three layers of shimmering cloth over It. I could feel the heat as it was summer. The lights that hit my eyes were blinding. I woke up after that and did what good men do after such dreams, scratched my head in wonder and lit a cigarette.

Captain P looked at me and said, 'Tell me about the glare.'

I told him the lights were so bright that for a while I could not see.

He smiled and told me that only those who have done the pilgrimage and are fortunate to be acquainted with those in power and in the know, can get so close to the Kaaba and know about the various shimmering coverings on the Kaaba. And only those who have actually stood near the Kaaba can mention the bright lights, as truly, with so many flash bulbs that light up the place, for a while it is difficult to see.

I began to go to Sarkar Makhdum Shah soon after, making at least one visit a month. Those days I had begun to do trance mediumship with the help of Meheru Gandhi. I was already into channelling for the past two years but wanted to experience trance mediumship.

I would go once a week, I think it was on a Tuesday or a Wednesday to Bandra, at Sorabh Adeshir's house, and first I would do a mediumship of healing, where people would come for various physical and emotional health issues, and then I would sit along with one or two others who were getting ready for trance mediumship.

That particular day, I had done two hours or more of channelling at my parent's home in Dadar. Then I did an hour or more of very heavy healing sessions, which always work. But that day I felt that my body had got affected. I could sense it in my gut that something had not gone right, so that day I decided not to sit for trance mediumship.

I asked Meheru Gandhi if I could be excused for the day, but she shut her eyes and looked back at me and said that she had been told, 'Yeh theek nahi hain.'

She told me, 'They feel this is not the right attitude.' What the good lady could not have known was that 'Yeh theek nahi hain' could also have been interpreted as 'This damn idiot isn't well.'

I said fine, let us do it. During the trance mediumship, first Sai Baba of Shirdi would come through. Then Avatar Meher Baba and then would come through this powerful surge of energy, only for emergencies and black magic and stuff like that. I never could figure who the energy belonged too.

Meheru had said it belonged to Makhdum Shah.

Anyway I was feeling depleted. My breathing had become sort of irregular and I sat and we said our prayers and then Baba Sai came through just for a short time and then Sarkar came through. You must understand, when in a trance, you really don't know what's going on. I would feel as though the voices were coming through a fog and I could hear myself speaking and it would sound so unlike me. It is a surreal feeling.

It seems Sarkar Makhdum Shah fired the hell out of everybody present. Poor Meheru got a real harsh scolding. It seems Sarkar told one and all that, 'We told you he is not well and yet you all allowed him to go through the mediumship. His very *praan* (life) is at stake. There is a burn out taking place as We speak. Stop this now.'

Anyway, I came back to my senses (or my non senses) and I looked around. Everybody who was around seemed rather shell-shocked and worried. I really didn't know what had happened. I looked exactly as how Adam, 'the genius with the unhealthy hots for the apple', must have appeared, when the good Lord, with his holy hands on his holy hips, tapping his holy foot, watched our man go all out at the controversial apple and between mouthfuls ask the Lord, 'Now what have I done?'

I reached home, sleeping on the back seat in Yezad's car. That night my entire mouth till my throat within had got covered with ulcers. It was a painful time. I could not talk (which for any married man is a rather normal state of affair), I couldn't eat or drink or even swallow my spit. The worst part of it all was I couldn't laugh. That hurt me.

Four days later I was asked to take a blood test. It was an expensive blood test and when the result came through, the doctor asked me to come over. The doctor was in Dadar so my dad came along with me. I was weak and felt feverish as I had not eaten for four days. The doctor asked me what my profession was. I told him I wrote books and articles. He lifted his one eyebrow like any well-trained Hindi movie heroine. 'Your body has an army within which protects one from diseases. The WBCs protect the body. Your army seems to have gone mad and has begun to attack you.'

'This can only happen to my son. He gets affected with the strangest illnesses,' my all-knowing dad said, offering his medical diagnosis.

'I have researched this and have found soldiers fighting on the border experience similar situations. The body has been put through so much stress that it doesn't know what to do.'

'Your body has gone mad, my son.'

'I would require a biopsy to be done.'

My father's face went pale. I nodded. That night in prayer Baba Sai told me to pack my bags for seven days and go off to Khandala. No medicines. Just His *udhi*, to be taken thrice a day in a little water and that's that.

Next day we were in Khandala. Seven days later there was no sign of ulcers. I had lost fourteen kilos in twelve days. It took me six months or more to recover my strength. My inherent common sense never returned.

A few months later, I had another experience with Sarkar Makhdum Shah. I have mentioned this dream and incident before and it has been published in *The Ramblings of the 110th*, but I rewrite it to make the reader have a personal connect with Sarkar Makhdum Shah.

One night I had a dream where I saw my son, Pashaan, and I, in Hazrat Makhdum Shah's dargah. The Sarkar's shrine is in Mahim, Mumbai.

Now both my son and I were standing in the sanctum sanctorum, where the mausoleum is placed. In the dream I could hear Islamic prayers being chanted. Then the caretakers began to usher everybody out of the sanctum sanctorum, but told us to wait. The doors were shut. Only the caretakers of the dargah, father and son were present. They began to clean the floor with rose water. I could smell the fragrance. Hear the chant. I usually don't remember dreams but strangely I remembered and still remember it after twelve years or more.

Once the floor was cleaned, they cleared the holy tomb off all the flowers and also the holy *chaddar* or holy cloth, offered by devotees that the holy tomb is covered with. Then they removed the top covering of the tomb.

I always thought that the master was placed in the wooden or marble casket which is covered with a lid and that is then covered with the holy chaddar with flowers over it. I was surprised to see that the master's physical body was placed way below in a crevice. I couldn't see Hazrat Makhdum Shah, as it was dark within, but the caretakers put my son and me inside the tomb with the master. Then, the tomb was covered once again. I kept hearing the chants. I was within the tomb, yet I could see all that was going on outside the tomb. After a while, once again the holy chaddar was removed, the lid of the tomb opened, my son and I were brought out and then the lid was put back.

I woke up then.

I had no idea what the dream meant. I mean I had just begun channelling. This whole world of spirits and energy and the occult was new to me. It still is.

I decided to take Pashaan to Hazrat Makhdum Shah and pay our respect and bow down in love, some time in the coming week.

While praying at night I was told by Baba Sai of Shirdi to go to the bedroom and, in a short while the boy got his first convulsion. Within a few minutes, another convulsion.

We rushed him to the hospital and into the emergency ward. With Baba Sai's grace he did not get a convulsion en route. It didn't rain too, which was good as we were on a bike. It was about one in the morning. The moment we told the staff, all young doctors, that he had suffered three convulsions so far and his fever was only rising, I could sense defeat in the eyes and mannerism of the doctors. It was as though they were going through the motions but weren't all there.

They gave my son injections directly into his veins and even on his thigh. He began to have another convulsion and he was in my arms. I don't know why but I knew I was going to lose him. I prayed to Baba Sai of Shirdi and told Him that, 'This is Your child, if You want him with You take him with grace, don't let him suffer, that's all I pray.'

Then my son exhaled. Have you ever heard the sound of death? It is terrifying. It is the loudest sound you will ever hear, the sound of the soul exiting the body. My son rolled his eyes up and exhaled this sound. Then he went limp in my arms. The doctors stepped back. Nobody looked at me, leave aside looking into my eyes. My son, my little curly-haired boy had left his father through the physical body forever. His mother fainted.

It was the longest half a minute ever.

Then like a swimmer coming out of the water, my son came back to life, gasping for breath. The doctors for a few seconds didn't know what was really happening. I told them, 'Do something please,' and then they sprang back to action, confused, but I could sense more confidence now than before.

It struck me early morning that I had admitted my son into Hinduja Hospital. It is on the same road, a few minutes away from Sarkar Makhdum Shah's dargah.

My son was meant to pass over. Only those who have passed over, or as folks say, only those who are dead, are placed in a grave. My son, whose time had come, was placed, not in a grave, but in the master's tomb, and then removed again, well and secure.

His time had come and the ceremony of passing over had taken place, and I had experienced it, but all in the dream state. In the astral world, my son was put down under, but for some reason, he was placed in the master's lap, in the master's tomb.

All the masters are one. Thus, the chant—'La ilaha ill Allah'—in the dream, meaning, there is only one God.

Who is Sarkar Makhdum Shah? He has various titles, Qutb-E-Kokan, Hazrat Shaikh Makhdum Ali Paro Qutb-ul-Aqtab Qutb-e-Kokan, Al-Mahaimi of Mumbai, Hazrat Makhdum Shah Baba. He was at birth given the name Shaikh Ali, but for some reason I have always called Him Sarkar Makhdum Shah.

Sarkar Makhdum Shah's lineage can be traced right back to Prophet Mohammed.

The earliest trace of Sarkar's ancestors is Hazrat Jafar Taiyar who was Hazrat Ali's cousin. Hazrat Jafar was called *Taiyar* as He was known to be like a 'kind parent of the poor and the needy'. He must have been such a noble man that another very evolved soul, Hazrat Abu Huraira, has been known to say that after Prophet Mohammed came Hazrat Jafar Taiyar.

So, Harzat Jafar Taiyar migrated to Ethopia or some African country, where He preached about Prophet Mohammed and Islam to the clueless African king. He came back to the holy city in Saudi Arabia, Makkah Sharif. Prophet Mohammed was so pleased seeing Him that He kissed Harzat Jafar on His forehead and hugged the latter close with a lot of love and affection. The Prophet then said the famous words, 'Man is like fruits of different trees, but Hazrat Jaffer and I (the Prophet) are the fruits of one tree.'

So, one can imagine Sarkar Makhum Shah's lineage, as He comes from the same tree.

Those days when the Prophet physically walked on Mother Earth, war was raging amongst the various tribes in Arabia. He made it clear that if anything were to happen to Commander Zaid Bin Haris, then Hazrat Jaffar Taiyar would take the commander's place and fight the war. Zaid bhai became a martyr and the holy flag was handed to Hazrat Jaffar Taiyar.

In the war that ensued, Hazrat Jaffar's right hand was cut off. Bleeding and badly injured, Hazrat Jaffar dropped His sword and held the flag in His left hand. Unarmed but still marching ahead, His left hand was chopped off too. When both His hands were cut, He knelt and picked up the flag by His chin and rested the flag on His chest with His neck holding the rod of the flag and marched on. He was killed at the age of forty-one and is known as the first martyr in the Islamic jihad and legend has it that instead of His arms, the Lord in His mercy, bestowed Hazrat Jaffar with wings studded with gems and pearls when He entered paradise.

Sarkar's forefathers came to India, like Zoroastrians, to flee from tyranny and to safeguard their religion and culture. Sarkar's family belonged to a tribe called Naita and resided in Medina but had to flee due to the cruelty of Jajjaj Bin Yusuf. Mr Jajjaj Bin Yusuf for some reason lost his head and went nuts and began to kill all saintly folks. In a fit of insanity he killed more than five thousand scholars and saintly folk and thus seeing no other option, many of the Naita tribe packed their belongings and came down to the mouth of the Indus river and made it their home. Those days Bombay or Mumbai consisted of a few islands, Mahim being one of them, and thus the Sarkar's tribe settled in Mahim, Mumbai, India in the ninth century.

Sarkar Makhdum Shah's parents were wealthy and also very pious. His father, Maulana Hazrat Shaikh Ahmad Sahib was a noble man, a scholar and was exceedingly spiritual. His mother, Fatima Binte Nakhuda Hussain later on known as Maa Saab, was an exceedingly God-fearing woman, who was constantly in prayer, even while taking care of Her family. The impact both the parents had on Sarkar Makhdum Shah is of great importance. It goes to show how parents can take an uncut diamond and through dedication, love and wisdom, make the diamond shine, its lustre gracing one on the physical plane as well as beyond the beyond.

Seeing the intelligence and spiritual inclination of Sarkar Makhdum Shah, both His parents decided to dedicate Their lives to bringing up the boy in a manner that He moved ahead spiritually. Thus, by the time Sarkar Makhdum Shah was nine years of age, He had been taught apart from the foundation of all education, complete knowledge and could recite the Holy Koran, with proper phonetics, understood the philosophy and the true meaning of the Koran. It was thanks to His parents that He could divine the true essence and the very heartbeat of the celestial song given by Allah to Archangel Gabriel who gave it to Prophet Mohammed. Sarkar Makhdum Shah wrote more than hundred books in His physical lifetime and even now scholars all over the world acclaim the books as bringing out the true essence of the Koran, the word of Prophet Mohammed and the Sufism of Islam. I guess if you remove Sufism from Islam, it is like removing the fragrance from a rose, the sigh from the heart, the glow from the sun.

Seeing that the spiritual, intellectual and moral foundation of His son was firmly entrenched and that His boy would now only soar higher and higher, Sarkar Makhdum Shah's father left His physical body.

Sarkar's need to learn and acquire knowledge only grew. After a while when He could take it no more, He approached His mother and sought Her permission to travel all over the world in search of knowledge. Sarkar's mother was intensely in love with Her son. She would have sacrificed anything for Him, but she was a wise woman. She knew that what the world teaches is only surface matter—the thin film on water. To go within, swim deep in the cool waters, and get the rarest of oysters. But, first of all to know where the oyster resides and then to learn how to remove the pearl and then the wisdom as to what to do with the pearl, no mortal can teach. This knowledge can only be imparted by Him and His merry band of winged scholars. So, She told Her son that there was no need to travel. She would pray and the teachers of teachers, the one who would be able to impart the ocean of knowledge would come and teach Her son personally.

Sarkar could not see beyond His mother. He agreed. That night Sarkar's mother, Fatima Maa, prayed with all Her love, devotion and faith.

The next morning, Sarkar went for His usual walk by the sea and He saw an elderly man sitting on a rock. Sarkar Makhdum Shah, a young lad, greeted the man and the man returned His salaam. He smiled and told the young lad that if He desired divine knowledge, there was no need to travel the world, the world to travel was within, where all knowledge reposes, and that He would teach Him all that is needed and he introduced himself as, 'I am the Khizr Alaih Salaam and Allah, the highest of the high, has sent Me to teach You all that is needed but You will not talk about Me or Our meetings to another soul.'

Khizr is the angel of knowledge and divine mysteries. It is said that all those who have truly wanted divinity to be revealed were blessed by Khizr's visit and grace. Many are of the belief that Archangel Gabriel is Khizr.

So, every day Sarkar Makhdum Shah would wake up early, recite His morning prayers and then go to the seashore to meet Hazrat Khizr Alaih Salaam and would be taught all that which is only worth knowing. The manner of teaching was different from the way we are taught by our esteemed schools and in a few days Sarkar Makhdum Shah was well versed with knowledge, both intellectual and spiritual.

One day His mother asked Sarkar where He went each morning and spent a long time. Obviously nobody but Sarkar could see Hazrat Khizr Alaih Salaam. Sarkar was in a dilemma. He had promised Khizr that He would never divulge to anybody Their secret spiritual rendezvous but He could not bear to either lie or keep anything from His mother. Thus, after a brief hesitation, Sarkar told His mother that He was being taught by Hazrat Khizr Alaih Salaam.

The next day when He went to the usual spot where His true education was under progress, He realized that Hazrat Khizr Alaih Salaam was not present. He realized because He had broken His promise His beloved teacher would no longer meet Him. He went back heartbroken and told His mother that the Khizr would never ever meet Him. His mother looked at Her heartbroken son and smiled and told the young lad to leave all to Allah, the highest of the high. If He wanted, Hazrat Khizr Alaih Salaam would have no option but to come back and resume His teaching.

That night again Fatima Maa prayed to Allah and I am sure She must have beseeched Him and also scolded Hazrat Khizr Alaih Salaam for breaking the heart of Her son, the very sigh of Her soul.

Next morning when Sarkar woke up and got ready for prayers, Hazrat Khizr Alaih Salaam met Him and smiled and took the young lad to Their beautiful spot of education, a rock by the sea. Hazrat Khizr Alaih Salaam put something in His mouth, chewed it for a while, and then took out the morsel and fed the young lad. 'Because of the love and prayers of Your mother, You have been blessed by the favour of Allah, the highest of the high, with the mastery of all branches of knowledge.' Hazrat Khizr Alaih Salaam blessed Sarkar Makhdum Shah and disappeared.

That evening, after the sunset prayers, it was as though Sarkar's heart had been wiped clean and every branch of knowledge known to man, angel, master and God, resided within Him.

So, how did the young lad who at birth was named Shaikh Ali, get the name Makhdum Shah? Once again, it was because of His mother. When Makhdum Shah was very young, one night, after Her prayers, His mother, asked for a glass of water. She was tired and thirsty and not well. Her son went to get water for His mother. When He returned His tired mother had gone off to sleep. When She woke up, She saw Her son, standing by Her bedside, holding the glass of water, waiting for Her to quench Her thirst. She asked Him why He was standing with the glass of water in His hand and for how long. He told Her that as She was thirsty and had asked for a glass of water, He had waited all night, as He didn't want Her to wake up and not have water around to be able to quench Her thirst.

I mean who does all this except Those truly filled with love?

Her son said, 'I wanted to serve You and do Your *khidmat* (seva).'

Hearing this from the deepest recesses of Her heart and soul, His mother blessed Him. 'Due to Your khidmat, I bless You that the world will know You as Makhdum (devoted servant) and Your love and devotion will make You a scholar of true wisdom.'

So, this is how Shaikh Ali came to be known as Makhdum Shah.

One of the first miracles performed by Sarkar Makhdum Shah was when He was ten years of age. He had a goat who He truly loved. One day the goat died and His mother didn't want Her young son to go through the grief of burying the goat. So She buried the goat at the seashore and when Her son inquired about the whereabouts of His goat, He was told that the goat had left the body. He was saddened and went to the spot where the goat was buried. The sand was still loose and He could see one of the legs of the goat. He went and said His prayers for the goat's well-being and safekeeping with Allah.

His Mother had sent Her maidservant to keep a watch on Makhdum Shah. She was aware of His attachment to the goat and thus was worried that the loss should not overly trouble Her boy. The maid was told by Him to stay away and knowing better than to follow openly, stood behind a rock and saw the young boy pray. After a while She nearly passed out. The leg of the goat trembled and then after a while, the goat came out of its makeshift burial spot. Makhdum Shah held the goat by the ear, spoke something to it, and took it back home. It became obvious to one and all that this child was filled with the divine spirit.

The most amazing thing was not about the goat. The maid, for some reason nobody seems to know Her name, began to have great love and respect for Makhdum Shah. When she would wash His clothes the first rinse would be done only with water. She would drink this water and then begin to wash His clothes with whatever was used in those days. Slowly, She too, began to get spiritual powers and divine knowledge and spent Her entire life serving Makhdum Shah.

Once Sai Baba of Shirdi, to teach His devotees after eating an onion, vomited it out. The strange part was that He had eaten it with relish but when He vomited, the whole onion came out. A devotee standing by His side dived at the onion and quickly ate it up. First Baba Sai abused and thrashed the guy and then smiled and nodded. He was happy with the man's devotion and love. The man evolved spiritually and became known for His powers and wisdom.

A number of lepers would drink and apply the water which Baba Sai had bathed with and they were cured of leprosy and other ailments.

The power of the giants is such that They need nothing to heal. It is the faith, love and devotion of the devotees and disciples that brings forth miracles and healing. All you need is love, love, love . . . love is all you need.

One day Sarkar Makhdum Shah told His maid to serve a man who had entered the mosque. He had seen the man, realized who He was, and told the maid to make sure that the man was fed. The maid got the food and searched the entire mosque but could not find the man. What to do? Sarkar had told Her to feed the man. She was not going to disobey Her master. She shut Her eyes, prayed and found Herself in Khana-e-Ka'aba in Mecca. How She had been transported only Allah and Her master, Sarkar Makhdum Shah were aware. She found the man, who Himself was a very evolved soul, fed Him, no ifs and buts, and She returned.

Sarkar Makhdum Shah was exceedingly generous. He loved to feed people. His home always seemed to be full of guests. The Hindus and Muslims loved Him. He was very liberal, unbiased and non-judgmental.

It seemed He loved fish, but when one day somebody wondered how a man of God could live a life with wealth, wear good clothes, stay in comfort and also enjoy food, this man was invited to join the Sarkar for a meal. Many had been invited and there was sumptuous food on the table and Sarkar made sure all ate to their hearts' content—He personally served them and then ate along with them. The main delicacy was fish. Long before the others had finished the food, Sarkar got up and went to wash His hands. The man followed Him and He saw Sarkar put the fish bones in the wash basin. He washed His hands and left. The man went to see why the fish bones had been left in the wash basin and then he saw the fish, nice, whole, overweight, swimming in the basin.

The masters operate from a state of detachment. Give Them fish or dry bread and They will eat it with equal detachment. Unless, you get a master to eat food prepared by a few folks I know. Then it would take Them to muster all their detachment and spirituality to eat a morsel! Hmm . . . that's another story.

So the man who doubted Sarkar went to apologize to Sarkar who told him something that truly makes all sense. Spirituality, and different kinds of wealth, are bestowed due to the wisdom of the One. What one deserves the One gives. His wealth, both material and spiritual, came from the One, according to God's mercy on Him.

Even here Makhdum Shah didn't talk about gaining wealth, worldly and spiritual, because of His past life's good deeds. He felt if the One decides, then through His love and mercy one is graced.

According to Sarkar Makhdum Shah, praying the 'Sura Fatiha' and the 'Durood', both the smallest but the most powerful prayers in the Koran, could lead mankind to the warm embrace of the Creator. Baba Sai has often advised those suffering from ill health, black magic, hopeless situations, to pray the 'Sura Fatiha'. The 'Durood' is a prayer one says for Prophet Mohammed. Both are short prayers but work miracles and Sarkar Makhdum Shah would advise one and all to say these prayers.

He would also often pray these words and it shows His humility, love and surrender to God: 'My Allah, You, alone, are my nourisher. There is no God worthy of worship except You. It is You that have given birth to Me and I am your slave. I shall remain firm on My promises to You to My level best. I seek Your shelter against My evil deeds and I do admit Your favours upon Me and I repent for My sins. You, please, forgive Me because no one will be able to forgive the sins except You.'

Here, we have Sarkar Makhdum Shah asking for forgiveness, calling Himself a slave and a sinner and one who has committed evil deeds. The touchstone of all masters is not the miracles They perform, or the knowledge and wisdom They posses, but Their humility, Their love, Their yearning for the One. They operate either as His/Her slave, servant, sinner . . . when in a good mood They permit Themselves to be called the One's child, and when in a state of oneness, and only in that state of oneness, They lose Their individual identity and then proclaim 'I am the One.' But when They come back to the state of duality, They once again call Themselves slaves, servants, sinners.

All the while Baba Sai of Shirdi would say, 'Allah Mallik' and 'Raja Ram' and that He was His servant and slave. Only when He merged into the stream of oneness, did He then proclaim His oneness and Godhood and then back to 'Allah Mallik', 'Raja Ram'.

Sarkar had the habit of going into a meditative state to the extent that apart from His mother's voice He was lost to the world. He truly loved His mother.

He performed innumerable miracles but His writings, more than a hundred works, are considered to be so profound, so simple, so beautiful that for many scholars His works bring forth the divine love, compassion and benevolence of God, Allah. He brought out the Sufism which is evident and still hidden in the Koran. His God was a benevolent God. If you loved Him, He reciprocated a hundred, nay a thousand fold. Thus, miracles on one side and His writings on the other made Him respected, loved, and popular, not only amongst the mango people of all religions, caste and creed (*aam aadmi*) but also with scholars and men and women intoxicated by God.

Sarkar Makhdum Shah is considered an Awaisi. According to Sufis, the one who receives divine knowledge and can penetrate into the divine world of concealment without the help of a physical guide or guru or saint is called an Awaisi and is considered as an elder in the realm of spiritual hierarchy.

He is considered the patron saint of the Mumbai Police, to the extent that there is a special room in the Mahim Police Station built by a senior British police officer, which is called the Makhdum Baba room, a room which contains all His holy relics like His bedsheets, shawls, dishes, and things used for Sandal. This room is not entered with shoes and the main Urs of Sarkar Makhdum Shah is undertaken by the police. Whenever a policeman or policewoman has an issue with law and order, a difficult case, even family issues that don't permit him or her to perform his or her job with utmost sincerity and dedication, tensions of the jobs, he/ she eventually goes and puts his or her petition to the Sarkar.

When Sarkar Makhdum Shah was fifty-nine years of age, on a Friday night in the month of February in the year 1431, He calmly shut His eyes and left His body. His mother Fatima Maa Saab for forty days and nights grieved for Her son and on the fortieth day She, too, left Her body to join Allah and Her very breath, Her son. Her holy tomb is just next to Sarkar Makhdum Shah's holy tomb and thus they have never left each other's side. The maid's tomb is outside on the southern side of the dargah. Nobody truly knows when the pious woman who served Sarkar and His mother, passed away.

Sarkar Makhdum Shah lived His life, like most masters, silently. Though He performed countless miracles, it really never is about miracles. It is about the love for God. It is about serving Him and Her and serving all creation in the Creator's name. Miracles will follow just as fragrance from fresh roses is inevitable. We forget that masters, too, are of the flesh. Their souls and spirit may be that of superhumans and demi-Gods or Gods Themselves on earth, but Their body goes through the same wear and tear as any being made out of the five elements. They bear the pain and tribulations, the hardship and the ridicule, to carry our burden and to show us the way. It is thus Their humility, Their love, Their soul song, that shines through. They will live on much after we have destroyed our Mother Earth, long after the new cycle of life commences and even when that withers away, Their Spirit, love, devotion and surrender will live beyond the beyond, for beyond eternity.

7

The Perfectly Mad One . . .
Baba Tajuddin

Illustration by Sumathi Shekhar

One day Baba Tajuddin, surrounded by hundreds of His devotees, looked at the heavens above and spoke softly, 'Allah, ask Me for an explanation regarding their sins and not them, for they are Mine.'

Only a mad man can have such love and thus Baba Tajuddin spent sixteen years in a mental asylum, certified by the world as a lunatic. If only the world was filled with more such lunatics, there would be paradise on Mother Earth.

It's the fantastically sane people who seem to be making the very heavens weep.

Baba Tajuddin, according to Avatar Meher Baba is known as the *taj* or crown of Sufis. He promised the very creation that till He did not evolve one hundred and twenty-five thousand of His disciples–devotees–lovers–children into saints, He would not rest in peace, either here or beyond.

He was clear that removing the suffering of one human being was more worthy than going a thousand times on the Haj and performing namaz or prayers at each stop of the pilgrimage. Though one must understand that according to Baba Tajuddin, offering prayers, each moment of the day, was the only way to live; no matter whether one was in isolation or one walked in the world as a householder. Prayers according to Him, were mandatory. But very often He mentioned that the best Haj or pilgrimage for a devotee is to win the heart of a person by selflessly serving the individual. 'Because man's heart is a thousand times better than the Kaaba.'

He and Baba Sai of Shirdi were very much made from the same mould. First and foremost, They, along with Baba Jaan, Narayan Maharaj and Upasani Maharaj, formed the five Perfect Masters of their era, who made Meher Baba realize His own Godhood and thus They gave creation once again an avatar.

Both were clear that oneness was more important than any religion. Both performed miracles, left, right and centre to safeguard Their devotees. Both cared nothing for their personal well-being. Their devotees saw Them in their family God they worshipped. They weren't very diplomatic with Themselves or the world around. They often abused and thrashed Their devotees. Their love for Their children was of an intensity that was not found in this world, far greater than the love of all mothers put together. They were worshipped by people from all communities and Their hearts and blessings were for all of creation.

Okay, so let me ramble a bit now. When I was young and less stupid, I most often stayed with my maternal grandmother or safely tucked away in a boarding school in Panchgani. Thus, I rarely stayed with my parents. On and off when I went to spend a random night with my parents, I would sit in front of the family temple, and see the assorted Gods, Goddesses and mad men. There was this small four-inch painting of a fakir, sitting on a veranda, looking at you. I would keep staring at Him and ask one and all who He was. My dad's father, who was a Sufi by temperament, had passed away, thus nobody could really name this man in green.

Fifteen years later, while writing *The Last Marathon*, I got introduced to Tajuddin Baba. Even then there wasn't much written about Him in the book. I had the five Perfect Masters along with Avatar Meher Baba's snap, but I never made the connect with the man in green.

Then something strange happened. Five years back, a friend called me and asked me: who was Tajuddin Baba?

I told him all that I knew. I asked him why the sudden interest? He told me something strange. He had a dream, this friend of mine, and in the dream he, along with his wife and son, stayed in a palatial place. I seemed to be part of his dream (which thus made it a nightmare, but anyway), in which he calls out to me and shows me piles of gold and precious stones strewn in the garden. Everybody is amazed at this treasure, which seems to have come out of nowhere. It seems I am smoking in the dream and I throw the cigarette and tell him, 'You want to see the greatest precious jewel, the virtual crown of jewels? Come.'

And then I walk to the bungalow, where there are creepers on the wall. I lift the creepers and there is a small door, which nobody but I seem to be aware of. I open the small door and enter. There is a staircase and the moment we open the door there is the sound of 'Ya Taj, Ya Taj, Ya Taj' and prayers from the Koran in the background. We walk down the stairs and there is a tomb. I walk towards the tomb and we slide open the covering of the tomb. There's sunlight streaming through the walls and the chanting gets louder.

Then this man comes out of the tomb. Now my friend had never seen the photograph of Tajuddin Baba, but he described Baba and there was no mistaking that my friend had truly been graced with Baba Tajuddin's presence.

So Baba Tajuddin comes out. He blesses my friend, says something about his health, then his son, and then his wife. I am standing a little away. Then Baba Tajuddin turns towards me. He walks towards me and my head is bowed down. He comes and according to my friend, 'This man, Baba Tajuddin, He is so tall and His face is long and beard majestic and He walks towards you and then embraces you, caresses you, like a mother would caress her child, for a long time and then tells me that, this child of mine has . . .'

So anyway, my friend told me what Baba Tajuddin told him about me. This was the first time He truly entered my life. Then again He came into another friend's dream and told me something else which I would rather keep to myself.

The third time was stranger. I get a call from a sage who tells me that his friend wanted to meet me. I said, 'Wookay . . . as long as I can sit down, have chai and cigarettes, I don't mind meeting your friend.' So this friend comes to meet me at a cafe in Pune where they specialize in mastering the art of making the most ghastly chai in all of the cosmos.

We get talking and I don't know what comes into me, but I tell the man a few things, some of them not very complimentary. The man smiles through my chatter but takes notes and says he would do as guided. While leaving he tells me, 'I meditated on Baba Tajuddin and last night He told me that the man you are meeting will tell you many things, listen to him carefully and do as told. So I asked Baba Tajuddin how would I know who the man was as I am going to meet a number of men and Baba Tajuddin said, this man would be carrying green fire.'

So I looked at this man and wondered, Lord love a castrated duck, what was the man rambling about, green fire and all—sounded like a horror movie gone spiritual!

'Don't you get it? You are carrying green fire! You are wearing a ring with a green stone. Your light is the colour green. Just behind you is this neon sign which is green in colour and symbolizes fire. And by the way, does your stomach and neck hurt?'

I nodded.

'Well He operates from the stomach and neck area and they are going to hurt a lot.'

'Tell Him thanks a lot. Much obliged. I shall convey this pleasant medical news to my doctors who will be ecstatic.'

So anyway, this is how Baba Tajuddin entered my life.

Enough of my ramblings. Wake up now and let's get back to the article.

So who is Tajuddin Baba?

Baba Tajuddin was born on 27 January 1861, in the town of Kamptee near Nagpur. He did not cry and the wise ones near the child thought something was wrong with the infant and keeping with the tradition of those days, the baby was branded with hot iron rods on His temples and soles of the feet. The child cried for a while and then looked around with strange bewilderment.

Baba Tajuddin's family came from Arabia, first stayed in Madras and then settled down in Nagpur. His grandfather was a Sufi sage known to many as Hazrat Imam Hasan and all His other relatives were considered holy men, whose shrines are still there in Madras (Chennai). Thus, Baba Tajuddin comes from a lineage of evolved Sufis.

Baba's father was in the army and he left the body when Baba Tajuddin was barely a year old and His mother passed over when He was just nine years old. Baba was taken care of by His maternal grandmother. He was put into a madrasa where He learnt English apart from Persian and Urdu. Baba Tajuddin was well-versed in English.

The day that changed Baba Tajuddin's life was when He was studying and Saint Hazrat Abdullah Shah walked in. He looked at Baba Tajuddin and then turned to the teacher and asked him why he was teaching the child who knew everything and brought knowledge from his past lifetimes. He then walked to Baba Tajuddin and chewed a date, removed it and offered it to the young boy. Baba Tajuddin ate the date. 'Eat less, sleep less, talk less. When you pray from the Holy Koran, say the prayers as though Prophet Mohammed has descended within you.' Saying this, He blessed the young boy and left.

From that moment Baba Tajuddin withdrew within. For three days tears gushed down His face and He was never the same ever again and I guess the realization of the very futility of this so-called existence and the illusion of everything material made Him go deep within. He began to eat less, interaction with others declined and His only focus was studying and self-introspection. He began to read a lot of literature written by poets and Sufis. One stanza particularly had a tremendous impact on Him, and all His life He lived with the philosophy of, 'Drink liquor, put fire on the Koran and the Kaaba, go and live in the marketplace, but never hurt the soul and heart of another being'.

The fact that a Sufi could say something so powerful, where the feelings of each and every individual was far more important than all the holy books and spiritual power houses, where it didn't matter whether you were spiritual or a part of the world, as long as you respected the feelings and treated each individual not on the basis of his or her financial power but as being another child of the Creator, equal and one with you, all was well. This philosophy always remained with Baba Tajuddin as nothing mattered to Him but the respect accorded to each being, man, woman, animal and all of creation.

Soon a flood swept away most of His home town and Baba Tajuddin saw what death, pain, tragedy could to do innocent people. To support His family, He joined, in the family tradition, the army as a soldier in Nagpur Regiment No. 13. He was truly close to His maternal grandmother and she reluctantly gave Him her permission. He travelled all over the country and even abroad, going as far as France. He began to coach Mr Ben and Mr Williams on the spiritual path and both made great strides in spirituality through their lives.

During those days in the army, He was always polite, punctual, disciplined and continued to pray five times a day, irrespective of where He was or how exhausted, despite the vagaries of weather or place. Then another incident took place which would change His life further.

The army was camped at Sagar and Baba Tajuddin would go into the forest to pray and meditate. There He met Hazrat Daud Saheb Hussaini, an extremely evolved soul. Hazrat Hussaini obviously recognized the oneness radiating through Baba Tajuddin. Both of Them would spend a lot of time together and Baba Tajuddin would serve the Hazrat. It was as though Hazrat Hussaini was only waiting for Baba Tajuddin. He gave the young man all His knowledge and power and then took samadhi. Even after His guru had left His body, Baba Tajuddin would continue spending the entire night in prayer and meditation next to His guru's tomb. He barely ate anything, hardly slept and was always looking within. He lived from the spirit where the body was just a casing.

His superiors and colleagues began to worry about Baba Tajuddin and some of them wondered whether He was on the right path or not, and where He disappeared every night. They wrote to His grandmother who thought her grandson had either gone the wrong way or had gone plainly nuts. She arrived and waited for her grandson. Then she followed Him at night and stood at a distance, seeing her boy pray and meditate near the tomb of the one who was obviously His guru.

In the morning, as soon as she saw Him, she realized the radiance coming through her lad. She embraced Him and told Him that she had got Him delicious food, all His favourites. He smiled and from His pocket removed stones and pebbles. He told Her, 'I always carry these sweetmeats (ladoos and pedas) for myself, so don't worry, I never go hungry'. She realized He was on another path, that lead only to oneness.

She left, and Tajuddin Baba continued His service to His guru. One day, after His meditation next to His master's tomb, He came back to the army camp, went to the senior officer and told him, 'You better take care of the men and your army, I am resigning.' Saying this He walked away, never ever to be connected with the material world again.

The army informed the grandmother once again and she returned to Sagar to see her grandson, roaming about the town, half-naked, unconscious of His very body or worldly presence. She thought that now He had gone completely mad and brought Him back to Kamptee, their home town. He was shown to various doctors, healers, exorcists, but obviously none could 'cure' the man from the most incurable illness known to creation—God-intoxication.

How does one cure a person suffering from God-intoxication, where the illness and cure are both the same: Him.

Baba's grandmother passed over, unfortunately heartbroken, with the false knowledge that now her favourite was beyond cure, little realizing that He was to be the cure for hundreds and thousands of individuals in His lifetime, and a thousand-fold more after He left His body. Baba Tajuddin's uncle took over and after a further course of treatment realized that Baba Tajuddin was beyond medical or spiritual or witchcraft treatment.

Thus Baba Tajuddin eventually was left to fend for Himself. This gave Him the perfect moment to go further into God-intoxication. Now He roamed around, sometimes half-clothed, sometimes naked, living under bridges, or wherever His innocent heart guided Him. Children would stone Him and knowing they got some perverse pleasure in doing so—He would Himself gather stones and make heaps of them, so that the stupid kids could pelt Him with ease. If somebody tried to stop the kids from hurling stones at Baba Tajuddin, He would get upset with the well-wisher, making sure that nobody came between Him and the children.

But slowly, Baba Tajuddin's powers began to show through. He randomly began to predict things and saved people from fatal calamities and changed fortunes of the people. Gradually, news trickled in like raindrops that became a raging storm, that this so-called mad man was in reality a truly evolved and powerful soul.

As His fame began to grow, Baba Tajuddin, realized that He had less time to pray and meditate. People flocked to Him for financial gain and for material comfort and the usual stuff all of us are so engrossed in. He would abuse and thrash people, and more people came, happy to be abused and thrashed by a master. He realized that hardly anybody came to Him for spiritual growth and evolvement. Everybody wanted just material gain while spiritual gain could boil its evolved head.

Tired of the crowds and their incessant demands, He realized that the best way to achieve isolation and at the same time still continue to live in His hometown and help the people and do His spiritual work in all the different dimensions, was to do something simple and effective. And hence Baba Tajuddin announced to a person who had come to seek His blessings that, 'It is time I got certified as a mad man and lived in a mental asylum.' The poor man didn't understand a word. He thought Baba was speaking in parables but Baba was stating a fact.

The next day, Baba Tajuddin went and stood outside a club frequented by the daughters and wives and mothers of the British regiment. The moment the women came out, they saw a tall, bearded man, standing stark nude, looking at them with the most benign smile. Some women I am sure must have passed out and the women complained to the men folk and that very day or the next day Baba Tajuddin was certified as mad and admitted to the Mental Hospital, Nagpur. He was thrashed by the Britishers and the Indian sepoys, but Baba Tajuddin only laughed and said, 'I am going to the mental asylum, put this mad man away.' He was thirty-one years of age.

The next week the same English women saw Baba Tajuddin walking about, with not a care in the world.

Aghast that the mad exhibitionist was roaming about on the streets in spite of being declared mad, she made inquiries and it was established that Baba Tajuddin could not have been roaming about on the streets of Kamptee as He was safely locked away in a cell. But a certain English officer, who too, had seen Baba Tajuddin on the street, rushed to the mental hospital, and seeing Baba Tajuddin in the cell, realized the grave mistake made by his people. Baba Tajuddin who spoke English well, told the young officer, 'You are doing your job, and I am doing mine, don't worry.' From that day onwards the English officer became a devotee of Baba and every Sunday would go to visit Baba, sometimes alone and sometimes with His family.

Baba began to perform miracles from within the hospital. Word spread but at least not many people could physically disturb Baba Tajuddin who was seemingly locked up in the mental asylum but who would materialize on the streets of Kamptee, as and when He wanted to. Terminally ill people were cured, those physically handicapped were all of a sudden able to use their limbs which they couldn't until then, disasters got averted, poverty was removed, injustice denied and all this lead to more fame and belief in the mad one. Food and gifts poured into the mental asylum, which was given to the staff and to the residents and also distributed outside to the poor. The doctors and the staff were in love with Baba Tajuddin and would wonder why He didn't go and live in a more comfortable environment. But Baba Tajuddin would refuse, and say that people like Him were mad and best suited for a mental asylum. The best part was that He never allowed any preferential treatment for Himself. He did all the work asked out of those lodged within and made sure His cell was always locked . . . though lot of good locking of His cell had done as our man was seen up and about everywhere, not only in Nagpur but in distant lands too.

Baba Tajuddin was in the mental asylum for sixteen years. In that period He was known all over the country. Dignitaries like Mr Antony MacDonald, the Chief Commissioner of Nagpur, Colonel Rowe, the Civil Surgeon, the Extra Assistance Commissioner, Mr Khan and the city Superintendent of Police, Mr Moti were devotees of Baba Tajuddin. But the most important, as well as the most humble, of all His devotees was Maharaja Raghoji Rao Bhonsle, a king and still one of the most ardent devotees who served Baba Tajuddin throughout his life, with not an ounce of ego, pride or showmanship. The Maharaja considered himself as a servant to Baba Tajuddin and even now his devotion to Tajuddin Baba is spoken about with reverence.

What is a guru without His or Her lovers? And can a guru live without His or Her disciples? If the disciples and devotees love and need their guru, the guru loves and virtually worships the disciples much more, for in them He sees Godhood waiting to manifest. Baba Sai of Shirdi would often say that He was privileged to serve His disciples and devotees.

The crowds increased and the authorities took advantage of this by charging an entry fee for all those who wanted to enter the mental asylum to meet Baba Tajuddin. This bothered Baba as He knew that there would be innumerable poor people who would not be able to meet Him. He began to be more visible outside to the people to the bewilderment of the authorities.

To show His displeasure, He showed Himself as Jesus Christ being crucified on the cross to an Englishman. The man recognized Baba Tajuddin. When he went to meet Tajuddin Baba, the authorities seeking money for entering the mental asylum, failed to recognize the Britisher. They sought money from him. The man was very influential and sort of hit the roof. Through his influence the rule of charging money was removed. He met Baba Tajuddin who looked at him and said, 'Yes, I am Jesus Christ.'

In the end, the Maharaja took permission from Baba Tajuddin, that if He was to be accessible to one and all, then it was time He gave permission to move Him out from the mental asylum. Tajuddin Baba looked at the Maharaja, knowing that only pure love emanated from this child of His. He nodded and gave His permission. The Maharaja paid two thousand rupees (in those days a large sum), and after sixteen years, Tajuddin Baba physically entered into the outside world.

The Maharaja had made all arrangements for Tajuddin Baba. A special place in the palace, a horse carriage, muscular men as guards, but no rules and regulations of conduct, from either the Baba or His devotees. The Maharaja would personally serve Baba Tajuddin without any ego, and through complete love and surrender. It's a beautiful love story of the king and the fakir.

But Baba would still sleep on the floor, still walk barefoot in the scorching sun. He would have tea at four in the morning and then leave early in the morning for a walk and keep walking sometimes till way into the afternoon. In a short while, shops selling flowers, sweetmeats and various things that could be blessed by Baba Tajuddin mushroomed up. Hundreds of devotees would gather around or walk with Him. People knew His whereabouts and stalls came up even in the forest where He would spend time. Sometimes He would sit in the horse carriage and would tell Heera Lal, who rode the carriage and who was also a staunch devotee of Baba Tajuddin, not to direct the horse, Bahadur. 'Let him take Us where he wants Us to go,' and the horse would gallop away and stop, strangely, at only those spots where people from far and wide had come to seek Baba Tajuddin's blessings. People would offer Him food and clothes and gifts which

He would touch and give to the hungry, the poor and the damned. Miracles were performed, like Baba Sai of Shirdi, at a drop of a hat, but it was always keeping in mind the spiritual well-being of the devotee. Nobody was too damned for Baba Tajuddin.

In fact, Baba Sai and Tajuddin Baba used to love each other. Very often Baba Sai would send devotees to Tajuddin Baba and Baba Tajuddin would sometimes tell devotees they had to go and hold the hand of the Sai. Baba Sai, before taking samadhi, had told one and all that it was Tajuddin Baba now who should be sought. So did Baba Jaan, who told one and all that, 'Taj is My successor, supreme ruler . . . What Taj gives, He gets from Me.'

Baba Tajuddin would call Avatar Meher Baba His 'heavenly rose' and when Baba Meher's group of disciples had gone to meet Tajuddin Baba, on Meher Baba's order, Baba Tajuddin had given each of the men Avatar Meher Baba's photograph and told them, 'Worship this photograph of Meher Baba' and Meher Baba would say, 'You have no idea who He was. I know who He is. He was Taj [the crown]!'

Often the masters would send devotees to other masters. Tajuddin Baba had sent numerous devotees to even Upasani Maharaj.

Duality exists only amongst dwarfs. The giants work in oneness.

Throughout His life, what made Baba Tajuddin so immensely loved by one and all was that He never judged or thought that anybody was beyond redemption. For Him, no matter how low an individual had stooped, there was always a way out, always a chance for the individual to come out of that dark hole. He is known to have forgiven the worst kinds of wrong-doers, knowing that in each one of us, was the spark of Godhood. Baba Tajuddin never lost sight of that spark of divinity in each and every one who came for His help. Thus, be it those who the world called criminals, the damned, those in disputes, those who were treated as abnormal mentally and physically, and untouchables and the sweepers, the so-called outcasts of society, all were treated with respect. For those gone astray, He always had belief and hope that there was light at the end of the dark tunnel.

Baba Tajuddin would also stay sixteen kilometres away in a poor Hindu devotee's place. The devotee was Kashinath and the place is called Waki. As usual, He would walk in the rain and let the clothes dry while still on the body or walk in scorching heat bare-footed. He had no connect with His body. All through the path there were devotees but then He was seen at many places at the same time. Once He told His devotee who drove the horse carriage, 'Come, let us go to Kabul,' and the next moment much to the shock and surprise of Heera Lal, They were in Kabul, something which was verified years later by the people who had come from Kabul and recognized Heera Lal.

For Tajuddin Baba, the duality between miracles and the mundane had virtually disappeared. Miracles were performed so casually that it was no wonder thousands milled around to meet Tajuddin Baba. He knew who needed what and no one who was true at heart ever went back without His blessings. Be it an untouchable who had made some humble food and tied the packet to a tree seeing the rich and mighty throng to bring Baba expensive gifts. But Baba still refused to touch anything but that parcel which hung from a branch. From a prostitute to a criminal to the handicapped to the poor and destitute to the rich and powerful to sages and fakirs, all came in droves.

At Waki, according to Baba's wishes, Kashinath made a camping site for devotees to meet Baba and that soon became so popular that people began to call it Chota Nagpur. He chose a mango tree and told one and all that those who sought medical help and refuge from physical or mental ailments, needed to just sit near or under the tree and use the soil as medicine. Miracles took place and still take place under this tree which He called 'the hospital'. Another mango tree He called 'the madrasa' for all spiritual aspirants. Here Avatar Meher Baba has spent considerable time. Another place was called 'kacheri', the court of justice, close to the madrasa, for obvious reasons. Then there is the 'high court', for those who were falsely accused and dragged into litigation. The 'school' was for children who wanted to do well in their exams and knowing Tajuddin Baba, whether they studied or not didn't really matter, as far as marks were concerned. If you prayed and gave your best, you were bound to succeed, irrespective of your capabilities. Faith over logic and talent, any day.

Baba had a dog called Sheru who loved Baba so much that he would take devotees who had come from out of town to Baba, wherever Baba would be at that time. Nobody would know where Baba was, but Sheru would. One day Sheru was not seen and later his body was found. The devotees told Baba Tajuddin about this and Baba said, 'Not possible.' How could His friend leave without His permission? Baba approached the basket decorated with flowers in which they had placed Sheru. Baba just said, 'Sheru, come,' and out came Sheru, prancing and wagging his tail. After a short time Sheru left his body, and Baba Tajuddin removed His shirt and covered His friend.

Another incident was of a devotee of Baba who left the body. But before that Baba was informed that this lady was very critical and about to pass over. So Tajuddin Baba, who was about to drink His tea, took a sip, and told His close disciple to go and make the sick woman have the tea. Our man went with the tea and was told that the woman had sort of gotten wings and taken flight. The love and faith of the disciple was so clear-hearted that he looked at the woman, lying horizontal, all dead and gone and told her, 'Wake up, Baba Tajuddin has sent tea for you, get up and drink it.' The woman, obeying the laws of the five elements, remained sleeping, lifeless. The disciple once again said the same thing. No response. Hmm. The third time he said this and poured some tea into her mouth. Up and about the woman became, finished the cup of tea and ran to Baba Tajuddin to thank her lord and master.

Once a businessman came to be cured. His feet were immobile and for years he had been handicapped. Baba Tajuddin looked at him with anger and told him with such firmness that, 'If you don't run away now I am going to come and give you the thrashing of your life.' There was such anger in Baba Tajuddin, that our businessman got up and began to sprint away—much to the amusement and wonderment of one and all. But Tajuddin looked on the businessman with love and a smile of a proud parent.

As time passed and miracles increased, Baba Tajuddin's name spread far and wide and along with it came about jealousy. Many folks claiming to follow Islam got jealous of the Maharaja's proximity with Baba Tajuddin. Money, gifts, food, flowed in, which went via the king's men and scrutiny. The money and gifts were distributed the way Tajuddin wanted and eventually at night, nothing would remain with Tajuddin Baba. The Maharaja loved Him so much that very often he would personally supervise all the creature comforts and demands of Tajuddin Baba.

People began to make life difficult for the Maharaja and eventually, Tajuddin Baba realizing what could happen if He continued to live in the palace, for the Maharaja's sake decided to leave the palace. He promised the Maharaja that He would take care of him and his generations forever and beyond, which was verified by the Maharaja even after

Tajuddin Baba took samadhi. He told the Maharaja, 'Who can take Me away from you? I and My bed will be in your house for hundreds of thousands of years.' Which is true, as even now Baba Tajuddin's special cottage called the Lal Kothi, prepared by the Maharaja for Baba, is still kept sacred and maintained in the same condition as when Baba was in the body.

One day Tajuddin Baba walked on a piece of land and told His people that the soil on the land was good and they should make a hut for Him on this land. Nobody understood the significance of this statement.

Slowly, Baba Tajuddin began to grow weak. His body was failing Him or He wanted to now leave this world. The Maharaja sent his best doctors to treat Tajuddin Baba but nobody could diagnose what was wrong with the ailing master. The Maharaja would come and serve Him, knowing that time was running out.

The evening of Monday, 17 August 1925, the Maharaja noticed a large flock of birds gathered at his place but they were very silent. Extremely quiet. Close by, in very humble quarters, Baba Tajuddin too weak, lifted His hands and prayed for the well-being of all, those present and those who loved Him. He then lay down on the bed and a soft gurgling sound came from His throat, and He shut His eyes and left the battered body forever. He always considered Himself to be the servant of Allah and His last whisper was, 'To God we belong and to Him we return.'

Far away in Pune, Baba Jaan softly spoke to those sitting near the master, 'My poor fakir, Taj has gone.' Nobody understood what the master meant. Only the next day, when the papers declared that Baba Tajuddin had taken samadhi, did Baba Jaan's disciples understand how close Baba Tajuddin truly was to the master.

The papers then reported that at the exact time Baba Tajuddin took samadhi, the statues of Lord Vitthal and

Rukmini Maa, in Pandharpur, shed tears for twelve hours. Newspapers like the *Madras Mail* and *Andhra Patrika* of 22 August 1925, in bold wrote that 'He, who was Lord Rama, had reappeared in the world in the soul of Baba Tajuddin Aulia and when His work was finished, He left the earth and He was recognized.'

The king had left His body. Long live King Tajuddin.

8

Ramakrishna Paramhansa . . . Maa Kali's Baby

Illustration by Pooja Bangia

I love Ramakrishna Paramhansa for His sheer child-like love for Maa Kali and His love for all of creation.

I remember reading about Him first, when due to a personal reason, Baba Sai of Shirdi first sent me to Shirdi, then to Avatar Meher Baba's Meherabad and eventually to Ganeshpuri, the land of Lord Nityananda. I was told not to leave Ganeshpuri for a few weeks. I stayed at an outhouse which was a dormitory, where one was provided a bed, a clean bedsheet, a blanket and a common bathing area. There were a few private rooms but that was way above my budget. We were provided simple meals and I remember the cost of all this was a hundred and fifty rupees. For me it was quite a bit of money.

So I would wake up at dawn, bathe and then walk a distance, the sky pregnant with countless stars, and then sit in the Muktananda prayer room. Muktananda is Lord Nityananda's successor and His samadhi actively reposes here. So, I would spend some time here, then walk a few kilometres to Nityananda's temple, sit there, then pay obeisance to Maa Bhadrakali, and then go for breakfast.

It was a strange phase. All that I had was taken away from me, and I was on a self-imposed exile. The outhouse had a few books and one day I sat and picked up a book on Sri Ramakrishna. I still remember it was an afternoon. Nobody was present. The sky was overcast. The book was a day-to-day account of the master's life. All conversations spoken and every activity indulged in. Something like

Lord Meher, the volumes on Avatar Meher Baba's life, recorded by His loved ones. I don't remember the title of Ramakrishna's book. Could be *The Gospels of Sri Ramakrishna*, but one sentence has stayed with me through these past eleven years: somebody in Ramakrishna's group was talking about liberation and moksha and merging with the Creator and Ramakrishna looks at the person and says, 'Let me be condemned to be born over and over again, even in the form of a dog, if I can be of help to a single soul, I will give up twenty thousand such bodies to help one man.'

I don't know why, I just began to cry. Tears gushed down and I shut the book. I really didn't need to read anything more.

So this is Ramakrishna Paramhansa. A master who in this one sentence has rubbished a few thousand years of philosophy, that the highest state is that of merging with the Creator and brought it down to something far more important, that till there is one person who suffers, He would come down even as a dog, to help the individual ease off the suffering.

This is the selfless love masters have for all of us, we the flawed amalgam of self-destruction, that even if They do not come down in the physical body, still They refuse to merge with the Creator, continuing to help, guide, guard, serve Their children, in the astral and causal dimensions; continue to be used as springboards for others to move forward on their spiritual journey and even reach the final destination, the final merger; while They, the masters still continue to work for the betterment of all of Creation.

Ramakrishna's life was a journey of love. His philosophy was simple. One could bring down or materialize one's God, Goddess and master, with the simplest of yogic methods . . . through the power of selfless love.

Thus when He wanted to experience Lord Krishna's energy, He realized that the only way this was going to be possible, was for Him to become the embodiment of Maa Radha's love for Krishna. He took this to another extent. He would become Maa Radha—how can one feel love for Krishna, but by becoming Radha? His mannerisms, too, would change, His walk, talk, everything would resemble that of a woman, in His case, Radha.

When He wanted to experience Rama, He became Hanuman. How can one love Rama without becoming Hanuman?

He experienced Prophet Mohammed as well as Lord Jesus Christ and all this through the power of love.

All His life anything that took place, however tragic or hurtful, He was clear it was Maa Kali's way of showing Herself to Him. Once in a state of spiritual ecstasy, He went into a trance and with nobody around Him, He fell down and dislocated a bone in His left arm.

He had a tendency in the latter part of His life to be more in the spirit plane, more in spiritual ecstasy, and He realized that the immense pain that He experienced due to the dislocation, brought Him down to Mother Earth, made Him body-conscious, which would force Him to focus on the work He still had to do while in the physical body. Also, He felt it was important that He fell down and broke His arm to realize that He was a medium, an instrument, a channel and this fall made Him realize His role with greater intensity and this time with more pain. He would make fun of those who considered Him as an avatar or divine incarnation. He would tell them, 'Have you ever heard of God breaking His arm?'

All He wanted was to help everybody experience the true love for the divine and mainly to realize the greatest reality, that the Creator was truly ever-present with each individual, wanting each one of us to realize our very own union with the Creator. He was clear that having the experience of all religions, by having direct realization of Gods, Goddesses, prophets and avatars, all paths led to oneness, that all religions led to the One, that there was no false way, but only different ways, and diet, clothes, languages, rituals, customs, prayers, may all differ, but eventually there was only oneness that existed; oneness was the only reality. All His life He tried to impress this one simple philosophy . . . the Creator, in active form was the Goddess (Shakti) and dormant form was (God–Creator–Allah–Ahura–Brahma), but both existed as One. He would say, a snake sleeping was like the male energy of God and a snake moving about was the Goddesses' energy. What one called the snake, or the dormant One, or the active One, didn't really make a difference.

He operated from such child-like love for the Goddess Kali that instead of quoting various philosophical stuff and scriptures, He would give simple answers. He was asked if God and mankind were in reality One, and what separated the two where love was concerned. For Him, there was one simple difference between the divine and mankind. He told the disciple that, 'If one does ninety-nine good turns to a person and one bad, the person remembers the bad one and forgets the others. But if he does ninety-nine bad turns to God and one good, the Lord remembers the good one and forgets all the rest. This is the difference between human and divine love. Remember this.'

He was like a child and often admitted that though He was a child He was not stupid. His innocence often was misconstrued as Him being simple (often mentally challenged) or just stupid. He was aware that His love, which was like that of a child, often like that of an infant, could never be fathomed by the world, only Maa Kali could understand it. That is why when He was suffering in His final months in the body and often His disciples wanted Him to continue to be amongst them physically, He would ponder, contemplate, whether He should or not, and then as always leave the decision to the Mother. 'She will take me away lest, finding me guileless and foolish, people should take advantage of Me and persuade Me to bestow on them the rare gifts of spirituality.'

For Him, spirituality was the rarest and the only gift worth seeking, the only miracle worth yearning, the only sigh of the soul worth emanating. All else was bollocks.

He was of the opinion that nobody was bad or evil. It was God operating in that form for His or Her own divine play. For Him, God and Goddesses operated in the pretext of the wicked, the pious, the honest and the fraud.

Everything was the embodiment of God, one just needed to love selflessly to realize His and Her presence.

He endured horrific pain in many of the last months of His physical life, and every sage made it clear that if He wanted to He could avoid the pain and agony. All He needed to do was to get His consciousness to His throat and within a few days or weeks He would be cured. When asked why He did not cure Himself, all He answered was, how could He bring His consciousness to His throat as His consciousness was only with and within Maa Kali? For Him, it was impossible to remove His attention from Maa, thus, there was no way that He could focus on His throat for days or weeks.

When He left His body, He called out Maa's name thrice—Kali, Kali, Kali—and then left the physical body.

Okay, now enough of my ramblings. So who is Ramakrishna Paramhansa?

Swami Vivekanand once said that, 'The time was ripe for one to be born who in one body would have the brilliant intellect of Shankara and the wonderful expansive, infinite heart of Chaitanya; one who would see in every sect the same spirit working, the same God; one who would see God in every being, one whose heart would weep for the poor, for the weak, for the outcast, for the downtrodden, for everyone in the world, inside India or outside India; and at the same time whose grand brilliant intellect would conceive of such noble thoughts as would harmonize all conflicting sects, not only in India but outside India, and bring a marvellous harmony, the universal religion of head and heart into existence. Such a man was born . . . He was a strange man, this Ramkrishna Paramhansa.'

Ramakrishna was born to good, kind-hearted, pious parents. His father at the age of sixty or above took a pilgrimage to Gaya in 1835. Gaya is the place where one goes to pray to Lord Vishnu/Narayan for the ancestors and appease them and try to convince the departed ones not to make a nuisance of themselves, but to go about calmly blessing those unfortunate enough to still infest planet Earth. It was in this auspicious place that Ramakrishna's father dreamed of Lord Vishnu who promised him that He, Lord Vishnu, would be born as his child. Virtually during the same period, Ramakrishna's mother who had not accompanied her husband on the pilgrimage, whilst praying to Lord Shiva, had a vision that she was going to mother a child filled with divinity.

Thus, on 18 February 1836, in a small town near Calcutta (before Mamata Banerjee gets an out-of-body experience let me rephrase and say Ramakrishna was born in Kolkata), and His parents named Him Gadadhar (as the dream had been envisioned while in Gaya), 'the bearer of the mace', Lord Vishnu.

Ever since he was a child, Ramakrishna would often fall into a spiritual rapture or trance. While enacting a religious play or talking about God or playing with friends, whenever there was any mention of God or the divine, He would either be filled with the divine presence or He would pass out due to spiritual oneness, where the body was too weak and young to be able to withstand the divine presence and energy.

He was filled with love for one and all and His parents and siblings feared that He was not going to be suited to handle the world and its strange cunningness and hypocrisy.

In 1866, at the age of sixteen, due to the contact and influence of His older brother, He was appointed as the priest of the Kali temple at Dakshineswar, a beautiful temple, on twenty acres of land, four miles away from Calcutta–Kolkata, dedicated to numerous Gods, but mainly to Goddess Kali, on the banks of the holy Ganges. Thus, began His journey on the highway to the absolute reality. The temple and the nearby estate was owned by Rani Rasmani and managed by Mathur Mohan, her son-in-law. They loved Ramakrishna and recognized the divinity in Him long before anybody else did.

He was so devoted and in love with Maa Kali that He became a small child, missing His mother. His belief was simple. If one wanted the grace of the Mother, one had to love Her as Her child. Not as a brahmin, not as a priest, not as a devotee, not as a disciple but as a child. He would weep, dance, sing, talk, feed the Mother.

He didn't care about what the world thought of Him. Rani Rasmani and Mathur Mohan stood by Him. It was as though the Goddess made them realize the divinity within Ramakrishna first, or else nobody would have allowed Him to stay, leave aside serve the Mother, in the manner in which He did—completely unconventional. Sometimes He would miss Her so passionately that He would put His head and face in the mud and weep for hours, crying out, 'My Mother, where have You gone?' Those who visited the temple would be heartbroken thinking that He was crying for His mother, who had given birth to his physical body. Often He would not eat for days and keep awake for nights. One day, distraught at the separation from Kali, He decided to kill Himself.

'I felt as if My heart were being squeezed like a wet towel. I was overpowered with a great restlessness and a fear that it might not be My lot to realize Her in this life. I could not bear the separation from Her any longer. Life seemed to be not worth living. Suddenly My glance fell on the sword that was kept in the Mother's temple. I determined to put an end to My life. When I jumped up like a mad man and seized it, suddenly the blessed Mother revealed Herself. The buildings with their different parts, the temple, and everything else vanished from My sight, leaving no trace whatsoever, and in their stead I saw a limitless, infinite, effulgent ocean of consciousness. As far as the eye could see, the shining billows were madly rushing at Me from all sides with a terrific noise, to swallow Me up! I was panting for breath. I was caught in the rush and collapsed, unconscious.

'What was happening in the outside world I did not know; but within me there was a steady flow of undiluted bliss, altogether new, and I felt the presence of the divine Mother.'

This is how Maa Kali graced Ramakrishna. His need to see Her only increased, and slowly He began to have more visions. Kali was no longer a statue in the temple. She was His Mother. He could see Her. Hear Her. Feed Her. Talk to Her.

Most people were convinced that He had gone nuts. When He prayed to Rama He became Hanuman and behaved like Him. He got a vision of Maa Sita, blessing Him for His love. According to Ramakrishna, Sita Maa entered His body and disappeared within, not before blessing Him that, 'I bequeath to You My smile.'

Imagine telling this to one and all. Immediately doctors were called, medication began and of course, nothing seemed to work. Rani and Mathur knew and believed in Him. In spite of a number of formal complaints about this strange loving, child-like mad man, they refused to remove Ramakrishna from His duties as the priest. In spite of the fact that once when Rani was in prayer, Ramakrishna had slapped her hard. Rani kept quiet as she realized that all through her prayer, her thoughts were on a legal matter and not on the divine and Maa Kali.

And Mathur, seeing his mother-in-law getting smacked right across the face in Her very temple, approached Ramakrishna and politely told Him (and I am sure at a safe distance) that there was a particular protocol even to rituals and taking care of the Goddess. He gave the example that even God did not allow 'flowers of two colours to grow on the same stalk'. Ramakrishna smiled as though He understood every word uttered by Mathur. The very next day Mathur was presented with two hibiscus flowers, glorious-looking, but on the same stalk, there was one red hibiscus flower and a white one.

Ramakrishna was consumed with the need to be devoured by the Mother's energy, not in bursts and spurts, but all the time. 'I do not know what these things are. I am ignorant of mantras and the scriptures. Teach me, Mother, how to realize Thee. Who else can help Me? Art Thou not My only refuge and guide?'

For me, His most beautiful prayer to the Goddess is: 'I have taken refuge in Thou My Mother Kali. Teach Me what to do and what to say. Thy will is paramount everywhere and is for the good of Thy children. Merge My will in Thy will and make Me Thy instrument, O Mother.'

What a beautiful prayer! This prayer itself can take mules like me and you through the sands of maya and the ocean of our personal daftness.

Everybody was of the opinion that marriage and sex would cure Ramakrishna from this strange obsession for Mother Kali and also make Him behave like so-called normal people. But here too, Mother Kali intervened. Yes, He was married at the age of twenty-three but to a five-year-old girl called Saradamani, who even at such a tender age only prayed that though the moon may have certain flaws, make Her nature flawless.

Ramakrishna showed no apparent improvement in His temperament and His love for Maa Kali. Finally, the intervention of two super souls, the first being a Brahmani, an adept in tantra and Vaishnava methods of worship, helped. She was fifty years of age and our Ramakrishna told Her that He, too, felt that He was losing His mind. After a brief interaction with Him and after meditation She informed Him that what He was experiencing was a phenomenon called Maha–bhava, which was considered as the most glorious ecstasy of divine love, recorded by sages, to have been experienced only by Radha Maa and Sri Chaitanya. She described His symptoms and Ramakrishna nodded and smiled like a child. He wasn't nuts.

It was She who openly announced to one and all that Ramakrishna was an incarnation of God, virtually an avatar. He learnt all about tantra and all that She had to teach Him in exactly three days. Then He merged with the Radha energy to experience and merge with Krishna too.

In a matter of few days, Ramakrishna accomplished what other sages took decades to experience. His philosophy was simple. There wasn't a mantra or a ritual that could replace pure, simple, child-like love for the One.

Ramakrishna spent three years with the Brahmani and then She realized that Her son would need a new guide and guru. The new master was Totapuri, whom Sri Ramakrishna called the Naked One, for the obvious reason—the master roamed about in the buff. He reintroduced Ramakrishna to the non-dualistic Vedanta philosophy, which basically believes that statues, rituals, ceremonies are all hogwash, the only thing that really matters is to tear the veil that separates the One from the individual, and to merge into oneness. Where the body played no role and it was all about the spirit and the merging of the spirit with the great spirit.

In a ceremony where everything had to be thrown into the ceremonial fire, the impressions of Gods and Goddesses, nothing but the formless absolute was to be focused on. Ramakrishna found this difficult. How could He remove His consciousness from His Mother Kali.

'Nangta began to teach Me the various conclusions of the Advaita Vedanta and asked Me to withdraw the mind completely from all objects and dive deep into the atman. But in spite of all My attempts I could not altogether cross the realm of name and form and bring My mind to the unconditioned state. I had no difficulty in taking the mind off all the objects of the world. But the radiant and too familiar figure of the blissful Mother, the embodiment of the essence of pure consciousness, appeared before Me as a living reality. Her bewitching smile prevented Me from passing into the great beyond. Again and again I tried, but She stood in My way every time. In despair I said to Nangta: "It is hopeless. I cannot raise My mind to the unconditioned state and come face-to-face with "atman." He grew excited and sharply said: "What? You can't do it? But You have to." He cast His eyes around. Finding a piece of glass He took it up and stuck it between my eyebrows. "Concentrate the mind on this point!" He thundered.

'Then with stern determination I again sat to meditate. As soon as the gracious form of the divine Mother appeared before Me, I used my discrimination as a sword and with it clove Her in two. The last barrier fell. My spirit at once soared beyond the relative plane and I lost myself in samadhi.'

He went into samadhi for three days. The huge master was spellbound. What had taken Him forty years, this frail, small man, with a shy smile had achieved in days, and that too, when He was in samadhi for three days.

According to Ramakrishna, the divine Mother then told Him not to operate from the absolute, as that would make Him redundant in helping mankind but to operate from Bhava–mukha, which is from the threshold of relative consciousness, the border line between the absolute and the relative. This meant to live and operate on the border of the absolute and the relative; to be on the threshold of merging and yet mingle with mankind and the physical world, which meant that He could experience love and devotion for Maa Kali but when needed, become one with the absolute authority, the Creator in the formless state. It was something that Avatar Meher Baba spoke about too. So did Sai Baba of Shirdi, who sometimes would say that He is the One and most often say that He was the servant of the great fakir, Allah Malik. A state of being a child, servant, slave and sometimes when the need be, God Himself—the worshipper and the One being worshipped in the same body.

As time passed His name and fame grew. Disciples came and so did devotees. (I have been made to write about His love for Swami Vivekananda at great length in my essay on Swami Vivekananda and there were many who loved Him as much or may be more than Vivekananda.)

Through His fame and name grew, Ramakrishna remained child-like. He would go into a trance and the state of samadhi in quick succession, which is rarely witnessed by anybody in the history of spirituality. (I am sure there must have been such divine cases but I am unaware about them, thus, I write from my relative and professional state of diving ignorance.)

Just after experiencing the absolute, He wanted to experience the radiance and divinity of Islam and He surrendered Himself to a Muslim guru, forgot all about Hinduism and Gods and everything, stayed outside the temple premises and three days later, experienced Prophet Mohammed approaching Him and merging within Him. He said that where Hinduism leads to, so does Islam, and they both lead to the One, the absolute.

A few years later He did the same with Christianity.
One day, staring at a painting of Mother Mary and Infant
Jesus, He felt Them come alive and divine rays entered
within Him. Christ possessed Him through and through and
He went into a state of samadhi. So strong was the power
that He cried out to Kali. 'Maa, what are You doing to Me?'
He didn't enter the Kali temple for three days. On the fourth
day He saw a man with the calmest of faces approach Him
and He realized that this man was none other than Christ
in spirit form. The One who suffered for all of mankind,
the Son of God who took on the pain and karma of all of
creation; Jesus Christ who is one with God and who was
love incarnate. Christ embraced Ramakrishna and merged
with Him.

Ramakrishna always believed that Christ was an
incarnation of God, and so was Buddha and Krishna.

As time passed, Ramakrishna segregated His followers
in two categories. One were householders and the other
were those who wanted to walk the path of renunciation.
For the former, the householders, the rules were simple. Do
one's duty, give it one's hundred per cent, but always do it
as your dharma, don't get entangled in it; one's main goal
is to serve the Lord and master and Goddess, and don't get
sucked into the politics and muck that surrounds home,
work and the world. Be within, but still outside. Don't
bother about the fruit of labour but do your work like seva
to the One you pray to and love. 'The wind carries the smell
of the sandalwood as well as that of ordure, but does not
mix with either. Similarly, a perfect man lives in the world,
but does not mix with it.'

For those who wanted to walk the path of renunciation
it was clear—avoid women and money. Nothing wrong with
either but their lure can pull you into the by-lanes of chaos.
But He believed that, 'The knowledge of God may be like
a man, while the love of God is like a woman. Knowledge

has entry only up to the outer rooms of God, but no one can enter into the inner mysteries of God save a lover, for a woman has access even into the harem of the Almighty.' (All women activists, Ramakrishna Paramhansa has taken samadhi.)

He believed that faith and love were two pillars that were mandatory for all those in search of God and to merge with God. Often He would cite the example of Lord Rama. When Lord Rama had to cross the ocean to go to Lanka and destroy Ravana and His army, He had to build a pathway. He had to walk His way to Lanka. But Hanuman had so much faith in Lord Rama that He could just fly across the ocean. He could only do so due to His faith in Lord Rama and the love He had for Lord Rama. 'Here the servant achieved more than the master, simply through faith.'

Baba Sai of Shirdi so often would say faith and patience are mandatory for all spiritual growth as well as to swim in the ocean of maya.

He was a friend, child, mentor, guru to all, but He never let anybody who came to Him ever forget that the goal is to move towards God and the Goddess. To realize that all are One and that oneness rocks.

His relationship with Maa Sarada was that of love and worship. When Sarada Maa was of age, He worshipped Her and made Her the living personification of the divine Mother and She too, wanted it no other way. It was a divine relationship. Fame, name, glory did not matter to Ramakrishna. Then came the last chapter of His life in the physical body. First, He broke a bone in His arm. It took five months or more to heal. Excruciating pain that was needed for Him to remain body conscious, to complete the work He had come to Mother Earth for. To spread oneness and make more and more people walk the path of seva, selfless love and worship.

Then came cancer of the throat. It started in April 1885. The spiritual ecstasy, the state of samadhi, the constant exchange of energy, the guidance, all took a toll on His frail body. He often spoke for twenty hours at a stretch. He only gave and gave Himself. The laws of the five elements that the body is subjected to, took its toll. Somebody had to pay the karmic bill. The pain was excruciating. The suffering was unimaginable. He, who had cured innumerable people refused to do anything that His Mother did not want Him to do.

The doctors advised Him complete rest and no more trances and spiritual ecstasy. But He had no control over all this. Yes, sometimes He would get tired of the relentless outpour of devotees and their needs and questions.

'Why do You bring here all these worthless people, who are like milk diluted with five times its own quantity of water? My eyes are almost destroyed with blowing the fire to dry up the water. My health is gone. It is beyond My strength. Do it Yourself, if You want it done. This (pointing to His own body) is but a perforated drum, and if you go on beating it day in and day out, how long will it last?'

But then moments later He would remind one and all that He would come back taking birth as a dog if it meant taking care of even one soul in need.

He was so child-like that once He told His loved ones. 'It was revealed to me in a vision that during my last days I should have to live on pudding. During my present illness my wife was one day feeding me with pudding. I burst into tears and said, "Is this my living on pudding near the end, and so painfully?" Ramakrishna Paramhansa became a skeleton. He could cure Himself but He made it clear that only if the Mother directed Him to, He would. Once He was hungry but couldn't swallow food. He shut His eyes and told Maa Kali that He wanted to eat but He couldn't. He then opened His eyes and told those near Him that Maa Kali told

Him that His children were eating food, which meant He had consumed the food, so why create such a noise about going hungry. He only smiled that sweet child-like smile.

On 15 August 1886, He spent time with His children and then went into a state of samadhi. His last words were 'Kali . . . Kali . . . Kali . . .'

The innocent drum of Mother Kali, eventually rested silently.

9

Haji Ali: The Prince of Waves

Illustration by Sheetal Gandhi Tandon

All those who live in Mumbai know of Haji Ali. For some the tomb in the water is a place of immense faith and devotion. For some it's a beautiful landmark. For many the very sight of Haji Ali dargah, about five hundred feet into the Arabian Sea, like a floating palace, brings forth memories, completely unrelated with God, master or the city.

Since I was born and brought up in Mumbai, Haji Ali dargah holds many memories. I spent nine years in a boarding school in Panchgani, the Billimoria High School and when in Mumbai, I lived with my maternal grandmother and cousins at Charni Road, which is opposite the ocean very close to Chowpathy.

The first time I remember seeing Haji Ali Dargah Sharief, was when I was fifteen years old. I had just taken my tenth exam and the results were a few weeks away. My track record in studies was way below sea level. I had even flunked in the ninth standard and my passing tenth grade was a very controversial, debatable, sensitive topic at home.

So one day my dad skipped work, came over to my maternal granny's place and the three of us got into a black-and-yellow Padmini Fiat cab. I remember my dad telling the cab driver, 'Worli, but take it from Haji Ali. We need all the blessings and prayers and miracles.'

The cab guy took one look at me and nodded his head in agreement with my dad. It was an old cab. Every nut and bolt in the car sang a strange song. I distinctly remember telling my granny, 'Forget my passing the tenth, this cab

149

proved God existed as the darn vehicle still moved.' I heard
a grunt from Dad seated in the front and a philosophical
smile from my grandmother.

Everybody was tense in the car.

'So where are we going, Dad?'

'We are going to see Nawab Saheb.'

'Why?'

'He is a medium.'

'That is wrong English and not very polite. One
should never judge a man by his height. Short, medium,
tall . . .'

'He is an instrument . . .'

'He is a medium instrument?'

'He is a medium or an instrument or a channel who
receives God's energy and answers questions.'

'So why are we going to see this instrument?'

'To ask Him how badly you are going to fail in the tenth
standard. Though why we need to go to a medium to ask
whether you are going to fail or not I still don't know as all
of Panchgani and half of Mumbai knows that you are going
to fail.'

'Hmm . . . Why has somebody made a house in the
middle of the ocean?'

'That is Haji Ali Baba's resting place,' my grandmother
informed me.

I saw my father look towards Haji Ali and pray
frantically. Then he turned towards me, rolled his eyes and
continued his prayers.

My grandmother prayed too. Seeing everybody pray,
even the cab driver bowed down in reverence. So I looked
at Haji Ali and told Him: whatever happens, let this strange
medium say I am going to pass or the coming return trip is
going to be highly entertaining for all concerned.

So I prayed to Haji Ali for the first time. 'I know I have
copied well but I don't know what I have copied Haji Ali

Baba. Please make sure whoever I copied from knew what she was writing.'

We reached Nawab Saheb's place. It was in Poonam Chambers or Apartment. A tall building and I remember it was truly a beautiful day and we sat in this nice hall and there were a few people waiting and my dad shut his eyes and looked as though he was in direct commune with all Gods and Goddesses, while my grandmother talked to me about my exams and I told her, don't worry, I had copied well and the girl really looked the intelligent and studious type.

Eventually our turn came. A really kind though tired-looking gentleman, must be in His early fifties or something, he walked and bowed and greeted my grandmother and my dad, and ruffled my hair.

We entered the room. I prayed to all the Gods and now included Haji Ali's name too.

Nawab Saheb asked for my roll number and then opened the tiniest of Korans. It was so small, I still remember looking at Him and the book, and was about to pass a comment when my dad coughed and I knew the sound of that cough; less bronchial congestion and more exasperation.

'He will get seventy-one.'

'Seventy-one what?' exhaled my father. 'You mean he will get only seventy-one marks out of six hundred marks?'

'No. He will get 71 per cent.'

'71 per cent! Him? Have you got his name and roll number properly. I just want to know whether he will pass. Please see again. He getting 71 per cent is not possible.'

Those days every second kid didn't get 99.9 per cent. In my time even a first class was really good.

'He will get 71 per cent. I know it's strange but They are never wrong, however impossible this prediction may sound.'

My dad came out and announced that Nawab Saheb had lost it. My grandmother was all smiles. On our way back I thanked Haji Ali. 'I know there's been a mistake in the prediction but at least for the next few weeks there will be peace, Haji Ali.'

I got 71.2 per cent. Forget my parents, all of Panchgani was shocked.

When I was twenty-three, I used to spend virtually every evening sitting on the parapet, with the water in front and then the Haji Ali dargah a little away, all lit up. I used to meet a close friend and we would sort of spend an hour or two sitting and talking and often involved Haji Ali in our talk too. We would go on and off and pray to Him within the dargah and just sit and gaze at the ocean.

I wanted to spend the rest of my life writing books but eventually had to take up a job. The Bank of Tokyo wanted somebody for six months. They must have been desperate as they didn't mind employing me. I remember I got this news while staring at the Haji Ali dargah. Should I take this job, Haji Ali? I mean I don't know jack about banking and accounts. And then it happened. Twice I saw the lights within the dargah go on and off. I sighed. Damn, that meant 'take the job'.

I nearly destroyed Bank of Tokyo, by once making a truly outstanding blunder. The entire management was on their toes, running around, while I sat oblivious to my mistake, writing a quote for my new book.

So who is Haji Ali?

There is not much information about Pir Haji Ali Shah Bukhari. All that we do know is that He is from ancient Persia, Iran, now Uzbekistan and that He was called Qutub-E-Zamaan (highest saint of His times).

One day when He was still in His hometown, He was in prayer when He heard a woman cry aloud. Something was obviously bothering her gravely as her loud cries could be heard by one and all. She was carrying an empty vessel and when He inquired as to why she was wailing, between her sobs she revealed that her husband was a very hotheaded man, prone to violence, and that she would not be spared as she had spilt all the oil she was supposed to take home. Haji Ali, a man of God and kind-hearted, couldn't see the plight of this woman. He told her to take Him to the spot where the oil had been spilt. He reached the spot and pushed His thumb into Mother Earth where the oil had been spilt, and in moments oil began to gush out of the sand; the woman collected her oil and happily went back home to her psychotic husband.

That night Haji Ali got disturbing dreams that He had hurt Mother Earth. He had done Her harm by pushing His thumb into Her. He woke up and found Himself sinking into sorrow and depression. It is said that He was a very affluent man but one can make out that He was tender, sensitive and the thought of hurting another being was beyond Him. The fact that He couldn't bear the plight of the crying woman or the sadness of Mother Earth shows how tender and compassionate Haji Ali must have been, is and will remain so.

There are various stories about how He landed in India. The most convincing one is that along with His brother, He had left for a voyage. I feel He went to Mecca to pray and seek forgiveness for hurting Mother Earth. Then He found His way to Mumbai, India. He wrote a letter to His mother seeking Her forgiveness and handed it over to His brother. His brother left for Iran and that was the last time His family saw Him. Though another legend says that His mother came to Mumbai, as she could not do without Her son and stayed with Her son, and in fact even outlived Him.

Whatever be the case, the fact is that Haji Ali spent the remaining years of His life in Mumbai. Always close to the very spot where His holy body has been preserved.

He spoke with all those who wanted His help and guidance; caste, creed, religion did not play a role.

He was of the firm belief that each day passes away like clouds in the sky and thus every time you have an opportunity, do good. Don't waste a moment of your life in doing wrong things, but focus on good and spreading inherent goodness to all of creation.

He also taught one and all that if one through love feared hurting God, then the individual would be free of fearing anything else. Don't fear God, love Him so much that one fears hurting God by one's thoughts, words and deeds.

His third philosophy was that if you go within and really know yourself, you will know God, as God resides within each one. So know yourself. Like Ramana Maharishi, he would guide one and all to go within and question themselves about, 'Who Am I?' The day you know your true self, that moment you know God.

In the year 1431, on 16 or 17 February, Haji Ali told His followers that when He left His body, they should put Him in a casket and release the tomb in the water in the Arabian Sea. Wherever the casket would resurface would be His final resting place. The place where His dargah is built is where the casket carrying Haji Ali Baba's body resurfaced.

Through all the floods and all the storms, Haji Ali's dargah has remained unscathed. In 1949, there was a storm in Mumbai which damaged most of the buildings far away from the seaface. But there was no damage to Haji Ali's dargah. In fact, there were people who were in the dargah and they thought there would be no way that they would survive the high waves. But however high the waves were, it was as though, when they appeared in front of the dargah, they bowed their heads and thus, those who were inside, people of all castes and religions, were spared not only their lives but it has been reported that even their property was left unscathed. That night countless diyas were seen floating on the water, in fact on the waves, although in reality, the wind, the waves and the storm should have made such a happening impossible.

In the olden days people would construct a makeshift path during low tide to visit the dargah. Later on, one day in the year 1944, Mr Mohammed Haji Abubaker, the trustee of Haji Ali dargah at that time, wanted to make a proper pathway to the dargah. He wasn't sure if it was going to be possible or feasible. He was undecided. One day an old man approached him and told him of a dream which he had a few nights ago. In the dream, Pir Haji Ali asked the old man why he had stopped visiting the dargah. The old man told Haji Ali Baba that since there was no pathway, he being an old man found it virtually impossible to go and pay his respect and offer his prayers. Haji Ali Baba told the old man that he could visit him as a proper road, a pathway from the main road to His dargah was now constructed.

The old man recounted the dream to Mr Mohammed and the latter realized that this dream was in reality a confirmation for him to go ahead and make the path and that all would be well with Haji Ali Baba's blessings.

Now the way to Haji Ali dargah is a proper pathway through the water. During high tide nobody can go in and those who are inside the dargah can't come out. Legend says that in earlier times every night, the high tide would come in and in the morning the pathway was free to be used for homage. I have gone often in the rains and it's beautiful. From there you can see Mahalaxmi Maa's temple and to the right there is another dargah, who many feel is that of Haji Ali's mother. The rumour is that Haji Ali's mother loved Her son so much that she wanted her resting place where she could see her son even from the tomb for all of eternity. Some say that the dargah is that of a woman who used to sit on that spot and pray for her son whose name was Haji Ali too. She had immense faith in Haji Ali Baba and wanted to be next to Him even after leaving the body. Both the stories are filled with love for Haji Ali Baba. Whether His mother or somebody else's mother, it is about a mother's love.

The last time I went to pay obeisance to Haji Ali Baba was with my two older kids. After that I haven't had the heart to ever go inside. I see Him when I pass by and say a short prayer and remember my first trip with my dad and grandmother; both have passed away. I miss those days, the loved ones, that beautiful Mumbai, those innocent times.

I remember a fifteen-year-old boy sighing on seeing the Haji Ali dargah, majestic and comforting, in the middle of the ocean, even then aware that all was well with Mumbai with Him surfing the waves.

10

Sant Dass: The Cobbler King

Illustration by Pooja Bangia

S wami or Sant or Saint Ravi Dass or Raidas (his followers today are called Raidassi and they have in fact made His teachings their gospel truth and their very own religion) was a class apart.

He was a cobbler (known in local dialect as a *chamar*), a profession and a caste which was considered rather down the rung in the social hierarchy. Of course we are talking about those days, in the fifteenth century, much before Jimmy Choo the very famous chamar and his colleagues put cobblers up the social ladder.

So Sant Dass and His folks were considered untouchables, and although eventually, kings and royalty as well as scholars and brahmins prostrated themselves, horizontal on the floor of His humble hut, Raidas continued to live and be supported by His profession, mending shoes, and sort of keeping head above water, body and soul together, just about barely.

So here we have an enlightened soul who refused to live by the grace and gifts of His followers and continued to work mending shoes, till He took samadhi, and the best part is that many scholars and researchers believe Sant Dass to have lived in the physical body till He was 125 years old and also that when He took samadhi His body sort of dematerialized. This was so dramatically different from our present-day highly enlightened folks, who make spirituality their business and become the boss-men of their own spiritual kingdom. We deserve the politicians and the spiritual CEOs we elect.

Sant Dass hobnobbed with Sant Kabir, the famous sage, who is considered by many as a prophet Himself and even Sai Baba of Shirdi, when questioned about which religion He followed, He said aloud, 'Kabir'. So Raidas and Sant Kabir lived as spiritual brothers, each holding the other in the highest respect. In fact, Sant Kabir considered Sant Dass as 'The most Saintly among Saints'. As I have often mentioned, the giants have gone, the bloody dwarfs reign now.

Much later, Sant Dass met Guru Nanak thrice. In fact, the Guru Granth Sahib (the holy book of the Sikhs) comprises forty-one verses written by Sage Ravi Dass and were handed over to Guru Nanak Babaji by the saint Himself.

And of course, Raidas was the guru of Meera Bai, the intoxicated child–disciple–lover of Krishna. Many scholars believe that Raidas's holy body was cremated in the compound of Mira Bai's Krishna temple.

What I truly like about Swami Ravi Dass is His complete disregard of everything that came between God and the disciple. Thus, for Him, one's lineage, caste, creed, sex, religion did not matter at all when merging with the disgruntled and selectively deaf old man known by many as God. He went about life in general and eons in particular floating about the galaxy with a trail of harp music following Him.

He was very clear that God wasn't the private property of any particular religion, creed, tribe or club. He was also of the opinion that to reach God one need not be a celibate or be adept at putting oneself in extremely exhausting yogic knots, or go on pilgrimages. According to Him, anybody who had pure selfless love for the divine, calm acceptance of one's karma, gave one's hundred per cent to one's duty and complete focus on merging with the Creator, was on the path to God, salvation, liberation and a life free of income tax and teenage children.

I really can't understand how anybody could be, and can be, so smug in their daftness, proud in their state of mental diarrhoea and spiritually so impotent, as to think that only their religion, (their diet, their language, their Holy Book, their caste, their clothing, and their hairstyle, no hair or hair covered with a skull cap, round cap, turban or a ponytail; or their full grown, half-grown, not grown beard; or the lines on the forehead, vertical lines, horizontal lines, dot of saffron or kumkum, or a black spot due to constantly touching the ground; or circumcised or not; oh God, with a throbbing in-grown toe nail), only has complete access to paradise/heaven/jannat/the ultimate club of nirvana.

Sant Dass all His life had to go through discrimination. Imagine it was clear to one and all that He was the man. His spirituality shone through. Miracles were common place. But mankind, the harbinger of imbecility, relentlessly tried to make the life of Sant Dass a living hell, filled with humiliation and snobbery.

All His life Raidas with dignity, pride and humility earned a meagre living as a cobbler, an untouchable, who lived in a small hut, with His wife and son. He mended shoes and was not apologetic about it.

If you live or have lived in Mumbai, you would have seen Sant Dass's poster at some cobbler's shop.

He was never made to forget till the very end that He was an untouchable and the funny thing is that He never made anybody else forget that He was a cobbler and an untouchable and yet the one who God favoured with His grace and blessings.

Very often He told one and all that to be blessed with the grace of the Lord all that one needed was to love the Lord, Goddess, master, with all of one's heart, to take the holy name and do one's duty to the best of one's ability.

In fact, historians are of the opinion that it was Sant Dass who initiated Guru Nanak with the 'Naam' or the importance of taking one's God, Goddess, master's name and through the chanting of the name, one went through life, karma, the entire scale of spiritual-astral-causal paragon and then beyond the beyond, and all this one achieved or got liberated through by chanting the name.

What name? Whatever lit your spiritual bulb? With what name did you refer to your God, Goddess, master, Creator, however you professed to call the One who was the father and mother of it all, didn't matter. With what love and intensity you chanted the name is all that mattered.

Chanting of the name with love and the sigh of the soul (preferably stick to one name), would take each and everyone, however lowly and damned the individual is, through the ocean of illusions and all, and free the individual from the clutches of both pain and pleasure, gory and glory, love and lust, ease and unease, and into the realm of oneness.

The very fact that He was referred to as Sant Dass, was clear that He was not only about spirituality and the other world, but the title Sant or Bhagat, was given to an individual who was a poet, social reformer, philosopher, traveller and somebody who toiled for the betterment of humanity, a complete saint. Those days one had to toil hard to be called a Sant. Now a thousand-feet ashram is constructed and the Charlie in charge is called Sant Sant Mr What Not.

Okay enough of my ramblings. Now who was Ravi Dass?

He was born in a family of cobblers who though well off, were still considered as untouchables. His date of birth is not certain though many feel He was born on the full moon of February, AD 1440.

Since childhood, He was engrossed in the devotion of God and used to spend His time with God-seekers who were beyond caste and creed. His family members were worried that He would get lost in the by-lanes of spirituality and become inept where worldly means were concerned and thus the family decided that the best way to ground Ravi Dass was to get Him married; the ideal way to snuff out all spirituality.

But He was made of calmer stuff and eventually the family threatened Him that either He forgot God and all His philosophy or He would have to sacrifice His family wealth. In short, either give up God or your comfort and wealth.

Ravi Dass decided that His only wealth was God and His permanent world was that with God and thus He was removed from His house and made to stay in a simple hut at the outskirts of His own home.

Ravi Dass began to work from this simple hut and continued to pray and preach about a God who cared not much about caste, creed, finance but only about love, devotion, duty and chanting of His name.

Those days the caste system and exploitation of man by man in the name of caste was at its peak. But Ravi Dass through His simple devotion began to win a lot of hearts and that became a major issue with the ruling brahminical society. They created major issues for Him and often He would be insulted, verbally abused and even imprisoned. But Ravi Dass never once doubted His own belief that the one who created everything was beyond prejudices.

He slowly began to attract a lot of influential people who had no option but to go to His humble abode to seek His blessings. Often they would hide from the world, as they did not want to be seen in the company of an untouchable, no matter how highly spiritually evolved or enlightened His state of being was.

His life was filled with creating miracles but the greatest miracle is to make people move beyond duality, into the ocean of oneness and to become better human beings. One of the most famous incidents that took place was when the brahmins complained to King Nagar Mal that this cobbler was creating discord in society by challenging the very fabric of the social structure. The king by now was fed up to the gills with these complaints and eventually to settle the issue once and for all, He summoned the brahmins and Sant Dass.

Ravi Dass would dress like a brahmin but would sit and mend shoes and this created more animosity amongst the brahmins. What they did not realize is that a brahmin in the true sense of the word was one who was engrossed and filled with Brahma, the Creator.

Anyway, the king placed an idol between the Brahmins and Sant Dass and then announced that whoever could move the idol towards himself without touching the idol was obviously spiritually more evolved. The brahmins did their stuff and the idol remained rooted to its place. Then Sant Dass shut His eyes and said this beautiful prayer.

Act not in such a way, O my Lord,
That my work may go wrong,
And Thou may merely watch,
Sitting at a distance . . .
Kanshi is crowded with a multitude of people
Who have come to witness the assembly of devotees;
Keep up or give up Thy reputation of being the saviour
of the poor and the lowly
Prays Guru Ravi Dass, the cobbler.
I have come to Thy shelter, O God of all Gods,
Have mercy on me, thinking me Thine own . . .
With confidence in Thy name, I have given up hope
of others,
My mind finds no comfort in worldly observances,
Accept the service of Guru Ravi Dass, Thy Slave
O Lord,
And manifest Thy Name, the purifier of the fallen ones.

All eyes were on the idol when suddenly the idol disappeared and when they looked at Sant Dass, the idol was comfortably resting on his lap. It seems there were eighteen thousand brahmins who were present for this spiritual duel and the king converted them all into following Sant Dass as their guru.

But Sant Dass continued to live in his modest hut, continued to work as a cobbler, refused all gifts and tokens and money from those who came to meet Him, saying His duty was to earn His own living and God would take care of His and His family's modest needs.

Okay, now back to my ramblings. First and foremost, saints and Perfect Masters and prophets had Their own way of working. There are enough saints and Perfect Masters who accepted gifts and money from Their devotees and this money was always passed forward to the poor and the needy. Some of the masters would ask for money and gifts and then distribute them to the poor and the underprivileged. Some masters would thrash anybody daft enough to offer Them anything. Some would not care if gifts and cash were given or not. Thus, it is important to note that each master has His or Her own way of handling the issue of gifts and money.

Secondly, where Sant Dass is concerned, I feel that He on purpose continued to live in the hut and earn from His profession as He wanted to make it clear to one and all that even an untouchable could become God's beloved and still live in the most humble surroundings. If He had accepted the patronage of the kings and royalty and the rich brahmins, He would no longer be an untouchable, no longer would He be poor, no longer would He be able to impress and influence the countless poor Indians to think that status, caste, creed, wealth, had nothing to do with God and His favours; that the poorest cobbler and the richest king was loved equally by God, who only saw pure love, surrender, devotion and nothing else mattered.

Anyway, enough of my stuff.

Meera Bai, who treated Sant Dass as Her guru, used to be ridiculed and made fun of for having an untouchable, poor cobbler as Her guru. When She could take it no more, She went to Sant Dass and offered Him a very rare and a bloody expensive diamond or some precious stone (researchers say the stone was as big as the Kohinoor diamond). She kept insisting that He take it and Sant Dass told Her, 'My dear child, I don't need it. Whatever I have attained, has been attained through My humble work. If it is below Your dignity to come to Me or if people are harassing You for coming to Me, You may stay at home and do Your devotion.'

But She insisted and placed the diamond on the thatched roof of his hut. After months She came to pay Her guru a visit and saw Him sitting at the exact spot, working, oblivious to one and all, in complete union with His work and His God, and the blasted diamond was exactly at the same spot where She had kept it. She realized the depth and greatness of Her guru and His love for His God and master (Rama, Hari, Krishna) and I would like to believe that His love passed on to Her and after a while She, too, became God-intoxicated and is now known as one of the greatest disciples and lovers of Krishna.

Sant Dass travelled the length and breadth of the country and scholars say He even travelled to parts of Arabia. Those days travelling did not involve too much cost but a lot of effort. But Sant Dass travelled with other saints and scholars and some brahmins who realized who He truly was, to spread the word of God, equality, devotion and untangle countless people who were caught in the web of caste and creed. He wanted the brahmins not to waste time and their spiritual growth and He wanted the poor to realize that God belonged to all and to focus on Him and make Him theirs for eternity.

It was in one of His travels with Sant Kabir that They met young Guru Nanak. Guru Nanak was with His friend Madira, and Nanak's father had given Him twenty rupees to go out in the world and make a good deal. Babaji met

Sant Dass, Sant Kabir and three more saints. Guru Nanak sat Them down and took care of Them and went back to His father saying He had made the best deal ever. I am certain Guru Nanak's father had a lot to say about this very strange business deal. It is said that Sant Dass met Baba Nanak thrice and in fact initiated Him in the glory of the holy name.

Little wonder that giants like Sant Kabir, Guru Nanak, Sant Ekanath, Sant Haridas, Sant Dadu, Sant Tukaram and many more saints considered Sant Dass to be the sage of sages.

Even now scores of people worship Sant Dass as the messiah of the downtrodden. There is an entire new religion that considers Him their Prophet and their God. Countless Sikhs call themselves Ravidassis and worship Ravi Dass. Ravidassis have a number of gurudwaras all over the country and even in the United Kingdom.

I love this poem of His the most.

If I did not commit any sins, O Infinite Lord, how would You have acquired the name, Patit-Pavan (redeemer of sinners)?

You are My master, the inner-knower, searcher of hearts. The servant is known by his God, and the Lord and master is known by His servant.

Grant me the wisdom to worship and adore You with My body.

O Ravi Dass, one who understands that the Lord is equally in all, is very rare.

Sublime.

He was such a simple man that once, when His disciples told Him that a particular day was very important, and that a dip in the Ganges was considered very auspicious, He stood up to go and then He sat down, and told one and all that He could not accompany them as He had promised to give a man his pair of shoes and as He had not done His work yet He would rather finish working on the shoes than take the dip in the Ganges. Then He smiled and said, '*Mun changa to kathauti mein Ganga.*' (If the mind is pure, the Ganga flows in the small, shallow earthen pot.)

And His disciples saw the Ganges flow in the iron casing in which all cobblers dip their wares and the leather and other stuff.

It is said that Sant Dass lived to the age of one hundred and twenty-five years while some scholars say He lived to the age of one hundred and five years. Anyway, one day Perfect Masters Kabir, Namdev, Tirlochan and Dhanna came to meet Him. They told Him that They had been divinely guided and that Sant Dass had achieved supreme liberation and that twenty-one days later He would leave His body to go to His Lord and master. Sant Dass served the masters and They physically embraced each other one final time.

Sant Dass called His family members and disciples to Benaras and informed them about the divine message. Then on the twenty-first day, Sant Dass after an early morning bath sat for prayers and meditation. With the name of God in His heart and soul, He took samadhi. Some believe He dematerialized and there was no physical form left while some say He was cremated in 1584 (AD 1528).

What is important is that the cobbler who was considered as an untouchable, touched the lives of countless people, helping them to go beyond social stigma and prejudices and realize that: The One who makes the thunder roar also hears a butterfly sigh.

11

Sadhu Vaswani: God's Whisper

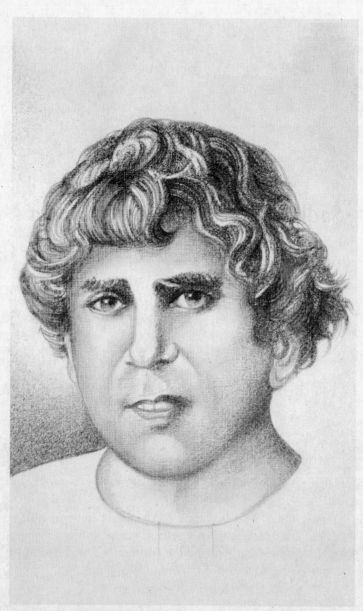

Illustration by Pooja Bangia

The first time Sadhu Vaswani entered my life was exactly twenty years ago. The Mumbai riots had left me heartbroken. To see mankind kill each other, all in the name of God, blind to the dictates and manoeuvres of politicians and the land mafia, I decided to get out of my beloved city, Mumbai.

I wanted to shift to Pune. Now, when I look back there was no logical reason. I did not know anybody in Pune. Financially, it wasn't going to be a great move, as those days Pune was still a small town, the bastardization of this beautiful town into a concrete jungle hadn't really begun. Thus, I shifted to Khandala, a beautiful hill station, midway between Mumbai and Pune.

Apart from alleged madness, we Zoroastrians have an access to lot of facilities, like beautifully located sanatoriums. There are so many Parsi sanatoriums all over the country that one wonders if we were a community of travellers or sick people, as the word 'sanatorium' is a polite or a gentler word for infirmary or a hospice. But our community elders, now all stars in the sky, in their benevolence and foresight, have built sanatoriums and dharamshalas all over the country.

Thus, as a mid-way point, Khandala was the ideal location. The place where we lived was opposite a small lake, and to the right, beyond the mountains, was an ancient temple. Those days the express highway wasn't conceived, so it was still a small place with maybe a few hundred-odd people living.

Financially, I was sort of barely managing to keep body and spirit together, but in those days even a hundred-rupee note went a long way.

Every day I would catch whichever train halted at the Khandala railway station and reach Pune. From there I would walk to *Maharashtra Herald*, the oldest English newspaper in Pune.

It would take me about twenty minutes or more to reach the newspaper office and I would pass Sadhu Vaswani's ashram. His birthday was around the corner and there were hoardings informing one and all that 25 November was Sadhu Vaswani's birthday and was declared as the International Vegetarian Day in His honour.

So each morning my train would arrive at the Pune station around 10 or 10.30 a.m. and then I would pass by Sadhu Vaswani's place and I would wish Him a good morning. I began to call Him Saint Veg. So every morning I would look at His photograph and say, 'Morning Saint Veg, hope You are doing well.' And then when I would walk back to the station to catch my 4.30 or 6.30 train I would say, 'Night Saint Veg, see You tomorrow.'

I remember one day while passing by the main hoarding I was asked to halt by two women and a man. I realized they were promoting some or the other cause.

'Today is Sadhu Vaswani's birthday,' informed the man.

'Happy Birthday to Him. My birthday was a few weeks back, too.'

I am all for friendly birthday chit chats.

'In His honour, would you like to pledge to become a vegetarian?'

I nearly swallowed the cigarette I was smoking. We Zoroastrians love our non-vegetarian food. I didn't know paneer or cottage cheese existed till I was twenty-four years old. We put mutton even in the sparse vegetarian food we eat. If nothing else, we would break eggs on vegetarian food to make it palatable. My family was more than convinced I was off my head in most of the decisions I had taken. If I turned vegetarian, they would bloody disown me.

'I am a vegetarian for nearly forty-eight days in a year.' Mentally I was trying to figure out how many Thursdays came in a year. I settled for at least forty-eight.

'Sadhu Vaswani would be happy to hear that at least I am not responsible for taking life for forty-eight days in a year. Right?'

They asked me to think about what my gluttony was doing to the animals. I promised them I would. At lunch I skipped chicken sandwiches from Marz-O-Rin. Dinner time I forgot, and had two helpings of fish.

Six years earlier, I returned to Pune. Around three years ago, one morning I went to buy mutton and saw a sight at the butcher's and when I heard the cry of the goats stocked in some small, dark unventilated locker, just below the slab on which our butcher sat and slit the throats of the goats and when I heard the wailing chickens and the plea of the animals, I walked out a born-again vegetarian.

But that's not the end of the story. Wake up, please. Good.

So that afternoon I was seated with a few of my friends at Prem's Café, and I was speaking about the sight I witnessed at the butcher's and told them I had turned vegetarian. One of my friends looked at me and said, 'That's strange, as today is Sadhu Vaswani's birthday, it is 25 November and it's International Vegetarian Day. It is a great day to turn vegetarian!'

And I couldn't help but smile. I remembered my walks and realized Saint Veg was having the last laugh.

Though I am the most disgruntled vegetarian going about, as I hate vegetarian food, I remembered Saint Veg today and decided to ramble about Him.

Sadhu Vaswani may or may not have performed miracles. I do not believe performing miracles is the sign of a master. His spirit was filled with oneness and compassion for all, and for me that is the true calling card of all masters.

Sadhu Vaswani's parents themselves were noble souls. His mother was a Guru Nanak devotee and disciple. She knew the entire *Sri Japji Sahib* by heart and would also recite the *Sri Sukhmani Sahib*.

His father was a Maa Kali disciple. The Mother had graced Him with Her darshan and He would pray to Her standing on one foot for hours. Through His devotion He had received the power to heal people.

He was a landlord but often the family had to go through tough times and when Sadhu Vaswani was born, the family was going through a financially lean period.

When Sadhu Vaswani was a young boy, one day, passing the butcher's shop He saw animals being ruthlessly killed and decided to turn into a vegetarian. The very thought of eating something by taking its life was not acceptable to the young boy. The parents tried their best to make Him change His mind but my Saint Veg stuck to His ground and the parents eventually relented.

From childhood He would worship the sun, seeking the sun to fill His body with its radiance and strength and pray to the moon to fill Him up with Her purity and calmness.

The first signs of His divinity came when He prayed for a relative who had lost his job and who couldn't afford to even feed his family. Every night for seven nights, Sadhu Vaswani prayed to God to give the relative a job and on the eighth night His mother told Him that not only had the relative got a job but got a job that paid the man forty rupees a month. In those days it was considered a huge sum. In these days, if one is lucky, one can procure a cup of ghastly tea in some restaurant with the same amount.

So initially, Guru Nanak and Maa Kali's influence and protection along with His parents' spark of divinity were His guiding force.

Then at an early age He read about Jesus Christ. When He read about how Lord Jesus Christ was crucified and the passage when the Lord Christ, thirsty for water says, 'I thirst,' and nobody gave Him a drop of water, Sadhu Vaswani felt a knife twist in His little heart and He began to cry. From that day onwards, Jesus Christ became a part of Sadhu Vaswani's life.

In fact, a few years later Sadhu Vaswani dreamt of Jesus Christ. This is what the dream revealed, in His own words, 'We spoke to each other. Jesus said to me . . . control your mind, unfold your heart that I may draw out tunes from your heart, even as a musician draws out melodies from the strings of the sitar.'

Even as a child He would help the poor with whatever little pocket money He would get. He would take food from home and feed the poor. He convinced His friends who were in awe of Him, as He was a naturally gifted leader and speaker and academically the best of the lot, to bring whatever they could to feed the poor.

He would spend hours at night on the terrace in contemplation and had realized the importance of going within. The breath and the process of going within made Him strong, courageous and bold.

Growing up, He read about the life of St Thomas of Acquinas. The saint would regularly flog Himself if He felt He had strayed even a little from the path of divinity and Sadhu Vaswani began to cane Himself too, whenever thoughts took Him away from the path. In fact, there was a time it seems when He would wear a garland of thorns and every time He felt He had strayed in His mind, He would pierce the thorns into His delicate skin till He bled.

By the time He had turned sixteen and excelled in academics, He had decided to turn into a wandering sage or fakir. He even voiced this plan to His mother, who had become a widow and she made Him promise to her that till she was alive in the body He would never become a sage or a fakir. He kept His vow for the next twenty-four years.

He won many laurels in His academic career and became a professor and headmaster too. But His mind was always on God and always on serving the needy.

He was also greatly influenced by the master, Ramakrishna Paramhansa, and Vivekananda. When He visited Ramakrishna's ashram and saw the picture of Jesus Christ which Ramakrishna Paramhansa had gazed at for years and was told that even the master was blessed with the Christ's love and vision, Sadhu Vaswani felt a kinship with the master. But the master had taken samadhi and Sadhu Vaswani ached and yearned to meet His guru.

He met His master, Sri Promotholal Sen, and His lifelong search ended. With the meeting of His master, His need to become a sage and fakir intensified, but His promise to His mother chained Him to His worldly profession.

When He was forty years old, His mother fell ill, a victim of a plague that had created havoc in that part of the country. Sadhu Vaswani nursed His mother but her spirit was ebbing. To assure His mother that she was going to be well, He drank from her own bowl of water. Nothing happened to Him but a few days later His mother passed over.

Hours after He cremated his mother, He resigned from His very well paying job as a professor and scholar and renounced the material world.

During His pilgrimages to all the holy places, Sadhu Vaswani was blessed with the presence of Lord Krishna.

He lived a very humble life. He would bathe from a common tap, which was located at a corner of a street. He would wake up early and meditate and then serve the poor. People began to see His Godhood and recognized Him as a saint. The sick, the needy, the anguished, flocked to Him and He opened His arms to all. To annihilate His ego, Sadhu Vaswani began to beg for His food. The greatest test was to go and knock at the door of His friend and beg for food, which He did.

For Him, it was all about the spirit, and the ego of the flesh had no place in His life. Then two meetings with two fakirs again impacted His life. One day, travelling from place to place He met up with a fakir and He began to speak to the sage. Sadhu Vaswani realized that this fakir was no ordinary man. He asked the fakir how to make the Lord happy and how to merge with Him. The fakir replied that one needed to become a moth. The moth has only one agenda, to merge with the flame. It is not bothered about death, hurt, physical anguish or annihilation. It only wants to merge with the flame.

Sadhu Vaswani then told the fakir that He was filled with imperfection and His greatest fear was that He would never please the Lord enough for the Lord to embrace Him and accept Him. The fakir told Sadhu Vaswani that the Lord is like the mother. The mother's love goes beyond all imperfections. All that the mother seeks is pure love. Thus, the only way to merge with the Lord and to gain His acceptance is to treat the Lord like the universal mother and to become a child to gain the mother's tender embrace.

Fakirs played an important role in Sadhu Vaswani's final metamorphosis. One fakir told Him that there were children who threw stones at Him but He endured everything as if that is what the Lord wanted, that He should suffer, so be it, He would suffer. Sadhu Vaswani had asked the fakir what gift God or the master truly treasured and the fakir replied that once He had asked his master what was the best gift the fakir could offer His master and God and the master had replied, 'The gift of an anguished heart.'

This sentence had left Sadhu Vaswani in a sort of trance-like state. For days He went into isolation. Days would converge into night and vice versa. Then Sadhu Vaswani met another fakir. The fakir sang songs and Sadhu Vaswani was

reminded of Lord Krishna and His mystical flute. The fakir
told Sadhu Vaswani who had prostrated Himself at the feet
of the fakir, to meditate on His *satguru* (though a Muslim
man of God, the fakir had used the word 'satguru', meaning
the Perfect Master) and said that only meditation on one's
Perfect Master and with the blessing of one's master can
one be blessed with the true treasure, which in reality is the
master's glance of mercy.

Mercy and compassion, two words meaning pure love
from the master can only unchain us from our ignorance
and free us from the wheel of karma. Baba Sai of Shirdi
often has said during channelling that only selfless love,
which comes from the realization of oneness and which
brings forth compassion, can release us from duality and
merge into self-realization of oneness and Godhood.

'We keep going from one place to another when in
reality all we truly need to do is to go within and let one's
God, Goddess, master manifest within us. To awaken
divinity that already reposes within us.'

Anyway, enough of my ramblings.

Then Sadhu Vaswani met another fakir who told
Him seven requirements to realize the oneness within
each individual:

- Have faith in Allah (which means, one's God,
  Goddess, master).
- Forgive the faults of your servants (which means,
  to forgive the flaws of all those who come in contact
  with you).
- Do not turn your face away from the truth (obviously
  this means, not only don't lie, but don't gossip and don't
  slander and malign as God is part of the conversation
  and He hears every word spoken or unspoken).
- Remember God every day (it really means every moment,
  as He is with and within each of us at each moment,
  never doubt this).

- Words of Allah when you leave your body will be 'I was sick and in pain and you did not care for me or serve me' (that means take care of the less fortunate and needy and those who are ill and less fortunate).
- Charity (give give give without any agendas; without the thought of karma or praise or ego).
- Love (eventually all comes to naught and is useless if one doesn't come from selfless love, compassion and oneness).

Sadhu Vaswani lived each of these tenets. All His life He served, and served and served. Even when in the last stage of His physical life, He had injured Himself due to a fall, He served the needy from the bed. He counselled, blessed and made sure countless girls were educated, as He knew that it is through education that one can dispel the darkness and surge ahead into His light and radiance.

Sadhu Vaswani lived humbly. All His life He desired to serve and be filled with the Lord's radiance. His arms were open for the poor, ailing, the anguished, the young, old and rich, caste and creed being no bar.

He was a special warrior of the light, softness personified and humility engrained in every cell.

12

Archangel Michael:
The Warrior Prince of Light

Illustration by Nilufer Marshall

The army of archangels and angels does not belong to any particular religion. Just as the words *Aum* and *God* do not belong to a particular religion.

The concept of archangels and angels came about through the first known prophet, Zarathustra. Thus, Zoroastrians have been praying to archangels and angels over thousands of years. Zoroastrians have seven archangels and thirty-three angels.

Archangels and angels have been there since the beginning of creation; long before mankind, and will be there long after we have plundered Mother Earth to rubble.

Archangels and angels are the light of God. If God is fire, archangels and angels are the light and warmth that emanate from that divine fire.

Okay, enough of my ramblings. Now let us talk about the prince of heaven and light, Archangel Michael, also known as Saint Michael.

Who is Archangel Michael?

In Hebrew, the name signifies, 'The One who is like God'. Though in the Bible Archangel Michael is called 'one of the chief princes' (Daniel 10:13) and 'the great prince' (Daniel 12:1), in the Bible, Archangel Michael is called and referred to as the 'Chief of all Angels', and as many scholars believe that there can be only *one chief*, thus, Michael is the only one who can be called the archangel. Researchers conclude that as the term 'archangel' is referred in the Bible only in the singular and never once in the plural tense, thus there is only one archangel and that is Michael.

That could be the reason why Archangel Michael is mentioned more often than any other angel in various religious scriptures, namely the Torah (the Old Testament), the Bible (the New Testament), the Koran and the Zohar (the Kabbalah faith). He is honoured in Catholicism, Islam, Judaism, Oriental Orthodoxy, Lutheranism and Anglicanism.

(Roman Catholics believe that Michael—the one who is like God; Gabriel—the power of God or the strong one of God—and Raphael—God has healed—are archangels.)

There are various dialogues on how many archangels are there. Some scholars and religious schools of thought say seven, some say nine, some say eleven. Some believe that there are seven archangels corresponding to the days of the week as: Michael (Sunday), Gabriel (Monday), Raphael (Tuesday), Uriel (Wednesday), Selaphiel (Thursday), Raguel or Jegudiel (Friday), and Barachiel (Saturday).

Archangel Michael is considered the enemy of Satan and is the one who defeated Lucifer and removed Him and Satan's followers from heaven or paradise forever. Eventually He will be the One who will vanquish Lucifer once and for all in the final battle between good and evil, for all of eternity.

The subtle element of fire is associated with Archangel Michael. The pure bluish colour one sees in the fire is His colour too. Nothing can corrupt fire, but fire symbolizes the physical pristine presence of the non-corruptible and thus, a glimpse of the Lord's love, warmth, purity and divinity. This divine fire burns away all that is not real, all that is not permanent, leaving the glow of divine radiance which is true, life nurturing and eternal.

Archangel Michael is also called the 'Benevolent Angel of Death', as He toils tirelessly to lead each one of us towards everlasting immortality.

According to the *Apocryphal Book of Adam and Eve*, it was Archangel Michael who followed the happenings of

Adam and Eve, when the couple sort of went cuckoo over an apple and thus were shown the door, for breaking the main tenancy act from the garden of Eden. It was Archangel Michael who taught Adam farming and also convinced God to permit the spirit of Adam entry into heaven.

The Church of Jesus Christ of Latter-day Saints believe that Archangel Michael is the heavenly form of Adam, the first being ever created by God in His own divine image.

Abraham's Testament, which dates back from the second century BC, clearly shows that Archangel Michael who being so close to God and through His intervention before God, can save the souls from hell and help them to reach heaven.

The love of Archangel Michael for the salvation of lost souls, those in the spirit world and those still occupying the physical body comes forth from Islamic writings too. In Islamic tradition, Archangel Michael has green wings made of topaz, his hair is golden in colour and is so long that it starts from the head and virtually touches the ground, and each strand has a million faces and every face begs in various languages and dialects for divine pardon and complete forgiveness for all the sins and acts of evil committed knowingly or unknowingly by those professing faith in God, as Lord and master.

There is literature which once again shows Archangel Michael this time with emerald green wings, not blond but saffron-coloured hair, but once again each strand of hair has a million faces, speaking different languages but all seeking forgiveness from God for all sins committed by every being.

No wonder He is known by many names. The angel of the burning bush, the angel of repentance, pity and holiness; the prince of the divine presence; the carrier of the heaven's keys, the archangels' leader and Jacob's guardian.

What is interesting is that early Protestant Christians, the Seven-Day Adventist and Jehovah's Witness are of the firm belief that Lord Jesus Christ was Archangel Michael before Jesus Christ took birth on Mother Earth to free mankind of their sins.

The above three faiths believe that Archangel Michael is another name for heavenly Christ; that is, before Archangel Michael became incarnate as Jesus. Thus, it is Archangel Michael in Jesus Christ's pre-human and post-resurrection reality.

The point to note is this: The Bible states that 'Michael and his angels battled with the dragon . . .' (Revelation 12:7) Michael is the chief of all angels and thus the leader of the army of angels that waged a war on Satan and his dark forces but the book of Revelation also insists that Lord Jesus Christ is the leader of the army of all faithful angels. (Revelation 19:14–16) So we have the Bible, which assigns the role of chief and leader of all angels to both Archangel Michael and Lord Jesus. (Matthew 13:41) Now, since in the Bible there is no mention of God, saying that there are two separate armies of angels that wage a war against Satan (the dragon)—one army of angels led by Archangel Michael and another army of angels with Jesus Christ in command—it thus makes sense to conclude that Archangel Michael is Jesus Christ in His heavenly avatar. Jesus is linked with the office of the archangel.

Scholars also believe that Jesus Christ is considered to be in charge of angels and 1 Thessalonians 4:16 states: 'The Lord himself will descend from heaven with a commanding call, with an Archangel's voice.' Thus, the voice of Lord Jesus is described as being that of an archangel. If Lord Jesus is described as possessing a voice of an archangel, if Michael is considered to be the chief of all angels, and if the chief of all angels naturally becomes the archangel, then through the interpretation of the scripture, it logically surmises that Lord Jesus Himself is Archangel Michael.

Could it be that this is the reason why the meaning of Michael is 'the one who is like God'? Who can be like God, if not His own son, Jesus Christ?

In his last recorded talk, Rudolf Steiner expressed concern about the 'great crisis' that all human beings would experience in the twenty-first century. He said, 'the (Archangel) Michael Power and the Michael Will (will) penetrate the whole of life' and that these 'are none other than the Christ Power and the Christ Will'.

Many Jews are of the belief that not only did Archangel Michael fight with Satan to protect the dead body of Prophet Moses, but it was Archangel Michael who was the teacher of Prophet Moses on Mount Sinai and it is very clearly mentioned in Apoc. Mosis, i. that Prophet Moses received the commandments written on the two tables through the intercession of Archangel Michael. In the Book of Jubilees (i. 27, ii. 1) it is believed that the angel who gave Prophet Moses the commandments called the 'Tables of the Law' is none other than Archangel Michael.

Archangel Michael has many roles to play. As mentioned above, He is assigned as the protector and the commander of the army of God against the dark forces.

In Catholic teachings, He is also considered the 'Angel of Death' and the 'Guardian of Souls', carrying the souls of all those who have passed over to heaven. (In Persia, He was and is still considered the prince of the stars by a select few. Archangel Michael is taken as a divine guide of human souls, guiding and guarding them towards eternal divine radiance.)

This role of Archangel Michael or Saint Michael as the guardian of the souls comes through this prayer dedicated to Him:

The holy house of God venerates you as Her guardian and protector;

To You the Lord has entrusted the souls of the redeemed
To be led into Paradise.

He is also depicted carrying a scale, which signifies Him weighing the soul's deeds, thus deciding how the scale tilts.

The Roman Catholic poetry dedicated to Saint Michael goes as below:

That you will gather the souls of the righteous and the wicked, place us on Your great scales and weigh our deeds.

That if we have been loving and kind, you will take the key from around our neck and open the gates of Paradise, inviting us to live there for ever.

And that if we have been selfish and cruel, it is you who will banish us.

It is believed that Archangel Michael comes forth just before one is going to pass over, giving the individual and the soul a chance to redeem itself. Archangel Michael takes upon Himself to make sure that very few join the legion of Satan and the band of dark forces. Archangel Michael is also prayed to by the righteous for protection.

Incidentally, in early days, Archangel Michael was considered to be the greatest of all healers and vast multitudes of people prayed to Michael for good health and to be healed of all afflictions—from minor to fatal illnesses. For example, Christians who lived in Egypt placed the Nile river, which was their 'be all end all' of survival, well-being and prosperity under the protection of St Michael and there were large festivities held for the archangel. In the early days, if there was an epidemic people beseeched Archangel Michael to heal them and rescue them from the disease.

It is also believed by a number of Archangel Michael followers and researchers that God after having created Archangel Michael, entrusted Him with the chiefdom and mastership of all the forces, of lightning, thunder, clouds, wind and the nature spirits. In his book *Michael's Mission*, Rudolf Steiner states the belief that the meteorite iron was hurled down on Mother Earth by Archangel Michael to neutralize all the effects of negativity created by human emotions.

In Arabic and the Koran, Archangel Michael is called Mīkhā'īl, Mika'il, Mīkāl or Mikal (ليئاخيم) who provides nourishment not only for all human beings but also for their spirit bodies and souls. In Islam, Mīkhā'īl is the Archangel of Mercy and the one who is responsible for rewarding noble people for the good that they have done in their physical life. It is believed that while on His deathbed, Prophet Mohammed stated that Archangel Gabriel would be the first to pray for Him and Archangel Michael would be the second to pray over Him. In the Koran, there is one mention of Archangel Michael or Mīkāl: 'Whoever is an enemy of God or his angels or his apostles or Jibrīl (Archangel Gabriel) or Mīkāl, verily God is an enemy of the unbelievers.'

There is this story that once Archangel Gabriel and Archangel Michael visited Prophet Mohammed who held a stick given to Him by Archangel Gabriel. All divinations that the Prophet had experienced were through Archangel Gabriel and the latter inquires of the Prophet: 'O Mohammed! Give it (the stick) to the oldest angel.' Prophet Mohammed gives the stick to Archangel Michael saying, 'God gave me two heavenly counsellors to help me teach my message—Gabriel and Michael.'

In fact it is believed that the Prophet would voice His concern for the fate of all humankind to both Archangel Michael and Archangel Gabriel. In Islamic tradition, in heaven, the one who gives the call for all to sit for prayer (muezzin) is Archangel Gabriel, and the leader of those who pray (imam) is Archangel Michael.

There seems to have been some issue between the Jews and Muslims over Archangel Michael and Archangel Gabriel. For the former were only in favour of Archangel Michael, as is evident in this story about Prophet Mohammed. It seems that one day the Prophet was questioned by a few Jews about His prophetic revelations and all was well till then, but when the Prophet revealed that it was Archangel Gabriel who was the medium and the bearer of His revelations, the Jews seemed to have gotten riled and spoke ill of Archangel Gabriel, and called the archangel the spirit of destruction and the enemy of Archangel Michael, who was considered as the angel of fertility. There is another story of Caliph, Umar, who inquired of a few Jew scholars as to how Archangel Michael and Archangel Gabriel were regarded by God. The Jews replied that Archangel Michael sat at God's left and Archangel Gabriel at God's right but that the two archangels were enemies. Hearing this, Caliph Umar answered that an enemy of either archangel was immediately an enemy of God.

Even Joan of Arc was a staunch believer in Archangel Michael and the army of angels. Her life has been described in the book, *In Her Own Words*, where she has been quoted about the angels and Archangel Michael: 'I have never had need of them and not had them come.'; 'Whatever I have done that was good, I have done at the bidding of my voices.'; 'I shall call them to help me as long as I live.'; where she clearly only mentions Archangel Michael:

'When I was thirteen, I had a voice from God to help me to govern myself. The first time, I was terrified. The voice came to me about noon: it was summer, and I was in my father's garden . . . I saw it many times before I knew it was Saint Michael . . . He was not alone, but duly attended by heavenly angels . . . He told me Saint Catherine and Saint Margaret would come to me, and I must follow their counsel; that they were appointed to guide and counsel me in what I had to do, and that I must believe what they would tell me, for it was at our Lord's command.'

Saint Joan always took the counsel, guidance and protection of Archangel Michael, Saint Catherine of Alexandria and Saint Margaret (Marina)—Her three spirit guides. Saint Joan also mentioned her meeting with Archangel Gabriel.

Saint Francis of Assisi truly sums up the magnificence of Archangel Michael. He loved Saint Michael as He referred to the archangel as a saint and felt deeply that one and all should praise and honour Archangel Michael as He truly wanted all to be on the side of God and because His duty was to present souls to God. In the words of Saint Francis: 'Each person should offer God some special praise or gift in honour of such a great Prince.' Saint Francis would fast for nearly forty days from the feast of the Assumption (15 August) to Saint Michael's feast day on 29 September in love and honour of Archangel Michael.

Archangel Michael is always on guard against evil and is also occupied in an incessant war against the forces of evil. He is the first and the truest warrior of God or the warrior of light. He is always there for the humble and for all those who fight alone against all odds, be it external negative forces or internal strife between what is right and wrong. When called out to, Archangel Michael comes forth in all His glory and stands in front, fighting the true fight along with each individual. He is there to fight side by side against injustice. When the odds are stacked against you, when you feel lonely and defeated, call out to Him and you will feel His presence, just as countless believers have experienced. His colour is blue, some say steely blue, some have experienced laser blue too. Cover yourself in the luminous blue light, imagining that womb of blue light to be His protection. Call out to Him and He will be there.

If you are being maligned, prosecuted, or have committed a major mistake and have realized your mistake and through repentance call out to Him, He will be there by your side. He is the one who you call out when you are attacked emotionally, mentally, physically or via black magic or the evil eye or physic attack. All He needs and seeks is that you fight with courage, never tiring, never fearing, never giving up or giving in to the dark forces. Many believe that by constantly beseeching Him to fill one up with His strength, courage and love for God, one too becomes a Warrior of Light.

I have taken the liberty of channelling a prayer through Baba Sai of Shirdi. There are many prayers one can pray to Archangel Michael and they can be easily got via the Internet.

Below is a prayer that you can pray to Archangel Michael that came through from Baba Sai of Shirdi.

Archangel Michael, Prince of Heaven and Light

I pray to Thou for protection.

First and foremost protection from myself,

Protect me from my own ignorance, foolishness, negativity, vanity, and ego

Let me help myself live a life filled with child-like joy and humble dignity.

I beseech you to protect me and my loved ones from the world outside

Those who visibly wish us harm and those who have a smile in their eyes and evil in their heart and intent

Protect me from those who wish me and my loved ones loss, humiliation and sorrow

Those who cannot see me and my loved ones happy, prosperous, healthy and in peace, protect me from them all, Archangel Michael; the Powerful One.

Protect us from magic intended to harm me and my lot

Attacks that we cannot see or protect ourselves from

Let Thy shield and sword be our armour and our protection,

Cover us and our physical, emotional, mental and spiritual bodies with Thy love and Thy embrace.

Surround and protect me and my loved ones with Thy army of angels

Let Thy glory and armour of protection be visible to those who wish me and my loved ones harm, so they withdraw forever

Bless the weak, the meek, the ailing, the lonely, the sick, the poor with strength, calmness and peace.

For those who have passed over, do not let anyone be earthbound

Let more and more join the army of the Light,

Let justice and oneness prevail for now and for eternity,

So be it as I pray, so be it as I yearn, so be it as I believe

In You Archangel Michael, the one who is like God, I trust,

Be with me now and hold my hand when I leave this physical shell

And with me be for now and beyond the beyond

Amin!

13

Ramana: The MahaRishi

Illustration by Pooja Bangia

The story of Ramana Maharshi, or as I like to call Him, Ramana the MahaRishi, is that of simplicity. Not only was this master, like all masters, child-like, but His philosophy, too, was straightforward.

He believed that it was the identification of oneself to the body and everything related to the body which was the bane of all issues. The more the individual identified with his or her body, the more entrapped the individual got with the outside world, getting mired in the quicksand of karma and its laws of cause and effect.

The only thing, according to Ramana, was to ask this simple question:

Who am I?

Am I the body or am I the consciousness in this body? The more one questioned oneself, the less hold karma and the laws of karma had on the individual, as then slowly one stopped identifying with the body, the desires, the emotions, the words, the actions that followed. The more one stopped to identify with actions, thoughts, words, deeds, the grasp of karma and its fanatically rigid laws loosen their hold over the individual.

The more one got absorbed in the silence within, the chaos outside first stopped having a vice-like grip on the individual and then slowly, the hold of karma and all that which plummets one's true flight weakened and finally, the individual realized the oneness of it all.

To achieve this state of oneness and to burn away one's karmic balance sheet, the only thing required was to be silent and still from within. Nothing else was required but the repeated query: *Who am I?*

Am I the body? No. Then am I the desires? No. Am I the thoughts within? No. Am I this and am I that? No. Am I what the divorce decree says I am? Hell, no. Then Lord love a defrosted duck, who am I?

I am pure consciousness.

Just as Baba Sai of Shirdi had shown Upasani Maharaj two selves in a vision—one body dark and negative, the other body, pure and shimmering. Then Baba Sai had destroyed the spirit body of Upasani which harboured darkness. But He told Upasani Maharaj, that it was only after He destroyed even the so-called purer body of Upasani, would Upasani really be free. As till there is a body, physical, astral, causal, pure, impure, it doesn't matter, one is really not free. It is only when one has no identification with any of the bodies, but just pure consciousness, does one truly soar on the wings of the archangels, homeward bound.

Ramana, too, believed that it was when the individual only dwelt within, not identifying himself or herself with either the body, the thoughts, the desires, the karma, actions, words, but only with his or her true form, which is pure consciousness, that the pull and tug of heart, mind, actions, words, fame, repute, slander, ill repute, everything would just drop away.

He did not advocate leaving everything and going away to some mosquito-infested cave in some remote area where a mobile network was a distant reality.

All He insisted on was to stop identifying oneself with the body, as we are not the body but the energy within the body. He was very clear that what is destined will take place, no matter what, and what is not destined, if desired, will remain confided in the womb for future materializations.

When an individual speaks, acts, thinks, without identifying himself or herself with the word, action, thought, that is the time the clock of karma begins to stand still. Karma cannot affect an individual who doesn't identify himself or herself with the action, thought or word.

For example, let us say, you give ten rupees to a beggar. You have given the money as you feel the beggar truly needs it. All is well till now. But the moment you feel good about it, the moment you feel your master has seen all this and is going to bless you, the moment you feel the beggar is going to bless you, or praise you or your karma might get a little easier to bear, you have identified yourself with the action of giving the ten rupees to the beggar. That moment itself the laws of karma get into motion. You have tied yourself with the beggar in a karma gig.

But let us say you have given the money to the beggar because you truly feel compassionate towards the beggar and just want to lighten the burden of the man or burden and that's it. No pleasing the master, no getting bonus points from Him, no thought or intention or expectation of reducing your own karma, no blessings, nothing involved, but sheer compassion and love for the beggar, then you have not identified yourself with the action and thus karma cannot have a hold over you.

If it has to take place, it will take place. But the moment you and I stop identifying with the action or the result, emotions, thoughts or word, then we are removed from the arena of karmic play.

When does this happen? Ramana was clear that this can only happen when you realize that you are not the body, you are not your thoughts, you are not even your desires and emotions. You are beyond all this. You are pure consciousness, having chosen to be caught in the web of give and take, consumed by impressions collected through lifetimes of identifying oneself with the body.

The moment you realize that you cannot possibly be the body, the thoughts, the emotions, but you are beyond all that, the true journey inward starts and culminates with Godhood.

Ramana was emphatic that all one needs is to keep questioning oneself: Who am I truly? For that one needs to just be still and go within. Keep asking yourself, who am I? Keep at it? Am I this? Am I that? If I am not the body, nor the thoughts, nor the desires, then who am I? And one day, through the womb of silence, the wave of self-realization will engulf the individual and then the truth of oneness will embrace you.

All one needs to do is sit quietly, eyes shut and questioning every thought that arises, every desire that pounds, every word that echoes: Am I this? No? Then who am I?

Slowly, silence will engulf you. Embrace you within its sigh. The world may collapse around you, but you will know this is the dance of karma, nothing personal, nothing that can do the real you any harm.

Ramana was of the belief that most of us operate from fear. The genesis of this fear has come most often through lifetimes of identifying with the false self. When one realizes that you cannot be affected, the real you cannot be harmed, slandered, betrayed, hurt, manipulated, killed—fears will slowly drop away. Yes, one will go through what one has to go through, but the impact and ramification will not affect you, as the real you sits quietly embraced by pure silence within.

Who was Ramana? He was born on 30 December 1879 in Tamil Nadu. His name was Venkateswara, but for some reason, whoever was filling His form during admission in school, spelt his name as Venkataraman.

Ramana was breastfed till he was five. There was a motherless child named Meenakshi, a close relative, who He was fond of. Ramana showed His compassion early on when He refused to be fed till His mother had not first breastfed Meenakshi.

In school He was only interested in sports and games. He didn't care much for studies but was so intelligent that somehow He would get good grades. Two things were noticed about Him which were different from the beginning. No matter how badly He fell down or hurt Himself, His body would not show even a scratch.

The second being, He couldn't stand bullies and would get into fist fights, and because He was tough, He would be the last boy standing. But there was a problem. When Ramana slept, He could sleep through a war or an earthquake. Even if He was thrashed to be awakened for school, He would continue to sleep peacefully. Later on He would wonder why His body ached. That was because either His family would thrash Him to wake him up or His friends would come in the night to thrash Him, to get even with Him for all the thrashing He would give them during the day, as He couldn't stand fools easily.

But strangely, neither Ramana nor his brother required too many hours of sleep. So they would stuff the bed with pillows, cover the pillows with a blanket and then scoot outside to be with their friends long into the night. This habit remained with Ramana even after He became Ramana the MahaRishi. His devotees would always worry about His health and Him not getting enough rest and sleep. So strict instructions were given to one and all to let this sage rest and to make sure this was achieved; they would periodically make rounds to see if their master was asleep and that nobody was disturbing Him. Little did they know that the master would stay awake late into the night talking to His helpers and those who were meant to take care of Him and whenever He would know from within that the surveyors were nearby, He would tell all to pretend to sleep, and once alone, they would all chat till late in the night.

Soon, He and His brother were sent away from home, as His father wanted them to be educated in English. Thus He was well-versed in English too.

Even as a child, He was a leader and His words meant a lot to His friends. Once when He saw His Muslim friend eat a non-vegetarian dish, He showed His displeasure of having to kill an innocent animal to appease one's taste buds. The Muslim friend turned vegetarian for the rest of his life. But the strange part was that many of His disciples and devotees have recounted that though He never told anybody to be vegetarian, spending a little time with Ramana, the desire to eat non-vegetarian food would surprisingly disappear for the rest of their lives.

The turning point in Ramana's life was when His father passed over. Ramana stood by the body of His father and realized that His father was not in the body. The body of His father lay near Him but Ramana couldn't identify with the body, as this body was not His father. His father had left the building, as one were to say. Later on, Ramana told one of His disciples, Paul Brunton, 'It was the "I" which makes the body to see, to run, to walk and to eat . . . I know this "I" but my father's "I" had left the body.'

It was after a short while of His father passing away, on the afternoon of 17 July 1896, when Ramana was seventeen years of age, that an incident took place which transformed His life and the journey towards oneness began.

For some reason on that day, Ramana got obsessed and terrified with the fear of death and dying. It was overwhelming and there was no real reason for such fear. But the fear wouldn't leave Him. No matter what, how hard He tried to shake the claws of death and the fear of dying, the terror of dying overwhelmed Ramana. He lay on the floor and imagined Himself dying. He enacted the whole drama of death to the extent of His grieving family putting Him on the funeral pyre and giving the pyre the lick of flame.

He imagined His body burnt to ashes and then the ashes consigned to the waters. And He realized that He was never in the body when He died. He couldn't have been. He was consciousness. He was energy. How could consciousness be consigned to the holy fire? 'So I am the spirit transcending the body. The body dies, but the spirit that transcends it cannot be touched by death. This means I am the deathless spirit.'

This experience was the turning point in the life of Ramana. He began to go deeper and deeper within Himself. His attitude changed. He no longer fought, He no longer criticized, He no longer challenged. He became within. He did all His duties but His observation and contemplation of 'who am I' never left Him for a moment.

It was then that Ramana realized He was not cut out for the normal world. His need to go more within Himself was overpowering. Just before the incident of His tryst with His own death, He had just read Sekkilar's *Periya Puranam*; the book was about the lives of the sixty-three saints who worshipped Lord Shiva. The love, the faith, the devotion that the saints had for the divine and the need for oneness with the Creator, was so overwhelming that Ramana realized that His time, too, had come to dive within and swim in the ocean of silence and embrace oneness.

Six weeks later, on the pretext of some assignment, He left home for Arunachala, in Tiruvannamalai. Ramana had been lately mesmerized by Arunachala.

I can vouch for Arunachala. In 2001, along with my then-publisher and now old friend, Sunit Banerjee, and his wife Meena, we had gone to Arunachala. I was editing *Om Mystic*, one of the first web magazines on spirituality in India. So we arrived in Tiruvannamalai and it was already late. We had some grub and then I entered my hotel room and though the airconditioner was on, I wanted to breathe in fresh air. I opened the windows and I saw this mountain, right in front of me. It was nearing sunset or it was twilight. And I sat mesmerized by this mountain. There was something about this mountain that was profound. I sat and looked at it and then did what most people do when humbled by divinity. I lit a smoke.

Unable to look away from the mountain I left the hotel, got lost, fifteen minutes later found myself again in front of the mountain. It was now dark but there were lot of folks with carts and a certain part of the mountain was lit.

I stopped a chap and asked him what was with this mountain. He told me something in Tamil, which didn't sound very parliamentary and the bugger walked away. I stood staring at the mountain and then a foreigner came and stood by me. He, too, looked at the mountain.

We looked at each other.

'You know what is with this mountain?'

'That's not a mountain. It's a hill. Yes, this is the place Bhagvan Ramana Maharshi got enlightened. He stayed here for a long time. He was really a dude, man,' he replied.

'Yes, that's what I have been told too.'

We both stared at the mountain, which I was recently told was a hill and after a while when I looked around, I realized the man had left.

The next day we went to the ashram and it was so serene and beautiful. I sat by His samadhi and I felt a deep sense of silence within me. A profound state of nothingness. No joy, no happiness, no sadness, just nothingness.

So anyway, Tiruvannamalai, situated at the foot of Arunachala, is a small town, around 120 miles southwest of Chennai.

Ramana called Arunachala the spiritual heart of the world and I truly tell you, I knew jack about anything, but the hill mesmerized me. There is something in that hill.

Aruna means 'red bright like fire'. Ramana said it signifies not mere fire but the fire of knowledge and wisdom.

Achala means a hill. Thus Arunachala means the 'Hill of Wisdom'.

The story of Arunachala goes something like this. Once, for some odd reason, Lord Vishnu and Lord Brahma got into an argument about who was greater amongst the two. Our two Gods got overtly involved in the argument and there was chaos on Mother Earth.

Lord Shiva was meditating in some place and realized that both Vishnu and Brahma were sort of creating the mother of all ruckuses and so He appeared to Them as a beam or a column of light and after hearing Them out, He told Them that whoever finds either the end or the beginning of His light would be the Boss Man.

Lord Vishnu took the form of a boar and began to burrow away like crazy but after a lot of burrowing He began to see within Himself the light that He was trying to find.

I feel what the legend is trying to say is something like this . . . ya ya . . . am rambling again . . . somebody has to . . . so this is what I think: Vishnu and Brahma though Gods, began to identify Themselves with Their actions and thus began to lose Their Godhood as it brought Them down to karmic entrapment. Vishnu burrowed inside . . . means when you go more and more within, searching for the light, you realize that you are the light. So Lord Vishnu realized the light burning within Himself. He began to see within Himself the divine light which in reality resides in the hearts of all.

Okay, enough of my rambling now, back to serious stuff.

In the meanwhile, Lord Brahma went upwards in the form of a swan and He saw a flower of some plant falling and decided to sort of cheat . . . naughty boy Lord Brahma . . . and declared that He was the winner.

But when Lord Vishnu praised Lord Shiva that He was the 'be all and end all' of everything and resided in everyone, in their heart, Lord Brahma confessed that He had cheated. According to Ramana, Lord Vishnu represents the intellect, Brahma the ego, while Lord Shiva is the atman, the eternal spirit which resides in every being.

As the legend goes, Lord Shiva then tells one and all, 'As the moon derives its light from the sun, so other holy places shall derive their sanctity from Arunachala. This is the only place where I have taken this form for the benefit of those who wish to worship Me and obtain illumination. Arunachala is *Om* itself.' Ramana too made it clear that, 'In the end everyone must come to Arunachala.'

So Ramana left for Arunachala six weeks after He went through the fear of death and realized that it is all about 'Who am I?'

Ramana reached Arunachala and He began to go into a state of samadhi. He would go so deep into the state of samadhi that for days He would remain in samadhi. The local boys would harass Him, throwing stones at Him. Very often Ramana's body would be bleeding but He didn't care. Once He entered a deep pit filled with scorpions, snakes, insects and thus sat in peace for days but the boys found His spot and continued to hound Him.

It was then that a senior swami, Seshadri by name, realizing who Ramana really was, began to watch over the young sage. Those who did not know Seshadri took the swami to be a mad man and He protected young Ramana. When he realized that the pit would be the ruin of Ramana's body, Seshadri with the help of a few like-minded people, picked up Ramana who was still clueless about His body and brought Ramana's body near the shrine of Subrahmanya. His body was badly bitten and pus and blood sprang forth from various parts of His body. Ramana was oblivious to what had happened to His body.

Then six months later He was shifted to a shrine called Gurumurtam. Ramana lived for years like this, being shifted from one place to another. His fame spread far but He was oblivious to it all. He sat for weeks on the floor with countless ants crawling all over Him, stinging Him, His body sometimes a mesh of bites and blood. Ramana did not speak for eleven years. His mother found out where He was and He refused to leave. He was beyond the calling of mortals.

Ramana then went to the Virupaksha Cave in Arunachala. This cave is very important for Ramana lovers, as it was here that He broke His eleven-year silence. This was a cave used by a powerful sage who lived in the thirteenth century and is shaped like the symbol Om. I believe it was here that Ramana came back to human consciousness with oneness from God-consciousness. It was here that His mother eventually came to live with Him and She became His follower and threw away all her prejudices and became the mother of all Ramana's disciples. It was here that she passed away with Ramana taking care of her and making sure she was freed from the bondage of karma. In this cave, Ramana dictated His profound works, *Who Am I?* and *Self Enquiry* and it was here that He was called Bhagvan Ramana Maharshi.

More than once Ramana and His devotees were looted by dacoits. Every time they robbed Him, they hit Ramana. Once they slapped Him and another time hit Him hard on the thigh. Both the times Ramana offered Himself to them, to be hit, requesting them not to touch His people.

'The snake bites, the scorpion stings, the bull buffs. Are we right in crushing them because they do so? We should try to keep away from them. Even so, the thieves think that it is their nature to commit theft. But to pardon them is our dharma, our sacred duty. True humanity lies not in returning violence for violence, but in forgiveness. Let us set the man free.' After the thieves left, Ramana told His followers with a smile, 'They have worshipped me also.'

Later on, an ashram was opened. Ramana remained who He was: a friend of animals, the downtrodden and the poor. Animals, birds, squirrels, flocked around Him. A cow once put her head on His shoulder and cried and He tended to Her broken heart by talking to her. Later on she died with Him caressing her and assuring her that she was free from all karmic bondage. He healed a broken egg, nursing it till the egg hatched and joyously played with the baby, got slapped by a monkey and humbly apologized to it, realizing that the monkey was the king of his tribe and thus needed that respect which Ramana accorded to Him. He never referred to an animal or a bird as 'it' but always 'he' or 'she'. He was very protective about them. It was as though He spoke to them and they spoke to Him. There are innumerable stories of His interaction with animals.

Ramana could never tolerate any discrimination. Till the end He made it clear that be it an animal, a bird, a poor person, an elder, a child, they had the first right over Him. He would make sure the poor were fed properly, the women were treated with equality, no preferential treatment was given to Him and that He was accessible to all who wanted to come to see Him or talk to Him. Nobody went without being fed or helped. No matter what ailed Him, He was always there, with a smile and compassion flowing through Him.

And then the master got cancer. He was seventy years old, but looked much older. The physical deprivation and the lack of regard to His body had taken its toll. A nodule appeared below the elbow of his left hand. The doctors operated on it but in a month's time it reappeared. Ramana joked with the doctors that the nodule kept rising up like a very loving Shiva's *lingam*. Surgeons from Chennai were called. They operated but without success. Once He went through the operation without anaesthesia. Somebody asked Him whether it hurt Him. He said yes, it hurt the body.

Nothing could hurt Him though. Eventually, the doctors advised that His arm should be amputated. He refused, and said that just a simple cloth covering would do. 'There is no need for it. This body itself is a big disease. Such being the case why should the hand itself be cut off? Let any thing happen. Let this hand die naturally.'

But through it all, He spent time with His animals and birds and the throngs of devotees who came to seek His darshan. He was in tremendous pain but He never showed it to anybody. The doctors wondered how such a frail man could function with so much ease when they were certain He was going through severe pain and agony.

Many of His devotees wanted Him to perform a miracle on Himself and cure Himself. He said the greatest miracle is to go within and find God residing within each one.

On 14 April 1950, He came out to give blessings to the countless devotees who kept thronging the ashram for His blessings. He was weak and though He didn't show it, He was in extreme pain. He looked at all and kept blessing all. It was evening time. He asked His helpers to make Him sit upright. His eyes were ablaze with glory. Tears trickled down His cheeks and then He breathed His last. At that very moment, the newspapers reported the next day, when the master took samadhi, a comet moved slowly across the sky, reached the summit of the holy Arunachala hill and disappeared behind it.

Ramana only wanted each one of us to go beyond the body. Not to identify with the body, but with the eternal spirit within each one of us. This is our reality, the spirit within.

All else is dancing with shadows.

14

Sai's Chosen One, Meher's Guru: Upasani Maharaj

Illustration by Pooja Bangia

U pasani Maharaj holds a special place in the hearts of all those who love and revere Sainath of Shirdi and Avatar Meher Baba.

Upasani Maharaj was Sai's most beloved disciple and Shirdi Sai's grace and love turned a man with innumerable demons within to become a Perfect Master. He was also the one who brought Meher Baba from being completely immersed with Godhood into the dimension of duality: God with human consciousness. From a man who was only God-consciousness into God who accommodated within the man, human consciousness too.

So who really was Upasani Maharaj?

Kashinath Govindrao Upasani (15 May 1870–24 December 1941) never really conformed to anything that was normal as a child. While very young, He was thrashed by a teacher; he decided then and there that formal education was a waste of time. He was thus educated at home by His grandfather, who eventually renounced everything and went into seclusion, in search of God.

Where Kashinath lived there was a woman who the villagers considered either mad or to be a sorceress. The villagers avoided her and the children harassed her. Kashinath was not an exception.

One day, young Upasani Maharaj began to experience unbearable pain in the stomach and within a few weeks the village doctor diagnosed the cause of the pain as incurable and death to be inevitable.

So Kashinath's family decided that if the boy was anyway going to get a pair of wings, there was no harm in going to the controversial witch and trying their luck.

The old lady saw Kashinath and told the family that hell could freeze over but she was not going to help cure the boy. The family pleaded, but the old woman was adamant, muttering that the boy had troubled her a lot and thus He had got this illness and that the village doctor, who usually was as accurate in his diagnosis as the local drunkard, had for some odd reason got it correct this time and the boy was going to die.

The young boy, I assume, must have got an out-of-body experience with fright, and pleaded with the suave senior citizen who was breathing fire, to forgive Him. She muttered a few things under her breath and said, 'On one condition.' If He was to live and get well, He would have to come and visit her every day and spend some time with her.

I am sure Kashinath must have pondered over which was more preferable, a quick death or a slow one, but better sense prevailed and the boy gave His word.

So every day, it must have been some sight for sore eyes, the witch and the small boy sat facing each other, sometimes talking and other times, the boy with mouth ajar observing the witch.

As time passed, the young boy began to get better and in some time was completely cured. No herbs, no medicines; nothing; just spending time with this strange woman had cured the boy's stomach pain. But she infected Him with something far more serious—the worst possible pain and ache in all of creation—the agony that comes with the realization of being separated from God. She was inflicted with that pain of duality and she, the kind and good woman that she was, put the seeds of longing for God in Kashinath's young heart.

Thus all His life, Upasani Maharaj hated His body as He felt His body caged Him and separated Him from oneness with the Creator. But strangely, all His spiritual growth was due to His body.

So His first step towards spiritual accession began with a stomach pain that forced Him to spend time with the old woman–witch–mast, in love with God.

Thus began His journey. He got more and more disenchanted with the world around Him and His own body. He began to meditate or contemplate on God. He was happy in His own isolation. The family, seeing such behaviour, decided the best course of action to bring Kashinath to Mother Earth and maybe end His happiness and His search for the elusive one, was sure and certain—to get Him married.

He was fourteen and the girl was eight years old.

Those days the elders didn't waste time. So Kashinath did the most sensible thing—every married man since Adam has contemplated this, but not many have put it to action. He ran away. His grandfather, already rather evolved, realized where his errant grandchild was and wrote Him a letter that His mother was critically ill. The ruse worked. Kashinath came back and realized He had been duped. His child-bride died a year later. The family those days didn't waste too much time in mourning and all that nonsense, and in some time got the clueless and extremely bewildered Kashinath married again.

He was in a very vulnerable state, since not known to all, He had begun to have spiritual experiences, to which He had no answer. He had also begun to hear a peculiar voice in His head which He could not shut out. He ran away again, but returned, and then, after a while on the pretext of work, He went in search of somebody or to find some answer to what was eating Him up. He was truly confused and agitated and distraught. He had an issue with His body. He was miserable, and that voice within Him, sometimes soft, sometimes really loud, was making Him lose His mind.

He had begun to harbour suicidal tendencies, something He fought against until Baba Sai removed all the angst from Upasani Maharaj.

So Maharaj, unable to get a cure for His spiritual predicament, in his late teens entered a forest, climbed a mountain and entered a cave. Nobody can truly understand how He did so, as it seems an impossible task for whoever has visited this cave. His intention was clear. Either He got some answers to the voice that spoke to Him about what was really happening to Him, or He intended to test the laws of gravity.

Upasani Maharaj spent nine months in the cave. Initially very frustrated, He slowly slipped into samadhi and blanked out from this very interesting world. He fasted for nine months, surviving on whatever little rain water collected in the cave. He was skin and bones, and was on the verge of dying. His throat was parched. He felt as though somebody was pulling out His tongue and His skin was torn. He had no strength to come down the precarious mountain and wondered how on earth He had entered the cave in the first place. He had gone without food for nine months and had not drunk water for as far as He could remember. He knew He could no longer kill Himself, but it was as though God had heard His plea to die, nine months too late. And then it began to rain and rain and rain and water began to enter the cave and though He couldn't move, somehow the water reached Him, wet His lips and slowly He began to drink the cool rain water.

It was years later that He found out that His Boss Man, Sai Baba of Shirdi, knower of everything, had heard His pleas and Baba Sai had instructed His spiritual workers in the astral plane to bring down the rains. These spiritual workers are also called spiritual agents or *abdal*s, who surround masters to do Their bidding. I can imagine Sai Baba telling His abdals, 'Okay, My son now needs Me. He is in that blasted cave for nine months, first wanting to die and now wanting to live, go and make sure water reaches Him and I don't want ifs and buts, now get moving.'

So They got moving and seeing that there was no way They could get water up to the cave, They got water down into the cave. Upasani Maharaj eventually got some strength and I am sure being helped by the abdals, He reached the village nearby.

It took Him a month to get well and He returned to His family. He was in a better state spiritually and thus mentally, and decided to get back to the world of mankind. He studied ayurveda and became a doctor and also became an editor of a magazine that dealt with health and ayurveda. A few years passed and He became a rich man, bought hundreds of acres of land, and then, as it happens to all those who are marked by the wise one, in a short period of time He became bankrupt again. By then His second wife, too, had passed over and He was married to His third wife, who understood Upasani Maharaj and His angst and did not pressurize Him to once again take on His medical profession.

Upasani Maharaj and His wife decided to go on a pilgrimage and one night, when Upasani Maharaj was in a deep state of meditation He experienced a jolt, some occult experience, and He fell to the ground, unconscious. He was thought to be dead but His wife revived Him. Upasani Maharaj regained His consciousness, but from that moment He began to experience difficulty in breathing. Something had gone wrong which had affected His breathing.

His search to get cured one day made Him want to meet one of the five Perfect Masters, Narayan Maharaj. The master was giving darshan and there was a long line of devotees waiting to take the master's blessings but Narayan Maharaj told one of His devotees to bring the young man to Him first. He treated Upasani Maharaj as one of His own and removed a garland that adorned Him and placed it on the young bewildered man. Upasani Maharaj was so humble that He could never understand why a Perfect Master would treat Him with so much love, little realizing that in a short time He, too, would form the band of the five Perfect Masters, headed by Sai Baba of Shirdi, and including giants like Baba Jaan and Tajuddin Baba.

His breathing was making it impossible for Him to live in peace. He went to a very renowned ayurvedic doctor who after examining Him, and treating Him with a lot of love, advised Upasani Maharaj to go to Shirdi and take refuge in Baba Sai. He told Upasani Maharaj that this wasn't a physical ailment but was caused by intensive and exhaustive spiritual practices and breathing *kriya*s; the body had not been able to withstand the power of the spiritual energy and thus it had blocked certain chakras which needed Baba Sai's blessings to restore Upasani Maharaj back to normal health. Upasani Maharaj refused, saying He was not going to a Muslim fakir, as He belonged to a very high Brahmin lineage.

He kept suffering, and went back to Narayan Maharaj, who once again showed great respect and love and made Him eat *paan*, telling Upasani Maharaj that now He, Narayan Maharaj had coloured Him from within with the divine colours.

The ayurvedic doctor kept pressurizing Him to meet Sai Baba of Shirdi and at last on 27 June 1911, the bird came back to the nest.

Baba Sai through various conversations with His devotees that were actually intended for Upasani Maharaj, made it clear that They both had lived together innumerable lifetimes back. From my understanding, both Sai and Upasani were brother spiritualists, and for some reason, Upasani got waylaid on the spiritual path while Baba Sai moved on. But Baba Sai truly loved His friend and fellow spiritual brother and had decided that enough was enough; He would make

Upasani Maharaj finish His karmic cleansing and make Himself realized and a Perfect Master.

Sages say that the difference that exists in the state of consciousness between a stone and a normal human being, is the same when compared to the difference between an ordinary human being and a Perfect Master.

When Upasani Maharaj met Sai, the former was a normal human being, still far away from Godhood and Sai realized that only He, Sai, stood between His friend's karmic doom. Baba Sai was the singer whose voice Upasani Maharaj had been hearing from years and years. It was only later that Upasani Maharaj realized it.

But Upasani Maharaj was worried for His wife and His normal life. Baba Sai tried to prevent Him from leaving, but He was insistent. So Baba Sai told Him to go if He must, but in eight days They shall meet once again, here in Shirdi.

So Upasani Maharaj left, and eight days later, He still was unsure of how He managed to come back to Shirdi. Some say He kept travelling about in circles. Others say He got lost, and the people willing to make Him reach His home first wanted His help to reach a place very close to Shirdi and once they were near Shirdi, it was but natural they wanted to meet our old man. Whatever the reason may be, Upasani Maharaj stood in front of Baba Sai.

'So how many days ago did you leave Shirdi?'

'Eight days.'

'How many days did I predict you will stand in front of me?'

'Eight days.'

And slowly, Upasani Maharaj realized that this old fakir was a king in a really humble disguise.

It became clear to all that Sai Baba was partial to Upasani Maharaj. And Baba Sai said, 'Whatever He is, good or bad, He is Mine. There is no distinction between Him and Me. Now, the whole responsibility for Him rests with Me.'

Baba Sai sent Upasani Maharaj to a temple a few hundred feet away from where He sat. It was an old dilapidated Lord Khandoba's temple. His instructions to Upasani Maharaj were clear. He was not supposed to come out of the temple. Food would be sent to Him. Only for evening prayers would He come out and once prayers were over, He would return to the temple.

Upasani Maharaj entered the temple, which was inhabited by scorpions and snakes. Baba Sai had assured Him that He and His wife and near ones were protected and taken care of and to worry about nothing but to obey His wishes and that He knew best for Upasani Maharaj.

To make Upasani Maharaj understand who He truly was, Baba Sai told Upasani Maharaj, then only known as Kashinath, that He would come for a meal, thus to keep something for Him to eat. Kashinath would prepare a meal for Baba Sai every day and as Baba Sai was yet to come for a meal, He would take the meal to Him and offer it to Him as prasad. He wouldn't eat it as Baba Sai had made it clear He was not supposed to increase His karmic bonds by meeting anybody, and eat only what He sent.

Three months later when Sai was presented food by Kashinath, Baba Sai told Him that He had come for food but He had been shooed away. Kashinath said it was impossible as His eyes only searched for Baba. Baba Sai then asked Kashinath if He hadn't shooed away a black dog who had waited patiently for Him to give it some food. He was that dog.

Once again Baba Sai said He would come for food. Some time later, Baba Sai told Kashinath, what the hell, again He had shooed Him away. Kashinath kept wondering. Baba Sai then reminded Kashinath that He had taken on the guise of a poor untouchable.

Upasani Maharaj admitted that yes, he had shooed away an untouchable; years of conditioning had made Him look down on untouchables and Muslims.

Baba Sai then told Him, God and He, were in one and all. You look down on anybody; you look down on God and Baba Sai.

That was the cornerstone in Upasani Maharaj's life. Not only had He recognized the voice which had haunted Him for years, but He also dropped all discrimination henceforth.

Upasani Maharaj was sent food once a day as per Baba's wishes. Then one day Baba Sai stopped sending food. He resumed sending food after thirteen or fourteen months and Upasani Maharaj fasted for those thirteen or fourteen months. Scorpions, snakes, starvation, thirst, jealousy, spiritual and occult happenings—and He stood steadfast as his master had ordered and directed Him to be steadfast. The first law of spirituality, I shall obey, everything else follows later, even love.

By the end of that period, Upasani Maharaj was skin and bones. People stopped calling Him Kashinath any more, but called Him Upasani Maharaj, as 'upas' means to fast. He had conquered food and water, and thus He was henceforth called Upasani.

For four years Upasani Maharaj stayed in Lord Khandoba's temple. He went through hell. He went through various stages of spiritual growth and then realized oneness.

Baba removed His obsessive disdain of the body by making Upasani Maharaj have a vision. In that vision He saw there were two of Him. One filled with negativity and hate. The other filled with goodness. Baba Sai killed the one filled with negativity and evil. Then Upasani Maharaj questioned Baba, that was He now only good; was only good left? And Baba Sai said, even goodness isn't enough. Nothing should be left. Not even the good body, as we are only spirit, pure consciousness, devoid of all bodies; physical, astral and causal.

Baba Sai began to send somebody to specially cook for Upasani Maharaj. He began to send devotees to pray to Upasani Maharaj and do His aarti. He had in four years removed all karma attached to Upasani Maharaj and conferred Godhood on Him. This is why He once told all around Him about Upasani Maharaj. 'There was no one else like Him. His value only God knew. His merit was such that if the whole world was put on one side and He on the other, He would be greater!'

This is Baba Sai talking about Upasani Maharaj.

In the four years Upasani, with Baba Sai's permission, travelled to a few places. He didn't care about His clothing. He usually wore a gunny bag. He begged for food, slept in the dirtiest places. Once He was seen petting a dead animal and lying down next to it. He roamed about in tatters. He lay in dirt. But He could fool nobody. In spite of all His Baba Sai of Shirdi-like behaviour, which often, in the most polite words, was erratic, eccentric, wild and often abusive and violent, countless people rushed to Upasani Maharaj, too, for blessings. But He would always wonder, why Him? He always said He did nothing. Only His master and the Lord were the doers, but that didn't stop people from worshipping Him. On purpose He would stay with untouchables, and still the rich flocked to him; those who despised the untouchables forgot all their prejudices and would sit in the homes of untouchables, eat and drink in their humble homes, as Upasani Maharaj resided there.

He was a big man and He could be very, how should I say it, undiplomatic and non-Gandhian in His approach if anybody dared to get on His wrong side. But all those who knew Him realized He was a child at heart, with a mother's love for all.

His philosophy was simple—not to trouble anybody in the least. To suffer for all of creation, and be useful to others. To remain contented in a state of *be it as it may*. He also often told one and all that if you can't eat crap there is no way you are going to grow spiritually.

He did not mind it in the least when foreigners made fun of Him. Once kids put a garland of shoes around His neck and for days He roamed about with the garland of shoes till somebody had the courage to remove that garland and put a garland of flowers. He was unperturbed. He would tell one and all to worship anything, even old and torn shoes, as everything was pervaded with God's energy and presence. It didn't matter what one prayed to as long as one prayed with the belief that God resided in that thing and thus that thing automatically became God itself.

Upasani Maharaj started an ashram in Sakori, which is only five kilometres away from Shirdi, as Upasani Maharaj wanted to be as close to His Sai as possible. Yes, there was tremendous jealousy directed against Him by those who wanted Sai's favour and love only for themselves.

In Sakori, once again He fasted for over a year but this time He locked Himself in a bamboo cage that was so small that it barely allowed His six-feet-two-inch frame any movement. He did everything in that small cage and His devotees tried their best to keep it as clean as possible but He didn't care. He told one and all that He did this so that the karmas of His devotees were cleared.

When He came out of the cage, a girl child called Godavari garlanded Him. She would be His spiritual successor. Upasani Maharaj then began to teach the girl children scriptures and made them evolved. He made them understand the scriptures and then spread the true word. He made the virgin brides (married to the Lord) perform religious ceremonies much to the chagrin of the orthodox. He would allow untouchables to become one with the flock and educate them. The jealous spread the rumour that He was sex starved, but He didn't care. Till eventually, slowly, people realized the truth. He would give sermons to one and all and yes, if He lost it, would abuse and thrash one and all. Once He nearly thrashed a group of Hindu priests who refused to do prayers as Upasani held the painting of Sai Baba of Shirdi. He didn't care. He loved the old man. When Baba Sai dropped His body in 1918 it was Upasani Maharaj who performed the last rites.

After years, when He went back to Shirdi, He cried like a small child aching for His father and mother.

If Baba Sai was His guru and all, Avatar Meher Baba was His most beloved.

How can one forget Meher Baba and Upasani Maharaj's association? When living in Shirdi under Baba Sai's guidance and protection, Meher Baba approached Upasani Maharaj, who threw a stone that hit Meher Baba exactly at that same spot, at the centre of His forehead, which Baba Jaan had kissed and which had begun the journey of Meher Baba's avatarhood. By throwing the stone at the same spot, Upasani Maharaj brought Meher Baba back to human consciousness but as the Avatar.

They spent two days in Lord Khandoba's temple.

When Upasani Maharaj sought leave from Baba Sai of Shirdi, as there was tremendous jealousy and also because Baba Sai wanted Him to continue with His spiritual work, Upasani Maharaj settled down a few kilometres from His guru, in Sakori. Meher Baba would sometimes spend months at a stretch with Upasani Maharaj.

Then for twenty years They did not meet. The last time when They met was at the insistence of Upasani Maharaj two months before He took samadhi. They met for half an hour on a hillock. Nobody was allowed to see the Perfect Master meet the Avatar. The guru had become the child, while the child had become God in physical form. After the meeting, both looked at each other, knowing They would not meet again in the physical form.

Upasani Maharaj was very emotional in the last meeting with Meher Baba. He told Meher Baba, 'You are Adi Shakti, the ancient one, the all pervading one.'

What did the Avatar tell Upasani Maharaj?

'Oh Upasani Maharaj, our repeated salutations to you! Your name will be revered for ages to come! You brought down the ancient one and gave Him the knowledge to wipe away the tears of Our age! I can bring down the stars . . . I now have full powers . . . Maharaj has handed over His side of things to Me.'

The man who had an issue with His body, who went beyond the body and matter, worked ceaselessly for the upliftment of the poor and the women and the untouchables and all those who sought spiritual growth, passed over calmly, knowing He was going, like all Perfect Masters, with His spiritual successor, Godavari by His side.

15

Nanak . . . The Prophet and the Peasant

Illustration by Sumathi Shekhar

The first time I was made aware of Guru Nanak Saheb was when I was a young boy. I had returned for my Christmas vacations from my boarding school, Billimoria High School in Panchgani. The school had decided that Panchangi was way too cold during the winter and we were given a two-month off, in the hope that we would now drive our families up the wall and let the teachers and staff recuperate.

My cousins and I used to live with our maternal grandmother and on and off I would go to meet my parents and paternal grandparents. I was very close to my dad's father. For some reason he truly loved me and has come into my dreams, once even showing me an ancient kundalini exercise, which I religiously followed for four days.

So I was walking along with my grandfather when we passed a building and he halted, said a prayer, touched my head, and then we walked along. I asked him why he had halted, muttered or prayed at that spot.

'This is a gurudwara. A place where Sikhs and those who follow the teachings of Guru Nanak come to pray.'

'And who is Guru Nanak?' I inquired, trying to trip a boy who was running too fast for his own well-being.

'Like Prophet Zarathustra, He too was a prophet. He started the Sikh religion.'

'What's a prophet? Sounds like the fish we ate today . . .'

'We ate a pomfret.'

'Yes, I love pomfrets. Do you know that my school has the worst cooks in all of the world. All of the world, Big Papa. My school searches all of the world and finds these cooks. They are so bad that a few days before I came home, my friends and I realized that certain plants growing in the valley tasted better than the food. Of course, we were all sick as dogs the next day, holding our stomachs. Anyway what is a prophet?'

'A prophet is a good man who through prayers and His own goodness shows us all how to become one with God.'

'My cooks in school will never become one with God.'

'So Guru Nanak is the prophet of Sikhs.'

'And He was a good man?'

'Yes. Like you. You are going to be a very good man, my son.'

'No, you are a good man, Big Papa. Everybody says, wherever I am, there has to be lot of trouble.'

'It is all the energy within you. It has to come out somewhere. When you are big, this energy will come out in a good way. I won't be there with you then, but you will remember me.'

'Where are you going to go, Big Papa? You will be here only.'

'No. I will be with Them. Anyway, the prophets were good men who wanted to become the best of men who walked the Earth and They were so much in love with God that eventually They did become the best of men. Try to become the best person on Earth, baba. Even if you don't succeed, at least you will become a very, very good man and that is good enough.'

'I don't think the prophets would like the food in my school, Big Papa.'

And both of us chuckled and we went about walking.

So this was my introduction to Guru Nanak Saheb.

It was after twenty-odd years, while writing my first book, *The Last Marathon*, I was reintroduced to Guru

Nanak Saheb. I was researching on life after death and spirit communication. I would go to Vira Kheshvala who used to channel Avtar Meher Baba and Guru Nanak, who would come through calling Himself Ciam.

I always felt His energy to be very soft, very meditative, full of love and always wanting one and all to focus on God, meditate and chant the Lord's name.

In fact, the book opens with snaps of Baba Sai of Shirdi, Avatar Meher Baba and Guru Nanak Saheb. The book ends with a profile of Guru Nanak Saheb and His thoughts on meditation, mind over matter, the third eye, the art of giving and many more topics.

After ten years, I got married into a Sikh-Punjabi family who pray to and worship Baba Nanak. I wonder what my Big Papa would have to say about that.

The founder of the Sikh religion, Guru Nanak Saheb, was born in the Gregorian year 1469. Though 17 November is considered by most as His day of birth, scholars, researchers and astrologers, are of the opinion that Nanak Saheb was actually born in April, date unknown, but the time was midnight. Researchers and scholars of Christianity, too, believe that though His birth is universally celebrated on 25 December, in reality Jesus Christ was also born in the month of April.

Guru Nanak—or Satguru Nanak, Baba Nanak, Nanak Shah Faqir, Bhagat Nanak, Nanak Kalandar—it seems did not cry when He was born, but like Prophet Zarathustra, smiled and laughed. I guess if you can smile and laugh when you are born, you certainly are cut off for Godhood, as life on Earth has little to smile or laugh about.

What I love about Nanak Saheb is the 'no nonsense approach' to spirituality. He did not care much about the customs followed by either the Hindus or Muslims during His time. He did not believe that God could be won over by formalities, bribes, rigidity, blind faith, or age-old customs.

He was against the caste system, widows being forced onto their husbands' pyre, pilgrimages to get worldly favour and even bookish knowledge. His main aim was to preach oneness. His entire life in the physical shell was spent in preaching oneness and love for one another and living each moment chanting the name of God and loving God by whatever name you wanted to call Him and Her. He believed in chanting the name of the Lord. Being in prayer. Giving life your best. Sharing your wealth. Protecting the weak. Standing up to tyrants and always working towards the betterment of the world around you. He was against anything that stood for discrimination, falsehood of all kinds, hypocrisy and blind beliefs.

Once He saw some sadhus offering water to the sun. Nanak asked the men why they did what they did. One man replied that he was offering water to his ancestors. Thus, every morning when the sun rose, he would look eastward to the sun and offer water to his ancestors to quench their thirst. So Nanak nodded, faced west and offered water in the west direction. The sadhu inquired why he was offering water in the opposite direction of the sun. Nanak Saheb told him that his fields were in the west direction, so he was watering his fields. When the sadhu asked Nanak how that was possible, Nanak Saheb told the chap, 'If you can offer water to your ancestors in the spirit world with the belief that the water would quench their thirst, why couldn't he water his farms, which were just a little away from where they stood?'

Nanak's closest companion was a Muslim man, who was supposedly from the traditionally accepted 'lower caste'. Since childhood Nanak and Mardana would meditate together and then for decades They travelled the length and breadth, not only of India, but of innumerable countries, spreading the word of oneness.

In fact, it was with His Muslim friend that Nanak one morning went to meditate and bathe in Kali Bein or the

Black river. Nanak entered the river, kept walking and then disappeared. For three days there was no sight of Nanak and His family and villagers feared that He had drowned. On the third day Nanak Saheb walked out of the water, declaring that there were no Hindus or Muslims, but all were one.

Though married with two sons, He left with Mardana for Their spiritual journeys, and many scholars believe that it was this close friendship between Nanak and Mardana, the best of both Their philosophies and religions, that shaped Sikhism.

Nanak always believed that God was one and that God had no form and also that God was as equally concerned about our spiritual growth as He was concerned about our worldly well-being. This went against everything ever taught by the prevalent religious teachers. Like Baba Sai of Shirdi would often tell one and all, 'First I will give you what you want and when you are satisfied I will give you what I want you to receive; with an empty stomach nobody can reach God.' Similarly, Baba Nanak too believed that God was interested in one's spiritual and worldly well-being.

For twenty-five years, Nanak and Mardana travelled to many countries. Pilgrimages were made to places as diverse as Haridwar, Kurukshetra, Benaras, Kashi, Maya, Baghdad, Mecca, Iraq, Sri Lanka, Afghanistan, Turkey, Burma and Tibet. He spoke and interacted with countless people; patiently heard their philosophy and espoused His. He was truly loved by those who were real spiritual seekers; obviously He didn't take to those who spouted religious verses but were hollow from within.

Nanak was a firm believer of living life to the fullest and never as a recluse. That one should live in the world and still be detached from it. That family life is as important as a life of a monk or a sage. That it was important to seize each moment and give it your very best, always, with the internal chanting or *naam smaran* and never ever forgetting your Lord and master. That is why, after His pilgrimages, the last eighteen years of His physical life, Nanak Saheb spent as a householder, along with His family.

Nanak, after His twenty-five years of pilgrimages, asked a wealthy devotee to donate a large tract of land where the prophet built a town called Kartarpur in Punjab on the banks of the Ravi river. His followers came from far and wide. The best part of it all was that His followers still remained Hindu or Muslim, or whichever religion they were born in, but they were also known as the Guru's disciples, or Sikhs. A Sikh is the disciple of the Guru.

The beauty of Nanak Saheb was that the moment He returned for good from His pilgrimages, He spent the remaining eighteen years of His life cultivating land. He offered His morning and evening prayers, spent time in building His community, preaching and building various institutions which propagated His teachings and His visions; where prayers, work, oneness and community, free meals were the backbone. But He was equal to all as a cultivator, often as a peasant who toiled on the land. So here you have a man who played the role of a prophet and a peasant.

Nanak was very firm on the abolition of the caste system. Thus, He began the institution of *langar,* or community meal sharing. This took care of two important things dear to Nanak Saheb's heart. First of all, the langar was open to one and all. There was no bar either to caste, creed, religion, financial status, men, women, children. All were welcome, which made certain that only those truly serious about Nanak's philosophy of oneness remained with Him. Those days the concept of untouchables was rampant; Nanak at one go made sure that those who thought that other human beings were untouchables had no place with Him, as the community meals were open to all. Nanak Saheb was big on sharing one's wealth with those less financially fortunate and that there was no place for caste, creed or religious discrimination. These langars taught those close to Baba Nanak that one had to share wealth with the needy and one had to treat each and everybody as equal and as one's very own. Nanak Saheb made it clear that His closest companion was Mardana, who initially was considered as a lower-caste Muslim, and those who considered others as lower caste, or untouchables, had no place in Nanak's world.

Not many people are aware that Nanak had a low tolerance for bullshit or tyrants. He made it clear that if life had to be lived with dignity, one had to fight not only against the evil within oneself but also against the evil around one. If there was somebody who tried to harm one's loved ones, friends, neighbours, one had to stand united to fight such outrage. The very revolutionary stature of the Sikhs thus originated with Nanak, who felt it was important to live in communities, without caste, creed and discrimination, but to also protect the interest and the well-being of one's loved ones and the community at large. The man was a rockstar, in short.

At a time when women were being ill treated and looked down upon, Baba Nanak was very firm on women's rights and equality, telling one and all that without a woman, a man cannot survive or thrive. Thus, He gave tremendous respect and importance to women.

'From woman, man is born; within woman, man is conceived; to woman he is engaged and married. Woman becomes his friend; through woman, the future generations come . . .' spoke Nanak.

In fact, Nanak was a Goddess worshipper. The very first line of the Guru Granth Sahib is:

The Primordial Mother came into being by Herself, mysteriously, and She created three deities: one was the Creator, one the Sustainer, and one the Destroyer.

And the beautiful words: *Wherever I look I see the Lord pervading there in the union of Shiv and Shakti.* (Sri Guru Nanak Dev Ji, Adi Sri Guru Granth Sahib Ji, 21)

Unfortunately, His followers have forgotten the Goddess now. There's a beautiful story where Bhai Lehna, who eventually was appointed by Guru Nanak as His successor to carry forward His work, was a staunch Maa Durga devotee. Once, Bhai in a vision, saw a woman dressed in a red attire serving Nanak. Bhai Lehna asked who She was and He was told that She was Goddess Durga and that She came once a week to do seva for the Guru. It was then that Bhai Lehna became Nanak Saheb's staunchest disciple, who Nanak eventually called Guru Angad Dev. Bhai Lehna approached Nanak seven years before He took samadhi and Nanak told Lehna, who was till then a Maa Durga worshipper, that He had been waiting for Him.

Nanak tested his two sons and Bhai Lehna for a long time before He realized that blood was thicker than water, but nothing was thicker than the bonds of love, obedience and surrender. His final test of Bhai Lehna should make one understand the difference between a disciple and devotee. For a disciple, the guru's word is the word of God and nothing else matters but the guru.

One day Guru Nanak told His sons to eat a corpse who lay under a sheet. The sons refused, even reprimanding Their father that He had lost His senses. Guru Nanak then told Bhai Lehna, who bowed and asked from which side should He eat the corpse. From head first or feet, and Nanak told Him from the middle. When Bhai Lehna removed the sheet there was no more a corpse but food. Bhai Lehna first offered the food to Nanak Saheb, then His two sons, and then of what was left, He ate. It was then that Nanak spoke: 'Lehna, You were blessed with the sacred food because You could share it with others. If the people use the wealth bestowed on them by God for themselves alone or for treasuring it, it is like a corpse. But if they decide to share it with others, it becomes sacred food. You have known the secret. You are My *janamsakhi* (image).'

Nanak blessed Lehna with His own hand *(anga)* and so he was named Guru Angad. Then Nanak placed a coconut and some coins in front of Him, applied saffron on Guru Angad's forehead, and told Guru Angad to occupy His seat, thus making it clear that Guru Angad would take Sikhism forward and also that Baba Nanak's time to leave His physical body had arrived.

Before Guru Nanak Saheb took samadhi, His followers, many who were Hindus and Muslims, asked Him, how they should proceed with the last rites. Nanak said, 'Let the Hindus place flowers on My right and the Muslims on My left. Those whose flowers are found fresh in the morning, may have the disposal rights of My body.'

Nanak then drew a sheet over Himself and took samadhi. Nanak Saheb was seventy years old in the body and took samadhi on 22 September 1539.

The next morning there were only flowers. As usual nobody really understood Him. He was not the body. He was the spirit within the body, which had merged with the eternal spirit.

A few years later a flood washed away even the flowers, which His followers had begun to worship. Nanak had the last laugh. All His life He had preached that God is One and that He is energy and that to worship anything else would be to stray from the true path. When He saw His followers again worshipping matter than spirit, He smiled and made sure His last remains in the form of flowers, too, were washed away.

16

Mehera Be Brave . . . The Avatar's Beloved

Illustration by Pooja Bangia

The beauty of Mehera Maa is in Her pure simplicity, in the way She loved and served Avatar Meher Baba. What I find most profound and divine is the humble, selfless, quiet manner in which She loved the Avatar. Most importantly, not only did She maintain this humility and silent grace when Meher Baba was in the body, but even after He dropped His physical shell. Never did She forget the importance of maintaining a dignified silence and humble grace, till the day She breathed Her last in the mortal coil and was laid to rest, next to Avatar Meher Baba's samadhi; even in this, She was content to be outside, adjacent, to the main samadhi sanctorum, silently lying down, to the right side of Her divine lover.

Mehera Maa was sixteen years old when She decided to spend Her entire life in serving and loving Meher Baba, who was thirty years then.

She first saw Meher Baba at the age of fourteen at Upasani Maharaj's ashram, where Meher Baba used to spend time. Upasani Maharaj, Baba Sai's foremost disciple, was entrusted with the heartbreaking and also one of the most privileged duties of performing the last rites of Baba Sai of Shirdi.

Baba Sai of Shirdi was the head of the five Perfect Masters along with Baba Jaan, Tajuddin Maharaj, Narayan Maharaj and Upasani Maharaj. This powerful gang of five were instrumental in bringing about the realization of Godhood in Meher Baba.

Upasani Maharaj was instrumental in bringing the Avatar back to human consciousness though operating from the universal consciousness.

In such a profound setting, Mehera Maa decided to spend Her entire life serving God and slowly realized that Her God was already with Her, in the form of Meher Baba.

So She saw Meher Baba, and I have a strong feeling She rose in love with Him and decided that She would live and follow the Avatar all Her life.

Imagine, a sixteen-year-old, who was born to a Zoroastrian family, studied in a Christian school, loved Jesus Christ, and also one who wanted to look and dress beautifully, taking this profound decision to live and love only the lord.

Mehera Maa was not only internally strong but equally stubborn. Just two years prior to this, when She was fourteen, She had refused to attend a very important marriage, which was to be attended by the who's who of Pune, only because Her mother refused to allow young Mehera to wear a saree, which She had set Her heart on.

So She refused to attend the wedding and in hindsight, one can only sigh with relief, as She was beautiful and those days, it was not uncommon to engage and quickly marry girls in their teens.

Two years later, Mehera Maa and Her mother were called to live with Meher Baba and His mandali or the inner circle at Meherabad. They, along with Meher Baba's sister, Mani were the first three women disciples. She met the Avatar in Meherabad, where the handsome one sang a song to all those who had gathered around Him. Meher Baba had a beautiful voice. When He prayed aloud, the heavens stopped all work to hear Him pray and when He sang, it seemed that the cosmos danced to His tune.

And She was in love with Him.

And the Perfect Masters were aware of this love.

'Baba Jaan hardly spoke, and when She did it was very softly. People would talk to Her, and She would sit and listen and nod Her head, sometimes turning to see who was sitting amongst the women. I remember one evening when Baba Jaan turned to look at the women. She looked at each one, and then a little longer at me. I was so surprised that She would look at me, and I felt very shy. Baba Jaan hardly ever smiled, but now as She looked at me She had a slight, very sweet smile on Her face, as if She knew me. Then Baba Jaan turned away.' Mehera Maa narrated this incident. Soon after this incident Meher Baba called Mehera Maa to live with Him forever at Meherabad.

Those like me, who treat and consider and acknowledge Meher Baba as the Avatar, thus naturally acknowledge Mehera Maa as the Goddess. You cannot have God roaming around in the body without His Goddess nearby. The most beautiful aspect of this union is that just by loving Mehera, and making it clear that She was His very existence, Mehera became Mehera Maa. There was no need for miracles to be performed. No need for fulgent auras radiating from Her. Nobody needed any proof. No predictions.

This is the power of true love and the word of the master. Baba often said that Mehera was His divine half, like Radha Maa is to Lord Krishna and Sita Maa to Lord Rama. Mehera Maa was all that, as without the Goddesses you can't have God.

She is the Shakti to Him. He may take all the accolades but She is the One. She is the tops. She is His heartbeat. The sigh of His soul.

But then it isn't easy or any less complicated to be God's most special loved one.

Mehera Maa began to live with the inner circle at the age of sixteen and immediately Meher Baba made it clear that She wouldn't be seen in the company of men or speak to men or hear their voice or even the radio. So Mehera Maa, though living in the ashram, began Her life of seclusion from the world, as the world has men all around. She was looked after by the inner circle of women, headed by Mani, the Avatar's sister.

Thus, for years, the only man Mehera Maa saw or heard or spoke to was Meher Baba.

And she was really young and divinely beautiful.

And she loved Him so truly and silently and selflessly that She never once showed the slightest trace of frustration of being virtually isolated from the happenings of the world around Her or being made to live a life of a recluse.

Meher Baba travelled all over the country and all over the world, often with His male inner circle, and Mehera Maa would spend time loving Him, making small surprises for Him, looking after His garden, away from all the accolades and all that which the world had to offer.

Isolated, but never alone, as Meher Baba made it clear that She is the one.

But can you imagine what it must have been like for Mehera Maa?

She must love the Avatar like very few can love.

Her silent devotion and taking a humble place in the background, reminds me of Mother Mary's love for Jesus Christ and the silent manner in which She went about loving and serving Jesus Christ.

So She first saw Meher Baba in 1922, came to settle down in the ashram in 1924 and it was in the late 1960s, virtually a year before Meher Baba took samadhi, when He gave Mehera Maa the permission to interact with His male mandali.

Yes, in 1937 He did take Her with Him when He travelled, but She wasn't allowed to interact with any male member of the mandali. Also, going about with Meher Baba was not for the faint-hearted. He travelled by third class, or in those days it was called the cattle class by those who had money but no class, and very often on foot. The journeys were back-breaking and Mehera Maa was allowed to accompany Him on those journeys to take care of Meher Baba. 'There were discomforts and difficulties, but Baba was with us. We were going through it for Baba, and with Baba—and that was all we wanted,' Mehera Maa humbly informed those who wanted to know what it was like travelling with Baba. The truth is, the journeys were really difficult.

When Baba would not take Mehera Maa with Him, She mended His clothes, took care of His garden and made small gifts called 'treasures for Him'.

And then Meher Baba stopped speaking for the last forty-three years of His life. What must have Mehera Maa felt, as She loved to hear Him speak and sing? Even here, Her love shone through; not once did she question Him. If this isn't love, what is!

In 1952, Mehera Maa accompanied Meher Baba to the USA where there was a serious automobile accident. Baba had predicted two major accidents, one in the West and the other in the East. This was the first of those. Baba was severely injured, but He first made sure Mehera Maa was put on into the first ambulance to take Her to the hospital much before Him. But look at how humbly Mehera Maa referred to this incident. 'Even though Baba was in very great pain and in need of help Himself, He thought of another at that time. How beautiful He was with His love to think of another person at such a time when He Himself needed help.'

Baba still was mobile and would travel extensively, meet innumerable people, work and make His inner-most circle work as though the world was going to end. Meher Baba was a hard taskmaster. His word was the law.

Then in 1956, Meher Baba met with another serious accident, which really made Him go through physical hell for the rest of His life. This accident took place in India, at Satara, where a very dear disciple of Baba succumbed to His injuries. He had always wanted to pass over when physically with Baba, and his wish was granted by the Avatar.

The funny part with devotees is that they feel the master should never be ill and face calamities or injuries like the normal mortal. If the master is with them they feel no harm will come to them. Little do they realize that the master knows best and often, the gravest of calamities come to those who have embraced the master a tad too tightly in their soul. Karmic cleansing is a heartless companion.

The next and the last twelve years of Meher Baba's physical life though was plagued with merciless pain, due to injuries which never left their embrace of His pure self. Mehera Maa began to nurse Him through the day and night, taking care of Baba's every need. But always in the background and always with silent class and grace. It is here that She stands out with her dignified silence, her humble and selfless love.

Meher Baba often told one and all that 'Mehera loves Me as I should be loved.'

The greatest sacrifice Mehera Maa made was to follow Meher Baba's wish not to be by His side when He left His physical body. He did not want Her to see Him suffer as He knew He would suffer. For days He had spasms which would lift His body off the bed.

'Baba had reduced His food intake about two weeks previously and Mehera did her best to provide nourishment by sending Him things like fruit, juice, grated apple and so forth. At first He said that He did not want the grated apple but Mehera would send word back that He should have it, and after taking a spoonful or two, Baba would offer the remainder to the mandali, much like prasad.'

Sometimes the spasms went on for hours at a stretch. The Avatar bore His crucifixion silently and even with humour, but what about Mehera Maa who had to obey Her Avatar and stay away? She was dying a thousand deaths not being able to be with Meher Baba.

Shortly before He dropped His body, Baba asked one of His mandali to take this message to Mehera Maa. The message was, 'Mehera, be brave.'

For seven days Meher Baba's body was kept for His followers to come and pay their last respects. One can only imagine Mehera Maa greeting them all, keeping Her word to Meher Baba to be brave. For seven days people flocked to see Meher Baba's body for the last time, and all those seven days, roses tended by Mehera Maa made into a garland and, adorned Meher Baba.

'Mehera and the other women mandali would then enter the tomb. To see Mehera Maa walking from Her room to the tomb in a dazed condition and crying was very touching. She would come to the north window of the tomb and touch Her head to the window. She would then bow at the west window. When she arrived at the entrance, someone would remove her slippers. She would stand at the doorstep as if dazed, with tears rolling down her cheeks, hands raised a little in adoration and completely oblivious to the thousands watching her. She would step inside the tomb to be followed by the other women mandali. The doors would then be closed and all we could then hear was sobbing.

'Just before the door opened for Her to come out, *"Avatar Meher Baba Ki Jai!"* would be shouted by all. She would come out of the door and again turn towards Baba, completely lost in Her sorrow. Someone would help Her with Her slippers. She would bow once, twice and again and again. She would not like to miss a glimpse of Baba for a second. She would take a step and turn back, look at Baba and shed a fresh deluge of tears and then slowly move on. The parting from Baba was an extremely painful one. In her farewell moments we could see how deeply she was moved. In thoughts or deeds, in stillness or action, alone or in multitudes, she will remain one with Her beloved Baba . . .'

The love Meher Baba had for Mehera came through even after He left His body. One day when He was in the body, Baba stood outside Mehera Maa's room, placed His hand on a tree trunk and said He loved this tree a lot. After His samadhi, when Mehera Maa was in mourning, I am sure wondering whether Baba felt Her love, one day when She woke up, She saw His face, engraved on that very spot of the tree. Baba's face was there for all to see for many years till growth on the bark faded Baba's impression but even now it is said that for a few fortunate souls, His face shines through the tree trunk.

Though Mehera Maa's birthday was in January, since 1968 it has been celebrated on 22 December, as that was the last time Meher Baba celebrated Her birthday according to the Zoroastrian calendar.

For Mehera Maa that was the only day worth remembering as that was the day Her beloved Meher was with Her in Her final celebration.

Mehera Maa dropped Her body twenty years after Meher Baba. She took samadhi on Buddha's birthday and His day of realization.

'Always hold on to Baba's *daaman* and love Him, that is the one real thing you can do in this life. Baba may seem to try to snatch His daaman from your hands, so be sure not to let go, be sure to hold on tightly. Be true to His love for you,' said Mehera Maa to all Baba lovers.

Thus, She lived the next twenty years obeying Meher Baba, with all Her love, all Her grace, all Her devotion, living up to Baba's last words to Her . . . 'Mehera, be brave.'

Be blessed. Jai Baba!

Baba Sai of Shirdi through channelling has given this prayer to be prayed to Mehera Maa, Meher's Mehera.

Avatar's Mehera please pray for us that we always love the Avatar like You used to and even now do:

Let us love Him selflessly, humbly, silently, with pure child-like devotion;

Let us also win the Avatar's heart like You have, Maa.

Teach us silent devotion, oh Meher's Mehera,

Teach us how to serve always keeping the Avatar's happiness and comfort in mind;

Bless us, that like You, we too serve selflessly without ego but always with selfless love.

You, who loved the beloved of the five Perfect Masters,

You, who the Avatar considered His divine half,

You, who gave up all, to obey and serve Him,

Pray that we too are graced with such love and devotion that makes the Avatar, the Perfect Masters and You, Meher's Mehera, happy and proud of us.

Make us brave, oh the Avatar's favourite,

That we can continue to hold on to Baba's daaman to the very end;

For You know how bereft we are without His physical presence and what it is to be away from His warm embrace.

Meher's Mehera, pray for us, to always have the Avatar's blessings, love and protection on us and our loved ones;

Your prayers, He can never not hear or not grant

For you, His Mehera, the One who truly knew how to love the Avatar.

17

Archangel Raphael . . .
The Shining One Who Heals

Illustration by Nilufer Marshall

L et it be made clear that archangels do not belong to any religion. They have come out of God to help, serve and intercede on behalf of mankind and all of creation. Prophet Zarathustra, who is known as the first prophet, who was born nearly two thousand five hundred years before Jesus Christ, introduced the concept of archangels and angels. According to Zarathustra, there are seven archangels and thirty-three angels. Judaism talks of mainly three archangels, Michael, Gabriel and Raphael. Christianity took it from there and mentions the three archangels and the league of angels. Islam mainly talks of the three archangels.

The role and duty of archangels and angels is to help us in our day-to-day life, concerning physical, emotional, mental and spiritual hardships and strife. They wait for us to call on to Them, as that is the law of the angelic world. One needs to call on to Them and it is only then They intercede on our behalf. I am certain this is not because of some major ego issue, but because this is how things have been planned out in the celestial and terrestrial world by our Old Man. Thus, it is important to call out to Them as They wait for the summons and then They work tirelessly to resolve the issue or if there is a karmic blueprint clause, which prevents the issue from being resolved, then they ease the blow, give us strength to withstand the storm, heal us and help us to dust our clothes, get back on our feet and continue to walk the path.

Though each archangel has a decisive portfolio (could be health and healing, protection and strength, divine messages and unlocking mysteries and so on) it would be inane to assume that for all other problems the archangel can do nothing much. Each archangel is head of a particular department, but as every department is interconnected, one can call out to the archangel for any and everything. There are legions of angels working with each archangel and thus it's one big, happy, feathery family. Also the main priority is clear to Them, to lead one and all to the divine radiance; to be filled with the divine radiance; to spread the divine radiance; and eventually to merge with the divine radiance. Thus, eventually all roads lead to the arms of the Old Man.

Archangel Raphael is known to be the master healer or the one that heals through the compassion of the Lord. Those who are suffering from ill health of body, heart, mind, spirit and everything connected to the physical, emotional, mental and spiritual realms, and call out to Archangel Raphael, have experienced His healing grace.

As I have written above, one needs to call out to Him and then leave the process of healing in His capable hands. It is imperative that you call out to Him with faith and then leave the process to Him.

Most people are under the impression that Archangel Raphael is only meant to be called out to when they are ill or their loved ones are not well and that is where one falters. He is not only a glorified doctor for physical ill health, but ill health of all kinds.

What is disease? The absence of ease is disease. This can be caused through physical, emotional, mental or spiritual disharmony. Financial strife could create mental unease and thus even that is an illness that needs to be addressed and our handsome angel, Raphael, can be called out to handle the situation.

Physical illness, anyway, most often is a bad marriage of emotional, mental, spiritual disharmony. Thus, perfect health means the body, mind and soul being in harmony, which is rare in this day and time. Thus, the need to be attuned with Archangel Raphael becomes all the more imperative.

When channelling, I have come across many who have been told by Baba Sai to seek Archangel Raphael's help to overcome various issues of ill health. Those who have taken to heart Baba Sai's direction of calling out to Archangel Raphael, have come back with miraculous stories, which have left doctors scratching their heads and other unmentionable parts of their anatomy. Cancer, constant headaches, issues of the eyes, abdomen, fertility, depression, anger, addiction and paranoia have either been overcome or kept in reign.

The simplest way of connecting with Archangel Raphael is to call out to Him. First believe that They, the archangels and angels, exist in reality, and are waiting to help, guide, nurture and protect. So, you call out to Raphael with the belief and faith that He will come to you along with His league of angels and helpers. I would advise always to call your master first, the Goddess next and then Archangel Raphael. In my limited experience, this Trinity works in tandem. Through my research I later on learnt that Archangel Raphael works closely with Mother Mary, the queen of angels. So call out to Them.

Speak to Archangel Raphael regarding the problem. It could be a physical issue; it could be issues of emotion; it could be a mental dilemma; a spiritual problem; but as harmony means a happy union of the body, mind and spirit, everything is interconnected, and as He is The Healer of God, The Face of God for all good health, He needs to know what it is that ails you.

Tell Him what is the issue and then leave it to Him to deal with it in a manner He deems fit. Don't treat Him as a compounder for God's sake. He is a master healer and He knows what is best. If you don't know what ails you, then be specific. Don't try and diagnose the problem yourself. Leave the diagnosis to Him.

If you call out to Him in faith, leave the solution to Him, and be calm in accepting His way of handling the situation. I can assure you things will change always for the better.

I remember once I had asked Baba Sai that how come when being used as a medium of healing, the more serious problems were solved, while some very inane issues never got resolved. He had told me very politely, 'My demented child, illness of any kind, if it has to be experienced, and it is in the master karmic blueprint, will not be resolved, so don't go about raving and ranting for a solution but rather pray that if the healing can take place, please let the child be healed, but if for whatever reason the child has to go through the process of unease, then give the child strength and wisdom to go through the experience with calmness and positive surrender.'

Later, folks came in and told me that though the issue still persisted, they for some reason felt better.

In the same way, don't order Archangel Raphael to solve the issue but rather leave the problem in His capable hands and let Him do what is best for you or for the person you are praying for. He knows best. Lord love a defrosted duck, Raphael is God's appointed healer, let Him do what He thinks is best.

It is then that you will see and feel His presence and experience His proficiency.

Archangel Raphael is considered to be the most accessible of all archangels. He loves His job. You will feel His passion to heal you or the one you pray for and experience Him in all His true glory. He is known to take His work seriously but is considered to be filled with joy and happiness which He passes on to all those He works with and heals.

He is known to heal all kinds of illnesses and He goes to the root of the issue. If financial strife is the bane of ensuing illnesses, He will work to bring about financial balance, which will automatically reduce the stress and lead to the removal of ill health. Thus, be it physical, emotional, mental or spiritual issues, call out to Archangel Raphael and let Him do what is best for you and your loved ones.

He also works wonders where addiction is concerned. Very often addiction is a sign of one not being able to face the world, or an escape route. Usually, those who have been abused take to some form of addiction or other. It is an illness of the soul rather than that of the body. Health means harmony, and addiction is disharmony. Scores of people who have grappled with issues of personal addiction or addiction problems faced by their loved ones, have experienced the mercy and grace of this compassionate archangel, the healer of God.

Archangel Raphael naturally works with all healers, doctors, psychiatrists, psychologists, channels, psychics, who call out to Him. He is said to work with those who want to bring about peace calmness, happiness to this ravaged planet. Environmental issues are close to His heart as the well-being of the planet, once again comes under His portfolio. Those who work and pray for peace and well-being of all creation are close to His heart as are all mediums of healing, professional or otherwise, striving for the well-being of one and all. That is something He works towards.

It is important to know that one never heals. One is merely a medium. Only God heals and God does so via one's master, the Goddess and Archangel Raphael. Be clear not to get personal or egoistic, as then your energy will be used and it will lead to a burn out. It is important to always remind yourself that you are just a medium and let the healing take place in whatever manner best decided by the wise folks up there and you accept their decision and handiwork. Do not get involved in the decision or the process of healing, as if you do, it could lead to your ill health. Ask Archangel Raphael to protect you from negative or dark vibrations clinging to your aura and seeping into your heart, mind and body. This is important. When you are a medium of healing it is imperative that you bloody well stay healthy. The maximum number of suicides takes place in professions where one is working for the well-being of society. Healers, channels, psychiatrists and psychologists top the sad list. Let Archangel Raphael decide what is best for the one you pray or work with and ask for His protection and sheath of auric clothing, to protect you from ill health.

Thus, if there is ill health and one calls out to Archangel Raphael, He will be with you and that is truly a comforting thought.

Archangel Raphael makes His presence felt in various ways. Many who pray to Him or seek His help, feel a warm tingling sensation in their body. Some see the colour green, which is associated with Raphael. Your intuition might just peak or speak or you might get a solution in your state of dreams. You might hear Him clearly all of a sudden too. Many folks, all of a sudden meet somebody by chance, who guides them to a solution for the ensuing issue that is causing unease. You might pick up a magazine and your solution might be staring right at you.

Somebody might talk aloud on the next table and you might realize your problem has been addressed and the solution is given. You might see a hoarding and then suddenly realize a way out of your situation. Remember, He has a sense of humour. He might materialize in front of you in spirit form, to shock the living daylights out of you; and after you pass out with shock and regain consciousness you might be healed or have the answer to your situation—ill health or unease.

The most important thing that Archangel Raphael does is to empower you to heal yourself. It begins with bringing peace within one's spirit, which then moves to calmness of the mind, which balms the ruffled heart, which then cures the malady of the body. It always begins with the spirit or the aura where the unease is stored.

Very often the illness or unease is something to do with one's past or one's past lifetimes. Thus, it is important when one prays or works with Archangel Raphael, one mentions about bringing a calm closure to one's past, either in this lifetime or prior ones. Most of our issues are either karmic, genetic, or due to the wrong use of free will. Tell Archangel Raphael to start off with bringing peace in your spirit, heart, mind and body, with all that which is associated with the past. Till there isn't a closure, rot will always seep into one's system via the auric body. All karma is stored in the aura, and thus, it is important that cleansing first takes place of the astral and casual bodies. So ask Archangel Raphael to first cleanse and heal the astral and causal body, yours or your loved ones and then cleanse and heal your physical body and heal the situation or the reason for unease.

Don't put the cart before the horse.

Archangel Raphael is also called upon when one is travelling. He is said to really take care of travellers. Whenever taking off on a journey, call on to Him to make your journey fun, safe and memorable.

Of course, even Archangel Raphael must have realized that making life easy for those travelling in India is something that is way out of His portfolio and, dare I say, His league. Try to drive a car in our country without some mad man or a normal woman trying to prove how painfully mortal you are and cut short your disgruntled stay on Planet Earth. Better still, travel by local train (where no self-respecting archangel will travel or even fit in). Archangel Raphael has thrown in His towel in India but usually He works like a charm in other more travel-friendly places around the globe.

He is known to be the remover of darkness and the rescuer of mankind from death. Once again, darkness means ill health of some kind. Usually, when the soul or mind is ravaged, darkness ensues. When one cannot provide for one's loved ones, there is the absence of light. When there is physical suffering or emotional upheaval, there is darkness. Thus, call out to Him to fill you and your loved ones with the radiance of the Lord and master. When one says He is the rescuer of death, it means, He brings the soul to the level of Godhood, and thus immortality.

It is important that when you sleep, you call upon your master, the Mother energy, and Archangel Raphael. Thus just before you sleep and begin to snore your head and the roof off, pray to Them, that They cleanse your emotional, mental, physical and spiritual body from all ill health and unease and that They fill you up with divine radiance and well-being.

Archangel Raphael has the serpent as His symbol. According to me, the serpent symbolizes the kundalini energy. There cannot be perfect harmony till this energy, which is like a celestial serpent, isn't awakened, and then doesn't rise up to the crown chakra and then goes beyond to make one realize one's Godhood. Archangel Raphael helps in raising this energy and thus freeing the body, heart, mind, aura, vibrations and oneself from the clutches of duality and into the embrace of oneness.

The colour green is associated with perfect health of the body, heart, mind and soul. It is the bridge that connects one from the physical (state of duality) to the spirit consciousness (the state of oneness). Green is the colour that the sages believe emanates from the heart chakra. The heart chakra is placed between the lower three chakras and the top three chakras—once again signifying a balance between the physical and the spirit, and the marrying of both to achieve a state of harmony through progression, universal consciousness and then oneness. Thus, Archangel Raphael symbolizes the middle path—by merging both the physical and spiritual together a human being finds ease and harmony, and thus good health.

Call out to Him. He is handsome, strong, with a whacky sense of humour, and wants you to be happy, healthy and filled with vitality. Believe that He walks with you and wants only the best for you and your loved ones.

He is Archangel Raphael, the one known as 'God Heals' and 'It is God who Heals'. Make Him your friend. When down and out, this one will be standing right by your side.

This is a prayer Baba Sai of Shirdi has given through channelling:

I pray to Raphael who the fakir has brought forth with His breath, to heal one and all,

To pass His radiance, grace, calmness and health to one and all,

I seek You Archangel Raphael, first and foremost for the well-being of all creation,

You Israfil, I beseech You to heal first Mother Earth,

She is ravaged and bruised and mutilated,

Heal Her first for She never complains and only gives,

With Your army of angels and spirit healers, heal our planet which has silently suffered and slowly Her light gets dimmer,

Heal Her first, Oh Raphael, You who are the face of the only one who truly heals.

Then, I pray for the ones who cannot speak for themselves,

The animals, the birds, the life that abounds, mercilessly being trampled by a race so bent on self-extinction,

But first making sure all else becomes cold, void, and extinct,

Heal the mute ones, the meek, the suffering, the voiceless, the innocent.

I pray you to heal then the children; ailing, alone, orphaned, abused, violated, hungry;

See their plight and heal them, You who are known as the mighty one who is against the very devil,

Heal the children as well as the hearts of those who mirror Satan,

How can the health of mankind prevail if our children are battered and abused and slain.

Heal the children, oh Raphael, as the innocent are dear to my Allah;

I pray for You to heal the women, young, old, infirm; those abused, those sold, those violated, those mauled;

Heal them, their spirit, their bodies, their heart and their soul,

They are violated, abused, torn by lust and by ignorance and power,

Heal the women, whose tribe have begotten Rama, Christ and Zorast,

Let them not be tortured and humiliated.

I call out to You, the shining one who heals to take care of the old and the sick; heal their hearts, mind, body and spirit,

Let Your band of angels be by their side and nurse them to health and respect,

Be there, oh youthful One, as mortals decay and stink.

Come Raphael, work on the men, heal those who toil all day to provide a meal to their lot,

Self-respect lies in the dust due to a destiny not meant to uplift their souls,

Heal the men, make them strong in spirit and soft in heart,

Make their shoulders strong but their eyes tender and tongue calm

Let them control their bodies and heal the anger brewing in their soul

Raphael, heal the spirit world

Let not anybody be earthbound

My ancestors, give them peace, the same way You give peace to the ancestors of Adam and Eve

Let all heal and move towards Raja Ram's radiance,

Towards Christ and Mohammed,

As You know all of us are one.

I pray for my family and friends and myself, Raphael the one who spreads joy and health,

Remove all that which Thou does not approve from heart, mind, body, spirit

All that which stands between us and well-being

All that which obstructs us from internal and external peace and harmony

All that prevents us from dropping the veil of duality and embracing oneness

Give us health and well-being of body, heart, mind and soul

And when the time comes to leave this ragged cloth, stand by me, Archangel Raphael, along with my master and present me to the One

Make me and my loved ones whole never to be broken or dual ever again

So be it, Raphael, the One who works with Mariam Maa.

18

Lahiri Mahasaya,
the Lord of Yogis and
a Very Good Accountant

Illustration by Pooja Bangia

I was seventeen when I read *The Autobiography of a Yogi*, written by Swami Paramhansa Yogananda.

My uncle, Jamshed Guzdar, one evening asked me if I was interested in reading a book which didn't involve guns, alcohol, and the occasional murder. I looked at him and remember answering him that as long as there was humour in the book I didn't care if it talked about the seductive craft of garbage disposal.

So he handed me a book, dog-eared and all, which had on the cover a handsome, long-haired, healthy-looking yogi, who looked back at me innocently. I remember I began reading the book at my uncle's home at Warden Road, Mumbai. I left my uncle's residence, stood at the bus stop, waiting for a bus to take me home, where I lived with my maternal grandmother, uncle, aunt, godmother and my six brothers and sisters (most of them my cousins but we were closer than a pack of thieves). I kept reading the book and smiling, and occasionally chuckling. In the background I did hear buses halting, the cling of the bell, and them departing. After a while I felt my uncle tapping me on the shoulder and telling me that it would be rather good for the blood pressure of the entire family if I obliged one and all by getting on the darn bus.

For the entire next week I was mesmerized by *The Autobiography of a Yogi*. I was already into yoga and meditation and loved all there was about the occult and the paranormal. Even now I consider this book to be the mother of all books where the paranormal, and the essence and love of the master, God, Goddess, are concerned. It reinforced my faith that if you possessed humour, every issue could be faced with calmness and all the mysteries (apart from the female of the species) could be unravelled.

Every five years I pick up this book and go through it and am filled with the same love, happiness, devotion and Oneness. I still laugh at the same lines that I found funny when I was seventeen. This either means reality and the force of trueness never cease to impress and amaze me, or that I haven't really grown for the past thirty years.

I remember, even then, on and off while reading the book, I would turn to the section where the photographs of various sages and yogis were published and eventually I would halt at the photograph of this old man, sitting in a yoga pose, eyes partially open, with the cutest and most goofy look I had ever seen—the epitome of grandfatherly love and the innocence of a child. I would look at the photograph and chuckle and tell myself, such a look can only be brought about when one was intoxicated by either the divine or good, old-fashioned booze.

The sage whose snap even now makes me smile is Sri Shyamacharan Lahiree Mahasaya, or as many spell His name, Lahiri Mahasaya.

I love Him for various reasons. The first being, at a time when spirituality was considered to be the prerogative of sages and celibates; at a time when one needed to be adorned by the uniform of religion and live in the mountains; when it was sort of taken for granted that spiritual grace and evolvement was the exclusive right of only those who had renounced the family, the credit card and the world, here was a man who humbly and silently went about life, defying all prejudices and dogmas created by spiritual dwarfs.

Lahiri Mahasaya was a husband, a father of five children, an accountant and the one who gave back to the world the lost science of Kriya Yoga, the most ancient form of meditation, where if one immersed oneself in this particular method of meditation, heart, body, mind and soul, one could burn away all accumulated karma collected over one's soul journey, in one lifetime and then merge with the One—the Big Daddy. One could be free of one's own petty self, and get immersed in the oneness of all things.

Like all prophets and Perfect Masters, Lahiri Mahasaya did not believe in renouncing family and the world to realize God. Godhood resides within oneself and to renounce the world is no barometer of one's dedication and love for the realization of Godhood. Baba Sai of Shirdi, in channelling, so often says that one does not need to detach oneself from the world to begin to glimpse God, but one must detach from one's own self to be able to breathe in God and exhale one's lower self. What is one's own self or one's lower self? All the base emotions, the yearning for the external, the need for power and the lust for gratifying the 'I-me-myself', is the handiwork of one's lower self. The false self. The self that identifies with the external and the material.

Thus, Lahiri Mahasaya with His sweet innocent smile brought about due to the union of God and His true self, taught the world, especially the rigid fanatics guised as sadhus, fakirs and yogis, that true renunciation was of one's base emotions and not of family, friends and the world.

Virtually all His life Mahasaya worked as a humble accountant in the Military Works Department, and just nine years before He took His samadhi, did He retire from this job.

The second most important reason according to me why Lahiri Mahasaya is such a spiritual giant is the manner in which He balanced home, work and His spiritual journey. The beautifully detached manner in which He went about in a matter-of-fact way, on one hand, a husband–father–accountant, and on the other hand, the king of yogis. He thus became an inspiration for thousands who wanted spiritual growth in spite of being immersed in the family and the world. He set free all those who were influenced and thus chained by the religious maggots who claimed that God, *sadhna*, kundalini, chakras, the spiritual dimensions and liberation were only the prerogative of those who roamed about in various religious uniforms.

Lahiri Mahasaya reintroduced Kriya Yoga or Raja Yoga to mankind. This God-given process of accelerating your spiritual growth and cleansing your karma via meditative and breathing techniques is a gift of God to mankind. It can, within years, make one reach supernatural states of realization and also without bearing the brunt of karmic cleansing, this technique can wash away one's karmic balance sheet. This sort of meditation had disappeared. Apart from teaching Kriya Yoga meditation, what Lahiri Mahasaya did was He made complex spiritual issues easy to understand. What was once beyond the reach of the lay person, Mahasaya through His inherent simplicity and humility made Him accessible to all those who came to Him to understand various facets of spirituality and went to the core of the matter in the simplest manner. He opened the doors that were earlier shut to the common man and accessible only to realized souls and those who had walked the path of gyan (the science of yoga and life). In simplicity, I truly believe, resides the Lord.

According to Paramhansa Yogananda, 'No Prophet before him had distilled the entire Raja Yoga system of Patanjali and the yoga teachings of Sri Krishna in the Bhagavad Gita into a number of uncomplicated techniques capable of producing the greatest self-realization . . . surely the Yogavatar (the king of yoga) reached the zenith of all wonders in reducing the ancient complexities of yoga to an effective simplicity within the ordinary grasp.'

Lahiri Mahasaya showed the way to all, that one can go about silently performing all roles in life, if one was centred, calm, and in the flow of cosmic breath, which is a fancy way of saying being conscious of one's breath, even when involved with external things.

Lahiri Mahasaya did something else that was unusual. He did not believe that meditation, the kundalini, the chakras, oneness through breath, was the prerogative of any one religion. Hindus, Muslims, Christians and whoever was inclined to learn and grow spiritually were welcome. This was unheard of at that time. Those days religion and caste issues were rigid and one could be easily excommunicated from society and all the nonsense associated with social life.

The Hindus and the Muslims, like today, stuck to their lot, and in each community various shades of caste discrimination prevailed. And here was this accountant and a family man, who sat in His home, after work obviously, and taught one and all certain meditation techniques, explained spirituality, and made it simple and practical, and helped all those who came with the most mundane spiritual queries to the most sublime, irrespective of caste, creed and religion.

He would often say, 'None is sinful or sinless. Everyone is equal. Since everyone is the son of God, everyone has the right to practise sadhana. Irrespective of sex or class all have the right to practise this *yogasadhana*. It is not meant for any particular class of society.'

Forget religious demarcation, He gave initiation into various spiritual practices to gardeners, kings, sages–fakirs–priests, householders, postmen, the richest of the rich and to those who supposedly belonged to the lower castes and those who lived on the fringes of society. It did not matter to Lahiri Mahasaya, who you were and who you believed in, as long as you had the thirst, love and yearning for the Creator. If you wanted to embrace God and merge in oneness, Lahiri Mahasaya was your man.

Also, I love Him, for the king of yogis, took upon Himself to teach the world how to live with grace and dignity, irrespective of the storms and ups and downs that life had to offer. He had on purpose taken birth, with the most turbulent and heart-breaking destiny, to show the world that if God and His realm was your reality, nothing could and should deter you from walking the path.

This man, this yogi of yogis, this accountant who helped you to finish your karmic balance sheet in the most calm and peaceful manner, Lahiri, who could materialize in various places at the same time, and still be found meditating in His humble home, who saved the lives of innumerable devotees and disciples not only from death but financial ruin, allowed Himself to go through immense tribulations.

His second son, Dukari, had an attack of insanity. One of His daughters who He got married, died of cholera and the other daughter became a widow at an early age and came back to live with her parents for the rest of her life. Though He had worked hard all His life, and even received a substantial pension, Lahiri Mahasaya continued to work to support His family by giving tuitions to the Maharaja's son. Here was a king of yogis, one who could without blinking an eyelid save scores of His followers from sorrow, death and financial strain, yet allowed Himself to go through it all, in order to show the world and all those who wanted to walk the path of oneness, that no matter what, if one's priority was set on the divine, nobody and nothing could come in the way of the one embracing the light.

That nothing mattered but one's love for the Creator and one's union with the oneness.

I truly believe this is what makes Lahiri Mahasaya such a jewel in the spiritual crown. He personified what the lotus represents. The lotus lives in mire but still keeps itself out of it, retaining its beauty and purity. Lahiri Mahasaya lived His life immersed in the world but still so out of it and managed to bring a diverse set of people from all over and make them fall in love with Him and what He stood for and embrace what He taught.

Shyamacharan Lahiri Mahasaya was born on 30 September 1828, on Dussehra, the most auspicious day for the worship of Mother Durga, in the village Ghurni, West Bengal. Baba Sai of Shirdi took samadhi on Dussehra, while Lahiri Mahasaya was born on Dussehra.

Lahiri Mahasaya's mother died when He was not even five years of age. The family was once very affluent but a natural calamity took away most of the landed property. They moved to Kashi and since childhood Lahiri Mahasaya was spiritually inclined. Babaji first met Lahiri when the latter was still a child and the great primordial guru promised Lahiri's mother that He would always take care of the blessed child.

Lahiri Mahasaya completed His graduation and was well versed in English, Persian, Urdu, Sanskrit and His mother tongue, Bengali. He got married to Kashimoni Devi when He was eighteen and She was still nine years of age. He fathered five children as I have written earlier.

At the age of thirty-three, Lahiri Mahasaya met Babaji once again, who by touching the former on His spine, reminded Lahiri of His past lifetimes and Babaji initiated Him into Kriya Yoga. Maha Avatar Babaji is the most ancient guru; for some He is the physical manifestation of the Creator, many associate Him with Lord Shiva in the physical body—eternally young and present. It is said that when Babaji decides to dematerialize His body for ever, the world will come to an end.

Anyway, what is this Kriya Yoga that I have been harping about? It is called the 'airplane route to God'. Imagine one has to reach the twelfth floor. If one were to reach the twelfth floor using the stairway, apart from being extremely breathless, in a foul mood and panting like a constipated mule, the climb would take time and a lot of effort, depending upon one's physical fitness and the urgency to reach the top floor. Using the methods of breathing and meditation techniques stated in Kriya Yoga, one would reach the twelfth floor via the lift or the escalator.

'Kriya is an ancient science,' states Paramhansa Yogananda. 'Babaji revealed this to Lahiri Mahasaya (about Kriya Yoga): "The Kriya Yoga which I am giving to the world through you in this nineteenth century is a revival of the same science which Krishna gave, millenniums ago, to Arjuna, and which was later known to Patanjali, and to Christ, St John St Paul and other disciples."'

According to those who have mastered it, Kriya Yoga through its step-by-step process leads the follower to a state of breathlessness (not to be confused with asthma). It is said that *breathlessness is deathlessness,* which results in cosmic bliss; the one who can be peaceful for long periods of time, without breath, reaches a state of deathlessness. It is all about the breath. Inhalation and exhalation is fine, but the bliss is found in the gap in between; the space between inhalation and exhalation is where one finds initially, glimpses of bliss and as one effortlessly masters this process one can eventually experience the state of samadhi.

Sri Krishna, Elijah, Patanjali, Shankaracharya and Jesus Christ were known to have mastered Kriya Yoga, and many yogis and mystics believe that when St Paul declared, 'I die daily!' He was referring to the breathlessness state leading to deathlessness, leading to the state of cosmic bliss brought about by Kriya Yoga.

That is why Lahiri Mahasaya would always insist that all knowledge, wisdom, spiritual growth and eventually, merging with the one, took place via the breath, the *prana*. 'Prana is the origin of all power. By practising Pranasadhana, all sadhanas can be performed. Whether you maintain a domestic existence or renounce the world, wherever you are, prana exists within your body; meaning God is within you. If He is absent, you are non-existent. As long as prana is alive in your body, you are alive. What is the necessity for renouncing the world when you have to search for Him in your body?'

Lahiri Mahasaya filled up twenty-six diaries where He has explained His philosophies as well as written on the Indian scriptures, including the Bhagavad Gita and the Upanishads. The diaries also contain normal day-to-day happenings and routines, which make a profound and heartwarming read. For instance, Lahiri Mahasaya would take in His tiffin to office, a little ghee and sugar for breakfast and he would smoke a hookah every night after dinner. He would travel mainly by boat to the court of the king to teach the king's son, after retiring from work, in order to keep the home fires burning.

Lahiri Mahasaya before leaving His physical body predicted that: 'About fifty years after my passing, an account of my life will be written because of a deep interest in yoga that will arise in the West. The message of yoga will encircle the globe. It will aid in establishing the brotherhood of man: a unity based on humanity's direct perception of the one father.'

Exactly fifty years later, *The Autobiography of a Yogi* was published and launched in America.

Lahiri Mahasaya fell very ill on 26 September 1895. He was surrounded by His disciples, and even then, was explaining to them the meaning of His favourite verses from the Bhagavad Gita. Suddenly, He stood up and told one and all, 'What am I doing here? Why am I wasting time? It is high time for me to go home to my real home.'

A few hours later, three of His very close disciples who weren't with Him when He left His body and thus weren't aware of their master having taken samadhi, met Lahiri Mahasaya. The lord of the yogis had decided to pay His children a visit, even though He no longer was in the body.

Lahiri Mahasaya's *mahasamadhi* took place in Benaras, on 26 September 1895, the day of *Mahastami*, the day for the worship of Mother Durga.

He was born on the day of the Mother. He became eternal on the day of the Mother.

May the lord of the yogis, the God of the householders, the cosmic accountant bless us all.

19

To Christ with Love

Illustration by Pooja Bangia

Jesus, the Christ, as well as Jesus, the Man, had a strange journey to make. For the Man, it was the last journey and for the Son of God, it was to reunite with His Father, once again.

Eventually, the journey for both, the Christ and the Man who held the energy of the Lord, the Christ energy, would be tested to the hilt.

Jesus the Christ, the Son of God, knew what lay ahead, that day, when His body was brutalized and His spirit tested nearly beyond endurance.

Judas never wanted Jesus to be crucified. When he realized that his betrayal was the cause of Jesus being condemned to death by crucifixion, he shouted to the High Priest that Jesus was innocent. 'I have sinned in that I have betrayed the innocent blood.' (27:4) Nobody would listen. He threw those thirty pieces of silver at the doorstep of the temple and then realizing that nothing would stop Jesus from being crucified, Jesus who He truly loved, but due to a moment of insanity had betrayed, Judas killed Himself. Hung Himself and forever was condemned for posterity to be the main villain in the story of Jesus Christ.

I can only imagine what must have gone through the mind of Judas. He had made a mistake. He had blundered. But He had not wanted Jesus to be put to death, and death through crucifixion, never. How many of us have not sinned far greater than Judas. Who are we to blame or hate Him for His mistake?

And if Judas had not done what He did, would Jesus Christ have got the opportunity to take on the suffering and sins of all mankind, and redeem us all of our convoluted karmic journey? So in the arena of karmic play, had not Judas agreed to take on the worst scripted role any human being would have ever wanted to enact, the heaven above would have had to find another Judas. Without Judas, Jesus could not have enacted His part of the script. And Judas loved Jesus. And like so many of us who love another but become that person's greatest enemy, all in the name of love, poor Judas too, walked the same path.

And if He had not, wouldn't the Lord and Jesus Christ have to find another soul, willing to take on the role of betraying Jesus.

Somewhere down our karmic pathway, how many times must have we played the role of both Jesus and Judas in a lesser intensity, the Lord alone would know.

The script was written and now only the motions had to be gone through. Pilate, who was in charge of the trial, tried his level best to protect Jesus but no, the Old Man had finished the script, and like pawns, all had to enact their part. Jesus, the son of Mother Mary and Father Joseph, had to be crucified for Jesus the Christ to be resurrected and to live on for all eternity and beyond.

So the date of birth of Jesus the Man may or may not be 25 December, but the true birth of Jesus the Christ was three days after His crucifixion.

So the sordid drama began. The soldiers first stripped Jesus in front of all those who were present. People spat on Him, jeered at Him and abused Him. The soldiers thrashed the Son of God, while the heaven above, the archangels and the Lord Himself, held back. The furnace of karmic cleansing spares nobody, not even God, Goddess or the Son of God.

If Jesus the Christ had to take on the suffering and sins of all of creation, then the law of karma necessitates Jesus the Man and the Christ to pay the bill.

They stripped Him naked, spat upon him, jeered and then the soldiers began to hit Jesus on His head. They kept hitting Him till a part of His face was unrecognizable. He was hit upon the head repeatedly.

Here it is; Jesus the Christ who could make the blind see, make the lame walk, cure the lepers, intervene on behalf of the dying and raise the dead, had to stand quietly, while Jesus the Man was being thrashed about, insulted, abused, mocked, spat upon, stripped, humiliated.

And the heavens watched. The archangels sighed. And the Lord said this has to pass and so be it.

They put on a purple robe on the battered body of Jesus, to mock Him, as purple was considered to be the colour of royalty. They wanted to mock at Him as He said He was the Son of God, and thus royalty.

And Jesus the Christ and Jesus the Man must have known that this was just the beginning of the last waltz.

Then they made Him wear a crown of thorns. His head and face were already battered, bleeding and He must have gone partially blind and deaf at that stage and then to force upon Him this crown of thorns, I cannot begin to imagine how much it must have hurt.

Did He ever want to call upon the archangels, Michael, Raphael and Gabriel, to put an end to all this misery and allow Him to show to the world that yes, He was the Son of God, and who dare touch Him, or the Man, the Son of Mother Mary.

He must have had to restrain Himself. All the pain and humiliation, and He could have made it all go away with a bat of an eyelid, but He did not.

To please His Father and to wipe away our sins and sufferings—didn't God and He know that Jesus the Christ was going through all this suffering in vain? We, mankind, are the scum of the species. We aren't going to change. Let Christ come and go. Let Him be nailed to the cross a hundred times over, we, dear God, are not going to change. Nope. You allowed your Son to be crucified in vain and You sat there in Your Heaven, chaining Your archangels too, and watched the son of Mother Mary be put through hell. Good going Boss Man, good going. Anybody down here would have told You, You need a better script writer, dear Lord.

He was made to wear a crown of thorns and the thrashing continued. They wanted Him to drink something that would ease His pain so that He would be able to carry the cross and Jesus refused. How could He let anything reduce the pain? That would not please the Lord, right? That would not fit into the whole karmic cleansing song and dance routine.

They made Him carry the cross and made another man, some say a dark-skinned man, help a bit. All through the journey He was mocked, hit, whipped, spat upon, while His devotees and apostles and disciples watched in silence. All the while Jesus the Christ had to control Himself from unleashing His power while at the same time Jesus the Man underwent the worst possible pain known to mankind.

The entire crucifixion took six hours. Each minute must have seemed an hour. And then they nailed Him to the cross. We are so used to seeing Him nailed to the cross, that we forget what it must have felt like with rusted nails being shoved and hammered into His hands and legs. When the tip of a needle pricks our finger it makes us grimace. Rusted needles being banged into His hands and feet . . . and our good Lord watched from above. Somebody has to pay the karmic bill, no ifs and buts. So what if He is Jesus the Christ or even an avatar.

Christ thus said the most famous words in any language, 'Father, forgive them, for they know not what they do.' I mean, come on, you need to be Christ to be able to say all this. I know what I would have told God to do with the chaps crucifying me. It would involve a certain part of their anatomy being nailed to the floor.

But this was the same Jesus Christ who preached that if somebody slapped you on one cheek, give the bastard your other cheek.

And what did He prove? That no matter what, don't resort to violence. Don't hit back, as God resides in the other person too, though in a comatose state. To forgive is the greatest act of spirituality. To let go and let be, and where does forgiveness come from? It comes from harbouring love and compassion for each and every living being or inanimate object. To be able to forgive means to be able to live in a state of unconditional, selfless divine love and humble compassion.

And then He told the thief who had faith in Jesus as the Christ, 'Truly I say to you, today you will be with me in Paradise.'

There were two thieves along with Jesus being crucified. The other thief kept taunting Jesus to prove He was the Son of God and that He could perform miracles and Jesus kept quiet. The other thief, when He saw Jesus forgiving those who were so brutal to Him and praying to God to forgive His tormentors, the thief, hardened from a lifetime of crime, his heart softened, seeing Jesus the Christ, with one side of His head banged to pulp, blood dripping all over His face and body, still forgive the tormentors.

When you are in the presence of pure compassion it is truly hard to remain closed to the selfless love of the divine. And the thief told Jesus, who was battered and bruised, one of the most heartbreaking words, 'Remember me when You come to Your Kingdom.' What he meant was, 'Remember me when I come to Your Kingdom.' If this is not faith and love, what is? And what does Christ tell the man? 'Today you will be with Me in Paradise.'

Then Jesus the Christ saw Mother Mary. Jesus would always make it clear that all were His brothers and sisters and all were equal and one in front of God, but here, for the first time Jesus the Christ starts attaching Himself to the body and to the gross world. For the first time Jesus the Christ gives way to Jesus the Man when He sees Mother Mary along with Apostle John. He doesn't see His other brothers and family, but sees His mother standing with Apostle John, and the boy and man and son within Him must have cringed with apprehension as to who would look after His mother, Mother Mary. So He tells both Mother Mary and Apostle John, 'Woman, behold your son . . . (John) Behold your mother.'

For the first time during the entire crucifixion, the man overshadowed the spirit.

Yes, one can also look at it this way, that even though in so much suffering, Jesus thought about another person's well-being; I am sure, I agree with you, but I will still go with my gut. Jesus the Christ, for the first time let Jesus the Son, of Mother Mary, come to the fore. It was Jesus the Christ who had once told a band of followers, when He saw Mother Mary and His brothers in the same gathering: 'Who is My mother and who are My brethren? For whoever does the will of My Father in heaven is My brother and sister and mother' and Jesus the Man, told John to take care of His mother.

This is why, I think, for those brief moments that slip over where the connection with the gross body overtook the connection with the spirit, Jesus the Man cried out *'Eli, Eli, lama sabachthani?'*('My God, My God, why have You forsaken Me?')

I am certain Jesus the Christ who connected only with the spirit, could not and would not have looked to the Heavens and rebuked God, His Father. Nope. It was Jesus the Man who did so, as for a brief moment, His human emotions, coming from the connection with the gross body superseded the strength of the spirit and the laws of silent obedience and blasted karma, thus He screamed out to God, asking why His Father had deserted Him?

Yes, it could also mean that Jesus couldn't bear the separation from His Father, the Lord, but I still feel it was Mother Mary's human son who called out to God.

Then He said, 'I am thirsty.' This I believe is Him slowly going back to His original Christhood, slowly going back into the spirit, disconnecting with the body. 'I am thirsty' could also mean He was thirsty to go back to His Father but for whatever my understanding is worth, I still feel He was slowly disconnecting with the body, feeling less attached to the pain and agony. Of course He could have just been thirsty; nothing spiritual, nothing paranormal, just bloody thirsty for water, after being put through one of the worst possible tortures known to mankind.

So Jesus goes within after being given a few tabs of sour wine droplets on his bloodied lips. So He regained His centredness, after the lapse of oneness with the spirit, shaken up by the love for His mother, Mary. It is said that Jesus came to India, stayed in some place in Kashmir, and intermingled with yogis and gained further yogic powers brought through with the help of certain breathing techniques. Whatever it may be, I feel He must have taken a few deep breaths, now more and more shallow due to the body slowly closing down due to the physical torture.

Jesus reconnects with His Christ self and then says, 'It is finished.' This was once again Christ in command. As the Son of God, Jesus, was in control of all the elements of nature and through compassion manipulates the laws of karma and takes on the suffering of all of creation via the incorrect use of free will, and clearing the sins of all through His selfless love. He once had told His followers, 'No one takes it from Me, but I lay it down of My own accord. I have authority to lay it down and authority to take it up again. This command I received from My Father.'

The meaning is clear, He had destiny within His control and it was Him, who through His compassion, took on this work of karmic cleansing, and when the work was over, He said, 'It is finished.' So here again we have Jesus the Christ.

When He was convinced that the work was over, His body, which was already bruised further by the constant abuse of his captors, even though on the crucifix, He said these last words, 'Father, into Your hands I commit My spirit.'

Now that His work was over, He was tired. He was taking on all the sins of mankind, freeing them all their misdeeds, but the captors still continued to hurt His body, humiliate him and do all that which goes against the grain of compassion and love. He must have known somewhere that mankind would not change. A small doubt must have crept into Jesus the Christ that this inherent wickedness and cancer like malevolence was ingrained in our DNA.

He looks up and tells His Father, to call Him back. Mission sort of accomplished. I know Christ could not have been blind to mankind's self-destructive nature and also I don't think Christ lived in denial, but He still gave it His all and hoped beyond hope that His sacrifice would inspire countless people to try and emulate Him; yes, there would be many who would go against everything He stood for, but still, one has to give one's best.

So Jesus, battered gruesomely, breathes His last, as His body gave in.

Three days later, Jesus the Christ resurrected. For forty days He showed Himself to His followers. He lived on and off with His followers those forty days where He could take the form of a human body and shared meals with them. Jesus the Christ had gone beyond not only the human body but even beyond the spirit bodies into pure consciousness.

The resurrection of Christ, three days later, was His new birth. Archangels protected the entrance, One sat on the rock that blocked His physical body. The archangels arranged for all the appearances and all that which followed once Jesus had left the body. They could not do anything to save Jesus the Man, as He had to enact His part. But Jesus the Christ, was Their leader.

I always wonder that when the Son of God can go through so much of pain, humiliation and suffering, why is it that we want a life where there is no pain, agony, illness and any kind of poverty of body, heart, mind and soul. Could it be that He allowed Himself to be crucified not only to take on the suffering of mankind and absolve them of their sins, but also to keep reminding us that if the Son of God was made to suffer, we should go through whatever is happening to us with as much calmness and grace as possible; it did not make God unjust or vengeful. Like Jesus hurt and questioned God, we too, will hurt and yes, question God (and in India we have as many as thirty-three crore Gods and Goddesses to question and accuse); thus, yes, we too, will hurt and we will question God and doubt His existence, but the important thing, the right thing, the wise thing, would be to reconnect with the spirit within, try to fill the heart with love and compassion, forgive, share, laugh and always remember that when you face the wind or adversity, you must chin up.

20

Hazrat Baba Jaan . . .
The Qutub and the Rose

Illustration by Sumathi Shekhar

The first time I felt Baba Jaan's loving energy was seven years ago. I wanted to shift to Pune for good. Each time I would initiate the move, something or the other would impede the process. I am from Mumbai but for two and a half years was living in Delhi. My youngest daughter Meher was born and I didn't want her to live either in Mumbai or in the capital city. I had made several visits to Pune to work out the transition but it wasn't happening.

One day in prayer, Baba Sai of Shirdi gently whispered that the only way my move to Pune would fructify was if I took permission and blessings from Baba Jaan, as S(H)e was the ruler of this beautiful city. Baba Jaan took samadhi (or left Her physical body) on 20 September 1931, but as the beautiful stanza says, 'Cycles change, the worlds rotate, but Qutubs never their seat vacate'; Baba Jaan's spiritual reign over Pune continues.

I was aware of Baba Jaan, as my first book *The Last Marathon*, was about Avatar Meher Baba, life after death and spirit communication. I was aware that Baba Jaan was one of the Perfect Masters who initiated the realization of Godhood in the Avatar.

I had often been to Baba Jaan's dargah, when I used to visit Pune. So I reached Her dargah, and as it so often happens, the chaps in charge of providing Pune with electricity, being prominent activists in the 'save Mother Earth' movement and big on conserving power and electricity, had shut off the electrical grids. The dargah was in partial darkness.

A small lamp was burning and headlights of the cars that passed by, on and off shed light within the dargah. I was all alone with Baba Jaan. I knelt down, and touching Her holy tomb, prayed. I told Baba Jaan that I wanted her blessings and permission to settle in Pune, but only if S(H)e thought the move was best for the overall well-being of my family and Pune city. The moment I had prayed to Baba Jaan, the dargah and all the nearby shops lit up, as the electrical power had been restored. I knew Baba Jaan had given me permission and blessings. I went and touched my forehead to the neem tree trunk, where Baba Jaan used to sit while in the body.

The moment I stepped out of the dargah, Pune Electrical Board sprung to action, and all around once again the state of semi-darkness returned.

Within a week all obstacles were removed magically and in a few months, after completing the book I was working on, we shifted lock, stock and a temperamental baby, to Pune.

Every time, a day before I have to travel out of Pune, I go and seek Baba Jaan's permission. There have been times when at the last moment, the trip has got cancelled. I know it is Baba Jaan's way of telling me, permission to travel denied. The moment I reach Pune, in a few hours I go to give my *hazri* to Baba Jaan. I would like to believe S(H)e is as happy to see me as I am, to be back with the old monarch.

Baba Jaan was born in Baluchistan, Afghanistan, and named Gulrukh (one who looks like a rose). Her year of birth has been debated, either 1790 or 1820. S(H)e is believed to be have been born in an aristocratic family of noble lineage and according to many biographers, Baba Jaan had the lineage of royal blood—obviously S(H)e was royalty, spiritual royalty. Baba Jaan at a very tender age, learned the entire Koran and thus was a hafizah (one who knows the Koran by heart), apart from being fluent in Arabic, Persian,

Urdu and her mother tongue, Pashtu. From a young age, Baba Jaan was more inclined towards prayers, meditation and silent contemplation. Between the age of fourteen to eighteen years, Baba Jaan's parents wanted to get their daughter married. Baba Jaan had other plans. On the day of the wedding, S(H)e ran away and reached Peshawar, and then Rawalpindi, which was then in India. One can imagine a young girl, from an aristocratic family, brought up in the rigid discipline of the *parda* system, running away, travelling all alone, to reach an alien country in order to continue the spiritual journey. Those days wars were common; bandits were a way of life. In a male-dominated world, that a young girl of eighteen managed to escape unscathed and reach India, itself was a miracle. God was with Gulrukh.

For a long time Baba Jaan continued with her spiritual practices till one day she met a Hindu saint, who then formally initiated Baba Jaan into various spiritual practices. It is said that after the initiation, Baba Jaan went into seclusion for seventeen months, staying up on a mountain just outside Rawalpindi, continuing with the spiritual practices and austerities passed down by the Hindu saint.

Baba Jaan, after the seventeen months of isolation then stayed for a few months in Multan. It was here that Baba Jaan met a majzoob, Muslim saint, who blessed the thirty-seven-year-old Gulrukh with God-realization. Baba Jaan returned to Rawalpindi, met with the Hindu saint once again, who was instrumental in helping Baba Jaan return to normal consciousness; which means that though the state of God-realization continues, Baba Jaan could also live a normal human life, by coexisting with normal human consciousness. This is of utmost importance for if the master cannot operate from normal consciousness, then the God-realization is of not much use to all of creation. It is like radiance, not to be shared, only meant for one individual; while God-realization along with human normal consciousness, means the divine light and radiance is spread to all of creation.

Biographers are undecided at what age Baba Jaan met up with the Hindu saint, but for many, nearly two decades had passed since the time S(H)e had left Afghanistan, while some say S(H)e met the masters when S(H)e was nearly fifty years old, and some claim Baba Jaan was around sixty-five when S(H)e became God-realized.

Baba Jaan then travelled to Iraq, Syria, Baghdad and Lebanon. It is said that Baba Jaan travelled to Mecca, though disguised as a man, via Afghanistan, Iran, Turkey and then back into Arabia. In Mecca, Baba Jaan used to offer the mandatory five times a day prayers and also visited the dargah of Prophet Muhammed at Medina, all the while taking care of the needy, the hungry and ailing pilgrims.

Baba Jaan returned to India, and reached Nasik where for a long time S(H)e stayed in Panchavati. After that Baba Jaan reached Mumbai. By now, wherever Baba Jaan went, people began to recognize the light and divinity that throbbed within and shone forth. In 1903 Baba Jaan made another pilgrimage to Mecca, returning a year later. S(H)e visited and prayed at Khwaja Saheb, Moinuddin Chisti's dargah in Ajmer.

Baba Jaan then spent many years in north India where S(H)e was already considered a saint. But Baba Jaan was facing problems there. Baba Jaan did not follow any set rules and norms prescribed by any sect of either Islam or Sufism. S(H)e walked the path of oneness and being a woman, revered and loved by the masses, the orthodox religious groups and leaders were bound to have their egos and power threatened by this quaint, small person, who still towered above all of them spiritually. Baba Jaan never belonged to any sect. In fact S(H)e doesn't belong to the Chishti order of Sufism either. Baba Jaan belongs to Him, the One and is only answerable to the One. Like Sai Baba of Shirdi, S(H)e too, walked along with the fakir.

One day, being God-realized, and in that spiritual intoxication of oneness and spiritual ecstasy, eventually led Baba Jaan to reach Pune.

'After being self-realized Babajan lived for some time... in Punjab. During this stay many people began to respect her as a saint. Her occasional remarks, declaring Ana'l-Haqq [I am the truth] upset the Muslim population, and fanatical Muslim Baluchi soldiers (sepoys) of a local military regiment buried Babajan alive. After a lapse of many years, during the First World War the Baluchi regiment was transferred to Pune, and in that city the same soldiers came face-to-face with Babajan sitting under her neem tree at Char Bawdi. Fanaticism was transformed into devotion, and as long as the regiment remained stationed at Pune, the soldiers came to pay their respects to Babajan.'

The Baluchi regiment in fact became Baba Jaan's personal bodyguards and it was after they revealed to one and all what had transpired that Baba Jaan began to be known as Hazrat Baba Jaan.

Before Baba Jaan came to Pune, S(H)e settled down in Bombay in 1900, and lived in Chuna Bhatti for five years. There, two Sufi saints very high up the spiritual order of Sufism, Maulana Saheb of Bandra and Abdul Rahman of Dongri, became disciples of Baba Jaan and the latter would address Them as 'My children.'

One day Baba Jaan met Hazrat Taj al-Din Baba of Nagpur, known as Baba Tajuddin, a Perfect Master, another powerhouse, who walked to the rhythm of the oneness family. It is believed that Baba Tajuddin advised Baba Jaan to go to Pune.

Baba Jaan settled down in Pune in 1905. By then, S(H)e was, according to some researchers, either eighty-five or over hundred years old, depending on what one took as Baba Jaan's year of birth.

Baba Jaan lived in the most humble manner, disregarding all physical comforts, which often saddened and troubled the thousands of devotees and disciples who flocked to her. When S(H)e came to Pune, she initially lived near the shrine of Panch Pir at Dighi. The entire place was ant-infested. Hundreds and thousands of ants were seen biting and crawling all over Baba Jaan. Eventually, when one devotee could not bear the thought of her discomfort, after many days of persuasion, he managed to take Baba Jaan to his house, and quickly he and his family toiled hard to clean and clear the place of all the ants. Baba Jaan was a fakir in the true sense. S(H)e refused to pamper the body and was so engrossed in the oneness that physical discomfort and the body was of no consequence.

Initially, before the Baluchi soldiers arrived in Pune and revealed how they had buried and presumably killed Baba Jaan, who they found happily moving about in spiritual ecstasy in Pune, the devotees called Baba Jaan Amma Saheb. Baba Jaan would get furious when she was called either 'Mai' or 'Mother' and tell one and all 'I am a man'. One of the quotes of Prophet Mohammed is, 'Lovers of God are males; lovers of paradise are eunuchs; and lovers of the world are females.' That is why Baba Jaan was called Amma Saheb (Mother Sir).

Baba Jaan then began to live under a neem tree near Bukhari Shah mosque at Rasta Peth. By then the number of devotees had increased to an extent that eventually the devotees began to request Baba Jaan to choose a place where S(H)e and they would be more comfortable. Baba Jaan refused till a banyan tree was cut down to widen the road. S(H)e then moved under a neem tree (even Sai Baba of Shirdi when He came to live in Shirdi stayed under a neem tree) in Char Bavadi. This place was a dangerous area, frequented by thugs and thieves; mosquitoes and filth abounded. Within a decade the same place became a hub of spiritual activity and a pilgrimage spot for devotees and disciples who frequented from all over India.

Dr Ghani who knew Baba Jaan personally has penned a beautiful description in his book *Hazrat Babajan: The Emperor of the Spiritual Realm of Her Time*. 'Short in stature, firm and agile in gait, back slightly bent with rounded shoulders, skin fair and sunburnt, face broad and heavily wrinkled, high cheek bones, liquid blue eyes possessing great depths, head covered with a silvery crown of thick white hair hanging loose to the shoulders, deep sonorous voice, all conspired to make her personality very unique and unworldly. Her attire was simple, consisting of a long apron extending below the knees, pyjamas narrowed round the legs and a linen scarf thrown carelessly round the shoulders. She always went about bare-headed; the luxuriant crop of white hair—never oiled or groomed—was for all practical purposes a headdress in itself.'

Baba Jaan, like most unique-looking masters was initially harassed by children who threw stones (and I met an old man a few days earlier who told me that his neighbour knew Baba Jaan, who would, when in the mood, also throw stones back at one and all). It is known that Baba Jaan called everybody '*bachha*' (meaning child) and spoke in Persian, Urdu and Pashtu. S(H)e had an extensive vocabulary of abuses.

By 1913 Baba Jaan was already revered by people in Pune and nearby towns and cities. It was that year when Avatar Meher Baba, a young lad then called Merwan, met Baba Jaan with tears gushing down His cheeks. S(H)e lovingly called Meher Baba 'my beloved son' in Hindi. In January 1914, Baba Jaan kissed Meher Baba on the forehead one night and told one and all that, 'This is my beloved son . . . He will shake the world and all humanity will be benefited by him.' In the same month and year Baba Jaan again kissed Meher Baba on the forehead and Merwan lost all consciousness of duality and became God-realized.

In Avatar Meher Baba's words, 'When the five Perfect Masters brought me down (to earth), they drew a veil over me. Hazrat Babajan was one of the Perfect Masters, and she unveiled me to my present form. With just a kiss on my forehead, between the eyebrows, Babajan made me experience (in May 1913) thrills of indescribable bliss that continued for about nine months. Then one night (in January 1914) she made me realize in a flash the infinite bliss of God-realization. At the time Babajan gave me the *nirvikalp* experience of my own reality, the illusory physical, subtle and mental bodies—mind, worlds and all created things—ceased to exist for me even as illusion. Then I began to see that only I (in the sense of the highest self), and nothing else, existed. The infinite bliss of my self-realization was, is, and will remain, continuous. At the moment I experience both infinite bliss as well as infinite suffering. Once I drop the body, only bliss will remain.'

Baba Jaan loved tea and shared everything with the devotees. S(H)e liked to hear qawalis. Baba Jaan did not speak much and when S(H)e did speak it was in a soft voice. S(H)e listened to all and would nod often in response. S(H)e cured the sick and even performed astral surgery. S(H)e would hold the affected area between the fingers, pray, order the entity bothering the ailing person to leave immediately and the sick person would recover and experience virtually immediate relief. S(H)e has been known to bring back sight to a Zoroastrian child, by mumbling a prayer and blowing her breath on the eyes of the child. The child recovered immediately. Women who couldn't conceive were blessed and became proud mothers. S(H)e let people take away (rob) all the meagre possessions S(H)e had or was gifted with. One night a thief was trying to take away an expensive shawl gifted to Baba Jaan by a devotee. Obviously the thief was finding the going tough, as part of the shawl was held underneath Baba Jaan's body. So Baba Jaan raised the back so that the shawl could be easily whisked away. Once somebody had gifted Baba Jaan two gold bangles and a thief snatched them away from Baba Jaan in such a rough manner that the wrist bled profusely, but nothing mattered to Baba Jaan. In fact S(H)e did not allow the thief to be apprehended and told the police to take in custody those who had created such a ruckus over two bangles.

It is mentioned that Baba Jaan would keep murmuring things and very often would say aloud, 'Vermin are troubling me constantly; I brush them away, but still they keep on coming and troubling me'. S(H)e would go on and on talking under the breath and move the palms of the hand all over the body, as though cleansing the body of dirt or something that was causing lot of discomfort.

Meher Baba gave the following reason for Baba Jaan's inexplicable behaviour: 'Annihilation of all *amal* (actions) good and bad, means *najat* (salvation) and Babajan being God-realized was much above the state of salvation. She not only had no amal to account for, but was in a position to destroy the amals of others. The physical body of a saint like Babajan, when working on the earthly plane after realization, becomes the focal point to which myriads and myriads of amals of the universe get attracted, and getting purified in the furnace of divinity that is, the body of the saint, they go out again into the universe as spiritual amals. . . . Perfect saints like Babajan give out more spiritual amal to the world than they destroy. Hence it is that living saints are a blessing and mercy to the world whether one knows it or not.' (*Hazrat Babajan: The Emperor of the Spiritual Realm of Her Time.*)

Also Baba Jaan often when consumed by divine glory would get upset and say aloud, 'Why do you torment and kill my children. They have done no wrong to you. Do I not feed you, and clothe you? What is it that you want? And still you carry on with all these atrocities on my children. What have I done to deserve all this?'

Meher Baba, when questioned regarding this explained: 'By children, she evidently meant the saints of the time (Awliyae-waqt), who are misunderstood, vilified and persecuted by the churches of all denominations, unmindful of the circumstances of which they are the outcome. Babajan was equally concerned about the enlightened and the ignorant, and hence her reference to feeding and clothing of the latter. She was as much for the material well-being of the world at large, as for the spirituality of the godly few whom she called her children.' (*Hazrat Babajan: The Emperor of the Spiritual Realm of Her Time*)

Baba Jaan lived in the physical body in Pune for nearly three or more decades. S(H)e continued to live under the neem tree. Devotees fought over where the master's body, after the spirit left, would be buried. S(H)e didn't care about all this. The devotees were worried that the Cantonment Board, managed by the military, would never give permission for a dargah to be made, bang in middle of the road, even for a master. Baba Jaan when told of all this high-level drama about the burial, I am sure after a few choicest abuses, told them, 'Get away from here. How can the dead show concern for the living? I am not going to leave this place.'

Eventually, S(H)e didn't leave the place. Even today Baba Jaan's dargah is under the neem tree. When still in the body, a nice room was made for Baba Jaan a few feet away from the neem tree. Initially, the British wanted Baba Jaan out of the area but realizing the public sentiment and also the presence of the Baluchi bodyguards, the British relented. They made the dwelling. All officials had come to inaugurate the new dwelling. Baba Jaan refused to budge, the reason being the neem tree was not part of the interior decoration plan. Eventually, the officials had to extend the room in such a way that the tree, too, was part of the new dwelling. Once again Baba Jaan had shown little regard to man-made rules and regulations. S(H)e never followed any norms where religious worship or spiritual dos-and-don'ts were concerned. Neither did she care much about the British or the army or anybody. From the time S(H)e had left home till S(H)e left the physical body, S(H)e lived by just His calling.

In 1930, journalist Paul Brunton (Raphael Hurst) visited Baba Jaan. He wrote the following: 'She lies, in full view of passers-by, upon a low divan. . . . Her head is propped by pillows. The lustrous whiteness of her silky hair offers sad contrast to the heavily wrinkled face and seamed brow.' They hardly met for a long time yet Paul Brunton had felt Baba Jaan's divinity. 'That some deep psychological attainment really resides in the depths of her being, I am certain.'

Hazrat Baba Jaan's spiritual status is that of a Qutub (though I am certain Baba Jaan would care little for all these titles). The Qutub literally means a pole; but spiritually, a Qutub is the heart–core–nucleus–focal point around which all of creation revolves.

On 18 September 1931, three days before S(H)e left the body, one of Baba Jaan's fingers had to be operated as it was obvious there was something wrong. It is believed that just a few days prior to this operation Baba Jaan had told those nearby that it was time 'S(H)e shut shop'. One of those close to Baba Jaan pleaded that S(H)e should not speak in such a way and Baba Jaan said these beautiful words, 'Nobody, nobody here wants my wares. Nobody can afford the price. I have turned my goods over to the Proprietor.'

The Qutub has left the building. The fragrance of the rose is here to stay for eternity and the beyond.

21

The Goddess Within

Illustration by Pooja Bangia

My association with the Goddess in this lifetime continued or began with my birth. I was born on Kali Chaudas night, which is Diwali and/or Laxmi Pujan day. My mother often told me that the doctors told her to hold on to me inside her, as it would be good for her child if the child was born on the night of Goddess Kali and the day of Goddess Laxmi. So I can imagine my poor mother holding on to me with her dear life and then, when the doctor gave her the green signal, letting go so that I could waltz out, with a perpetual frown and a look of 'damn it, not again'.

When my dad and I would banter, I would remind him that when I was born, fire crackers lit up the sky and there was celebration all around. He would sigh and say that I had got it all wrong—mankind wasn't celebrating, the Gods were rejoicing, having got rid of me at last, and at least, from the astral world for a while. When he was angry he would remind me that I was born on the darkest night of the year, and when happy, he would say I was blessed to have two mothers.

When I was around three or four years old, I used to go to a school at Charni Road, behind the Japanese Garden, Mumbai, and there were these beautiful statues of Lord Jesus and Mother Mary. Twenty yards away from the school, there was a statue of Mother Mary kept inside a stone cave and I would be mesmerized standing in front of Her.

While growing up, I would stand before Mother Kali's statue in awe. I am certain that if She was on your side, even God would have to really think hard before He confronted you for all your wayward use of free will and its ramifications.

There were these two small temples of Maa Kali and Maa Santoshi, fifty feet away from each other, and depending upon my state of mind, I would stand in front of the Goddess and have a chat of sorts.

Then I met Swamiji Naik, who was the medium of Maa Mookambika Devi. He took samadhi a few years back, but what a sage and a medium He was. I was privileged to write a book called *The Devi's Emerald* and I would frequent Maa's temple in Bangalore, to interview Swamiji and His devotees and disciples.

I have personally seen Her grace, mercy, love and protection. Karma and everything else gets tossed out of one's auric ambit if the Goddess decides to take mercy on you. I have shared divine moments with the Goddess and Swamiji; lots of grace, fun and food.

My association with the Goddess continues with Mother Mary, Ava Yasht and me going to Baba Jaan's dargah every week. I know that Baba Jaan—one of the five Perfect Masters—would be upset with me for acknowledging the Goddess within, as S(h)e insisted on being called a man, but I truly see the mother energy in all its glory in Baba Jaan.

Throughout my life I have prayed to the male energy of the Creator, but whenever I fall ill, or even trip, through sheer reflex, the words Maa come out from the old fog horn. So I guess no matter what, the mother energy of the Creator is always called upon when we need comfort, protection, nurturing, pampering, mercy and grace.

Okay, enough of my ramblings.

The first day of Nav Ratras is the beginning of the nine auspicious nights of the Goddess Durga.

Lord Rama invoked Maa Durga before He fought Ravana. Lord Krishna worshipped Goddess Durga before the Mahabharata war ensued, to gain victory for the five brothers, the Pandavas.

Durga means 'the one who removes all misery from the journey of life'.

During the research on Nav Ratras I have realized that the nine nights are not only about the worship of Maa Durga in Her nine forms, but also the worship of Maa Laxmi and Maa Sarasvati.

The first three nights are spent in worship of Maa Durga. The next three nights Mother Laxmi is invoked and the last three nights one seeks the blessings of Maa Saraswati.

The tenth day is called Vijayadasami . . . the tenth day of victory.

So the first three nights is in worship of Maa Durga, as it is Goddess Durga—Maa Kali, who destroys all evil and brings about a condition of purity and well-being to enter and flourish. Maa Durga is known to destroy demons who create a racket and havoc in paradise and trouble the Gods too. Basically, what we are praying for is that may Goddess Durga destroy all evil that lurks within us; all that which keeps purity and godliness away from us. That is why Durga Maa is called *Durgati Harini* . . . 'She who removes all evil tendencies.'

The legend says that Maa Durga destroys a demon called Mahishasura. The word 'Mahisha' means 'buffalo'.

What does the buffalo generally represent? Sloth and inertia. (I do not want to upset or disrespect any buffalo or animal activist. I have deep respect for the latter and enjoy sweetmeats made from the milk of the buffalo.)

Anyway, don't all of us have Mr Mahishasura within us? Don't we have the buffalo tendency of sloth and inertia within us? In spite of potential Godhood, don't we all prefer to dwell in dark corners and not make the effort to realize our Godhood and Oneness?

Maa Durga destroys all sloth, evil, lust, ego, greed, negativity, falseness from within—if truly prayed to with child-like innocence. When you approach the Goddess like a child, the maternal love that flows through the Goddess for you is beyond description. If you approach the Goddess like an adult, She will treat you like an adult, and as we all know, adults are a messed-up species.

So the first three nights, one worships Goddess Durga to clean us up from all that which is enveloped in darkness and dark energies and negativity.

Once the soil is cleaned up, Mother Laxmi is prayed to for the next three nights, so that She in Her grace bestows upon us true knowledge of oneness, pure selfless love, divine wisdom, complete well-being of body, heart, mind and soul. Of course, nowadays Maa Laxmi is called upon to bless us with many smiling Mahatma Gandhis . . . preferably on thousand-rupee notes; gold too is most welcome. But Maa Laxmi is the Goddess of wealth, not hard cash. Maa Laxmi when prayed to can bestow on us the greatest blessing, true well-being, which can come about through noble thoughts, words and deeds; and one who is blessed with this, is blessed with true wealth for one's soul.

The last three nights one prays to Mother Saraswati. Maa Saraswati brings about joy of appreciating 'the song and dance of life'. It is Maa Saraswati who bestows on the individual (after the basic instincts are dealt with by Maa Durga, and a state of centredness and well-being is granted by Maa Laxmi), divine knowledge of one's own self which is self-realization of oneness with the Creator.

Thus, these nine auspicious nights are also a journey of the soul, from mire and muck to divine radiance. First cleansing is done, followed by nurturing of the soul and then realization dawns.

When one goes through the nine nights, the tenth day is that of victory, Vijayadasami/or Dusshera or Dusa-hara (cutting of Ravan's ten heads). The head usually stands for the mind; the mind usually is the warehouse of all the mess and all the crap and all the falseness and darkness; from pride to jealously to greed to ego. I don't need to spell it out. We are all too well acquainted with these ten heads. At least I am.

When one achieves self-realization through the grace of Maa Durga (Shakti–Parvati), Maa Laxmi and Maa Saraswati, then there is victory of the soul, through self-realization, oneness and ultimately, Godhood.

The Goddess is the energy within us all; man, woman, child, and all that which lives in all of creation. But approach Her as a child. Even God thinks twice before displeasing the Mother. And the Mother can't see beyond Her child.

Jai Mata Di. Glory Be to the Divine Mother.

22

The Storyteller's Rambling

These profiles on God, Goddess, gurus and archangels are not the all-composite biographies or life sketches, with dates, important events, miracles and data which are normally expected of a book that purports to write on the oneness family.

If you are looking for every little detail and all the historical facts then you have obviously picked up the wrong book. I am not a historian or a proficient biographer. I am just a storyteller. A hobo on the highway of life, meandering through bylanes in search of other beach bums like me.

I have written my personal take on the oneness family. My relationship, bond, connect, experiences in various forms with Them. During channelling, in the countless hours and since years and years, Baba Sai has come through (or at least I would like to believe that He comes through, with beautiful messages, sublime thoughts, debatable wisecracks, gems of information, huge boulders of wisdom and a whiff of His fragrance, His *khusboo*, a strange configuration of *udh ittar*, *loban* and tobacco mixed with some herb) and through my childhood, since I can remember I have walked through various alleys where They have left behind Their fragrance and radiance.

So this book is about my take on Them. I hope that this is the first volume of countless such volumes as They are so many within the oneness family. The ones on whom I have written are truly dear to me but please understand, All are dear to me. If you do not find the ones who are dear to you, it is because I am lazy and have time and again not written on Them when I should have. Also I would like and want that there should be many volumes on the Perfect Ones, so please forgive me, but there is no personal agenda in my writing on some and not writing on others.

This book is akin to dipping your fingers in cool water, before taking the plunge into the ocean of oneness. It only gives a glimpse about Them. A whiff. A caress. A faint rainbow in the cosmic sky. There is far and far and far more to Them than what I have written.

I have not focused on Their miracles. I mean performing miracles are a mandatory part of the spiritual kit of each one of Them. If you are a God, Goddess, guru, archangel, why would I focus on something which is as obvious as my inability to truly grasp Their magnitude and realize Their presence in our every throb, sigh and very breath? Why would I say, today I had a bath with water? Is that not obvious?

Anyway, enough of my ramblings. If you are reading this book, welcome home dear friend. If you can feel Their love for you and for all of us, am so glad you have finally woken up to Their love. If you can realize Their oneness, ahhhhh, my salutations to you. Make Them proud, is all I can pray for you.

What life offers each one is as important as what one takes out of life. You can play the victim and spread your darkness or you can be a warrior of light and become part of the radiance. You can be a whiner or you can be the harbinger of happiness. You can live your entire life with your beautiful head tucked deep into the recesses of your rectal opening or you can smell the fragrance of the earth when you bow down in obeisance. You can soar with hope or be bludgeoned with doubt and negativity.

You can wait for a miracle or you can become and live the miracle.

I leave it all to you. Baba Sai often says that the highest form of surrender is when honour and dishonour mean one and the same thing for disciple and child of each master. This is because when honour and dishonour mean the same, you have truly detached yourself from yourself, the highest form of detachment, and you have surrendered prestige and ill repute, both at the feet of the master.

It must be a truly groovy place to be in, this state of detachment. If this book and the many pages of ramblings I have indulged in, can make you take the first step on this road of complete annihilation of your lower self and make you smile and feel a child-like love and oneness for Them, then this storyteller, who is a phenomenally daft demented dork, will smile, light a cigarette and sigh *Jai Baba, Jai Maa, Jai Oneness Family*.

Be blessed always, my friend.

References

1. Sai Baba . . . My sigh . . . My Sai
http://www.saibaba.org
http://www.saibaba.ws/avatar/lifestoryshirdi.htm
http://www.saibabaofshirdi.net/satcharita
http://www.saibabaofindia.com

2. Nav Durga Namho Namho
http://hinduism.about.com/od/festivalsholidays/a/
navaratri.htm
http://rampuri.com/navdurga-navratri/
http://hindupad.com/navadurga-or-9-forms-of-durga-nine-
goddesses-of-durga-navratri/

3. Archangel Gabriel . . . The Master's Voice
http://angels.about.com/od/Famous-Archangels/f/How-Do-
I-Recognize-Archangel-Gabriel.htm
http://www.thesongsofhafiz.com/legends.htm

4. The Silent Avatar . . . Meher Baba
http://www.avatarmeherbaba.org
www.lordmeher.org
http://www.meherfilmworks.org/ghf/english_script.html
http://www.meherspiritualuniversity.org/meherbaba.html

5.   Lord Mahavir
http://www.cs.colostate.edu/~malaiya/mahavira.html
http://www.jainworld.com/education/level2/lesson20.htm
http://www.jaindharmonline.com/tirthan/tir24.htm

6.   Sarkar Makhdum Shah Baba
http://www.makhdumalimahimi.org/
http://www.auliasworld.com/2011/07/hazrat-makhdoom-ali-mahimi-ra.html
http://www.aulia-e-hind.com/dargah/Mahim.htm
The Life History Of Hazrat Shaikh Makhdum Ali Paro Qutb-ul- Aqtab Qutb-e-Kokan, Al-Mahaimi of Mumbai

7.   The Perfectly Mad One . . . Baba Tajuddin
http://tajbaba.com
http://www.tajuddinbabawaki.com

8.   Ramakrishna Paramhansa . . . Maa Kali's Baby
http://www.ramakrishnavivekananda.info/gospel/gospel.htm
http://www.belurmath.org

9.   Haji Ali, the Prince of Waves
http://www.hajialidargah.in/
http://auliyaallah.hpage.co.in/haji-ali-baba_41525491.html
http://www.aulia-e-hind.com/dargah/Mumbai.htm#2

10. Sant Dass: The Cobbler King
http://shrigururavidasji.com
http://www.sikhiwiki.org/index.php/Bhagat_Ravidas
http://ravidassiasamaj.com/ravidass_biogra.php

11. Sadhu Vaswani: God's Whisper
http://www.sadhuvaswani.org/
http://www.sadhuvaswanimission.org/

12. Archangel Michael: The Warrior Prince of Light
http://www.amazingfacts.org/media-library/book/e/85/t/
who-is-michael-the-archangel.aspx
http://www.whyangels.com/archangels_michael_gabriel.
html#.VPnHK3yUeSo

13. Ramana: The MahaRishi
http://bhagavan-ramana.org/
http://www.sriramanamaharshi.org/
http://www.arunachalasamudra.org/ramana.html

14. Sai's Chosen One, Meher's Guru: Upasani Maharaj
http://www.shreeswami.org/avatars/shri-upasani-baba-
maharaj
http://trustmeher.org/meher-baba-perfect-masters/upasni-
maharaj
http://www.saibharadwaja.org/books/saibabathemaster/
theoffshootsofsaibaba.aspx

15. Nanak . . . The Prophet and the Peasant
http://sikhism.about.com/od/tengurus/tp/Life_of_Nanak.htm
http://www.sikh-history.com/sikhhist/gurus/nanak1.html
http://www.sikhiwiki.org/index.php/Guru_Nanak

16. Mehera Be Brave . . . The Avatar's Beloved
http://www.meherameher.com/html/AVframe.html
http://www.sheriarbooks.org/bios/bioMehera.html
http://trustmeher.org/meher-baba-mandali/women-
mandali/mehera
http://www.avatarmeherbaba.org/erics/earlymehera.html

17. Archangel Raphael . . . The Shining One Who Heals
http://angels.about.com/od/SearchAngelsMiracles/p/Meet-
Archangel-Raphael.htm
https://theangelichealer.wordpress.com/

18. Lahiri Mahasaya, The Lord of Yogis and a Very Good Accountant

http://www.yoga-kriya.com

http://www.babajisannidhan.com/people/priyayukteswar.htm

http://hinduism.about.com/od/gurussaints/p/swamiyukteswar.htm

19. To Christ with Love

http://www.jesuschristsavior.net

http://christianity.about.com

http://www.lightsource.com/ministry/leading-the-way/articles/seven-statements-from-the-cross-12686.html

http://www.biography.com/people/jesus-christ-9354382?page=3

20. Hazrat Baba Jaan . . . The Qutub and the Rose

http://meherchowk.wordpress.com/2013/08/10/of-meher-babas-realization-centenary-celebrations-in-meherabad/

http://www.avatarmeherbaba.org/erics/holykiss.html

http://www.lordmeher.org/print.jsp?nextJsp=pages/15.html&pageNo=15

http://www.bhaukalchuri.org/ChatWebcat.html

21. The Goddess Within

http://www.sascv.org/ijcjs/snehlata.pdf

http://edugreen.teri.res.in/explore/water/river.htm